HACK

Sex, Drugs, and Scandal
from Inside the Tabloid Jungle

GRAHAM JOHNSON

D0242354

SIMON &
SCHUSTER

London · New York · Sydney · Toronto · New Delhi

A CBS COMPANY

First published in Great Britain by Simon & Schuster UK Ltd, 2012
A CBS Company

1 3 5 7 9 10 8 6 4 2

Simon & Schuster UK Ltd
1st Floor
222 Gray's Inn Road
London
WC1X 8HB

www.simonandschuster.co.uk

Simon & Schuster Australia,
Sydney

Simon & Schuster India, New Delhi

A CIP catalogue for this book is available
from the British Library.

ISBN: 978-1-84983-877-1

Typeset by Hewer Text UK Ltd, Edinburgh
Printed and bound in Great Britain by CPI Group (UK) Ltd, Croydon, CRO 4YY

For
Emma, Sonny, Raya
Connie and Clara

Also by Graham Johnson:

Darkness Descending
Powder Wars
Druglord
Football and Gangsters
The Devil
Soljas
Gang War
The Cartel

Contents

Introduction

The phone rang. It was Rebekah Brooks.

Acting Editor of the *News of the World*. Cold-eyed corporate killer. Supreme Top Operator.

At the other end of the line was me. Tabloid extremist. Prolific story-getter. Fleet Street's Next Big Thing.

I knew why she was calling – she wanted to find out for herself whether the photographs were real or fake. The conversation opened up something like this:

Rebekah: 'Hi Graham. How's it going down there?'

There were golf balls of stress in my shoulders. I was pacing around a chintzy, overheated hotel room on Bodmin Moor in Cornwall. This was the most important conversation that I would ever have in my life.

If I could blag my way through it, there would be glory beyond my wildest dreams. Triumphant return home. Fortress Wapping at my feet. But if I fucked up, there would be untold doom. Disgrace. Unemployment. Exile. The stakes were stratospheric. Just the way they always were.

For a brief moment, I zoned out trippily, even though she was still on the other end. I had to be honest with myself. Mad though it was, deep down, at that moment, I didn't really care about either outcome. I was oddly detached. Success was the preferred option, of course. But all that I really wanted to do, in my heart, was to please her. Make her think nice things about me, even if it was just for a short while. I was consumed with an unstoppable and irrational craving to give her good news. Like many corporate functionaries, I was in the grip of a modern phenomenon – an unnatural and slavish desire to satisfy my superiors, even if it was not in my interests to do so.

My other motivation to get through the conversation fast was fear, fear of nothingness. Of just existing. Of thinking. I just wanted to get to the next stage of the caper ASAP. I moved at 800 miles per hour, at all times: the mean velocity of a tabloid terror-ist, whether I was coming through your door to destroy your life, filing copy or irritably phoning my mum once every six months. I had so much latent nervous energy coursing through my veins that I was often charged with static, even when I was crashed out in a heap. I got electric shocks every time I got into a car. I worried so much about stories, that within two years of becoming a jour-nalist, I had a stomach ulcer. Like a German tank column, I only ever ate on the move, mostly out of 24-hour garages – Ginsters curry pasties, Lucozade to dissolve the exhaustion and a couple of Zantac popped for dessert. I had the thousand-yard stare of a soldier who couldn't take much more. My mind was so disturbed with passion and vice, I took beta blockers in an attempt to make it still. I was in my twenties.

On top of all of that, I had the impatience of a rapist – and I don't say that lightly. I myself had a conviction for Section 47 assault for pouring boiling water over a fellow degree student my girlfriend had accused of raping her. A fitting end to my gradua-tion ceremony that signaled the start of my working life. The wounds were still smarting. Not for her, I was worried my bosses would find out that I had a criminal record and it would hold me back from my jet-powered journey up the greasy pole to the top of News International. These were the degenerate impulses that powered my warped ambition. Aristotle found impatience to be a vice. The World's Biggest Selling Sunday Newspaper nurtured it as a virtue. So when Rebekah called, I just wanted to get through it and then for something else to happen, even if it meant the end. Experiencing nothingness is agony for a red-top reporter.

Rebekah carried on with her call, getting down to business: 'I've seen the pictures of the Beast of Bodmin.' She said they were amazing or something like that. The Beast of Bodmin Moor was a mythical big cat that roamed the ghostly hills of North Cornwall, according to folklore – and the local freelancers who made a few hundred quid every year selling stories about mysterious sightings. There were tales of the Beast spooking tourists with blood-curdling roars from across the moon-washed, foggy fields. During the nineties, the Beast had etched itself into the national tabloid psyche, quickly becoming the equivalent of the Loch Ness Monster for Britain's godless Generation X that also believed in crop circles. What's more, no one had ever tracked the Beast down, and papped it close up. Nor got irrefutable evidence of its existence. Except of course for Yours Truly. Earlier that day. Wow!

'They're great pictures,' Rebekah continued. She buttered me up a bit, by saying that when she had sent me down to Cornwall a fortnight or so earlier, she'd never expected me to nail the Beast, to stand the story up. High praise indeed, because at the end of the day, that's what great *News of the World* reporters did week-in, week-out – they stood up stories that were impossible to stand up. They made their own luck. They beat the odds.

'But we've all had a good laugh,' she went on, turning subtly. My spider senses picked up the tremors. Rebekah had a unique talk-round trick, one that would take her right to the apex of the News Int. pyramid. She often spoke through a wry smile that laced you up with condescension. This had the effect of locking both parties of the conversation into a narrow relationship of superior – inferior. She was also nimble enough never to allow her prey to move away from the submissive role. However, here was the rub – Rebekah used the sealed confines of this channel to love-bomb her target like a cult leader. She made them feel like they were the only person in the world.

Rebekah said something like: 'I can take a joke like everyone else. But c'mon, the joke's over now. We've all got a sense of humour here, in the office . . .'

These conversations were always very tricky because each party was trying to suss the other person out, decoding the nuances. Then she tried to outflank me.

'By the way, I've got the phone on loudspeaker.' She was bringing in the big guns to test my mettle.

'Stuart Kuttner's sitting in with me . . .'

Kuttner jogged in with a 'Hello Graham' in his clipped, whiney voice, an East End drawl that had been machined for full spectrum dominance by elocution lessons. Stuart Kuttner. Known amongst the reporters as Cuntner. Or simply The Cunt. By day, the Screw's Managing Editor. By night powerful Fleet Street fixer.

At that point I realised for definite that Rebekah was trying to blag me. Kuttner – a sense of humour? He looked like someone who slept on a stainless steel mortuary slab. He may have been one of Murdoch's Angels – the inner sanctum of British consigliere that had helped the proprietor build up his empire from the early days – but he had deathly, sunken eyes and a blank expression.

I also noticed Kuttner had used my name in his opening gambit; he was trying to be nice. But, at the same time, obviously taking the Beast of Bodmin issue very seriously. There's no way he'd want to be sucking up to me with a first name unless he had good reason to.

Rebekah carried on with her patter: 'If you say to me, "It was all a joke – we took the pictures for a prank," then that's fine. No harm done and we can move on and everyone can forget about it.'

She had sprung her first trap. Like all the best blags, it was half crude/half clever. She wasn't confronting me directly, by asking outright if the pics were spoofed-up. That would be seen as a gratuitous frontal assault on my integrity. *News of the World* reporters were assumed to have impeccable credentials. In truth, executives rarely challenged the integrity of reporters directly because it was a no-go area. Simply because many of us had no integrity at all. We lied for a living, cheated members of the public and broke the law routinely. Direct questions threatened to penetrate the Chinese Walls that were supposed to protect executives from contamination. The same nuclear-strength, labyrinthian walls behind which executives stood for so long during the phone-hacking scandal that blew up 15 years later.

Rebekah was trying to coax me into an admission by using the sugar-coated joke-line as bait. That was the crude part. She was also giving me a pretend outro, by claiming that if I said it was a joke, then all would be forgiven. That was the carrot. But of course, she was lying on all counts. The situation was already out of control. If I said this was all a joke, it would have meant instant dismissal.

Back against the wall, I would have to try and blag her that it was all true. The problem was Brooks was a top blagger as well. She'd started out as doe-eyed secretary on *Sunday*, the *News of the World*'s glossy celeb supplement. Seven years later she was the Deputy Editor of the paper. And everyone knew she was being groomed for a top slot in the corporation.

It's hard to blag a blagger. But I launched into it anyway. First of all, I deferentially confirmed to her that my sighting of the Beast of Bodmin wasn't a joke. Humbly, I said that it was all true and the pics were genuine. I played a little hard done-by, as a result of her attempts to undermine me, but not too much because that would have been to show disrespect. To disagree with what your superior had said, even when she was trying to trap you, was political suicide.

Following my denial, I then started to tell her the story of how I'd managed to track down the Beast of Bodmin so that it could be photographed. It was a whopper of a tale that involved a six-foot-long puma jumping out of a bush and going for me. At the right points in the yarn, to heighten the drama, I let the blag breathe. But during the adventurous bits, I machine-gunned the words into the phone, reacting to and embracing what Rebekah was asking and saying, the two of us twisting and turning in an elaborate merry dance. I paced the floor animatedly like a big cat stalking its prey, throwing all my effort into convincing her. The excitement of the story contrasted with the depressing backdrop of the room – the bog floor selfishly littered with piles of dumped newspapers. A half-eaten Full English on a wood-effect tray. An unmade, wanked-in bed. The trademark hotel detritus of the Lone Wolf reporter on the road.

The story was very far-fetched but she went for it anyway and at the end of the conversation I was sure that I had persuaded her that the pics were real. I can't claim all the credit for her swallowing it, though. The reason was simple – she wanted the Beast of Bodmin to be true. She was desperate for it to be true. This week she was in charge. The real *News of World* Editor Phil Hall was away on holiday and she was in the hot seat. She wanted a big story to kick off with. She wanted to have an impact. She wanted his fucking job. The whole Beast of Bodmin scenario had been her idea in the first place. It was on her direct orders that I'd been sent down here, dressed as Sherlock Holmes, for fuck's sake. Now that it had worked out, she wanted to claim all the credit. Who was going to spoil the fairy tale? I certainly wasn't. Silently, and without expressing it explicitly, it seemed we had agreed to believe in each other. In my mind, a manufacture of consent had been consummated.

1

Star Wars on Earth

Two years earlier, my job interview at the *News of the World* had been secretive and shadowy. I entered through a side-door, so that I wouldn't be seen. Straight into a rat-run of roller-shuttered filing cabinets that gave me cover until I got to a blacked-out room in the corner of the office.

Many years later, in the fourth line of her resignation letter, Rebekah Brooks spoke of 'her desire to remain on the bridge' as she exited this room for the last time. The newsroom looked like the bridge on the Death Star – a grey, airless state-of-the-art office bathed in 100 per cent unnatural light. An ominous hum lurked in the background – hushed voices, subdued ringtones and the tapping of keyboards. The audible holocaust of lives being destroyed by remote all round Britain. Well-groomed functionaries glided purposefully between green screens on long Formica-topped workstations, arranged in parallel, like a war room. An all-pervasive terror emanated from the aloof, powerful executives bunkered up in the glass offices around the perimeter. Some of the reporters dared to look up at me as I hurried past. What were they thinking? Were they quietly praying for my soul as I entered their lair? No, I knew what they were thinking: 'Who is this scruffy cunt – and is he after my job?' This was the black heart of the Evil Empire – and I craved to be part of it.

Fortress Wapping was largely windowless and cashless. Security doors on permanent lockdown. Red signs in the corridor warned of threats and attacks because of 'the business we are in'. Like the Death Star, the atmosphere was drenched in fear and repression. Dread so powerful at times, so tangible, that it weighed down on the bodies of reporters like the atmospheric pressure under the ocean, often crushing them.

A good example was Sean Hoare, the former *Screws* whistle-blower who was found dead during the middle of the hacking scandal. I first met Sean around Christmas 1995, a few weeks after my job interview. He was a showbiz reporter at the *Sun*. He was a laddish, rough-and-tumble journo who often arrived to work falling out of the back of a builder's van. He was ideally placed to ride the wave of the *Loaded* generation that had just broken into mainstream popular culture. Sean was dating a gorgeous, shiny-haired secretary in my department. Noel Gallagher's mobile was keyed into his Nokia 2120 and he was high on life.

A few years later when I last saw him, Sean was rattling like a smack-head. He had the body of a doddering, Alzheimered-up pensioner. Speech slurring Ozzy Osbourne-style, and I could see slo-mo thoughts framed on his face, thoughts that he found frustratingly difficult to express. He had the kind of bag-head teeth – blackened and corroded by cocaine acids – that you only find on a working girl banging it out on the street.

As someone who had been in theatre with him, I recognised the symptoms of the Fleet Street equivalent of Gulf War Syndrome – the limp unfocused gaze, the soul shrivelled by years of lying for a living, darkened by the abuse of cruel, torturous bosses that had left this hulk of a man timid like a runt dog. Then the injustice of being disposed off when he had passed his use-by date. Cause: driven to drink and drugs by the constant pressure to deliver stories. Verdict: bullied to death by News International.

Back on the bridge, my 'job interview' was about to begin. Enter Darth Vader. Feature's Editor Ray Levine. Today's interrogator. I was guided to a black leather chair, rammed tight up to his paperless desk. A glaring table lamp shone in my eyes, so close I could feel the heat on my cheeks. Slivers of fluorescent rays, from the blinds that fronted his office, dramatically striped parts of the room by the door, giving it the appearance of a death row cell in an old black and white film. But these were quickly extinguished as the door shut tight, until Ray Levine was reduced to an amorphous umbra in the shady recesses of the room. Moving around me like a CIA inquisitor at Guantanamo Bay.

Foolishly, I had brought along a cuttings folder, photocopies of my previous stories to show off. I was very proud of them – Ray fucked them off immediately. Ray was a dark-skinned Iranian of Jewish heritage with an incongruously boyish grin. I'd known a few Israelis and like them, Ray was tough, cocky and loud.

'What type of stories do you like doing?' he asked, without looking at me and busy doing five other things. It was a Saturday afternoon. The next day's paper was being put to bed and Ray was hunched over his laptop, answering last minute subs' queries, legals and niggly demands from the Editor.

'I like turning people over, stitch ups – drugs, vice that kind of thing,' I replied deferentially. 'I've also done a lot of brothel stories.' Referring to a genre of journalism that I would later come to know as 'investigations'.

Dan Collins, the Deputy Features Editor, stood over me and picked up a handful of my cuttings. I didn't let his cherubic Harry Potter-face deceive me. His bookish, straightforward manner masked a paper-cut wit and an unnerving eye for detail. He looked more like a Cityboy than a junior news exec – double-cuffed, stripy shirt, dark suit, textured leather shoes. Murdoch paid his officer class well.

'Why haven't you got the originals?' he fired at me, referring to the copies I'd shadily made from the office cuts' book the day before. Dan was probing to see if I was blagging it. To suss out if

I'd ripped off someone else's exclusives to pass them off as my own.

'No time,' I said. The sub-text of the answer was this – I spend every waking hour booting in doors and chasing stories – no time to make a fucking scrapbook of them. Not *Blue Peter*, mate.

Dan parried: 'How come you haven't got any bylines on these stories then?'

He was just trying to rattle me – he knew very well that lowly-paid agency reporters rarely got credited for their hard graft.

Dan scanned a bondage story I'd done for the *Sunday Mirror* about a sado-masochist party at a club owned by former Tory Defence Minister Tom King. King hadn't known about the sex party but the fact that it had been held at one of his business addresses made it worthy of a spread. To get the story, I'd had to go under cover as a rubber fetishist, disguised in skin-tight plastic trousers and a homoerotic black string vest. I looked like the secret fourth member of Right Said Fred gone wrong. Very embarrassing, especially on my pale, battle-fatigued frame. Ray looked half-interested because of the *Screwsy* sex angle.

I told them how I had done some sneaky stills on a Canon Sure Shot of a semi-naked girl hung up on a meat hook being whipped – a difficult task in low light whilst being overlooked by pervy bouncers. Even so, Ray's expression was half 'I wouldn't wipe my arse on that story in the executive bogs down the corridor' and half 'So fucking what?' This was a Fleet Street legend who had hidden in a bedroom cupboard to catch another minister – David Mellor – shagging in his Chelsea kit (allegedly). Ray had served his time on the *Sunday Sport* in its 'London Bus Found on The Moon' heyday. *Private Eye* dubbed him Ray Latrine.

'Yes, nice one,' he said diplomatically. 'But how come you gave this to the *Sunday Mirror*? Why didn't you offer this to us first?'

'We did – we offered it to you first. Well, News anyway,' I explained naively. 'Words and pics – but they knocked it back. So we moved it on, to the *Mirror*.'

'Cunts,' he spat.

'Who? The *Sunday Mirror*?'

'No! Fucking News.'

'Oh!' I said.

'We're not fucking News. We're Features. Putting it up to them is hardly giving it to us, is it?'

I'd just walked into a political minefield. One wrong move and I'd be confined to a journalistic wheelchair for the rest of my life. I should have realised. But how was I to know? I didn't know anything about office politics anywhere, never mind at the vipers' nest that was the organ read by a quarter of all the British population. No one in my family, nor anyone I had ever known, had ever worked in an office – except a betting office. So it wasn't something that came naturally.

Later I found out that the two main editorial departments at the *NoW* – News and Features – were fierce competitors that would have gladly sent each other to the gas chambers. They sabotaged each other's stories. They doubled-up on jobs, each assigning reporters without the other knowing. They bid against each other on buy-ups. They tried to fuck each other at every turn. They robbed each other's stories. They would have robbed each other's women, if they could.

What's more, I was astonished to find out, the cut-throat rivalry was a deliberate management tool, based on the arrogance of being a market leader. The *News of the World* was so powerful that they didn't even consider rival papers like the *Sunday Mirror* and the *People* competitors. Ray wouldn't wipe his arse on them in the executive bogs down the corridor. Even though he'd earned his spurs on the *People* under Phil Hall. Phil Hall later moved to the *News of the World*, bringing Ray across with him, before becoming Editor. Rival papers' names were never mentioned. The management's ethos was: 'Well, if there's no one to compete against, we'll just have to compete against ourselves.' That's what Ray later told me, anyway.

2

Street of Shame

The interview was dragging on in newspaper terms, almost 20 minutes gone. Dan was still holding the S&M story. 'So was there any shagging at this party then?' he asked, throwing me a line, and a hand grenade at the same time. Our eyes met for a second, and then I looked away. The moment of truth. Or rather, the concealment of it that always happens when a tabloid reporter is quizzed about an undercover sex story by his peers. When quizzing another myself, I always looked for the clues that were a window onto a man's soul. The bad breath. The horrid smile. The lead forehead. Subliminal signals, put there by Mother Nature, to get the moral measure of a man. Indicators as to what had really happened in the masseur's cubicle when the tape recorder had been deliberately turned off. I wondered whether I was emanating signals of my own.

'No, just kinky stuff,' I replied, trying to brush it off. 'It's weird. That crew aren't really into sex', glancing back up at both Ray and Dan. 'It's all about power and domination.' Today, I was the gimp. I could see Ray's leathers hanging-up in the corner. He liked to ride high-powered motorbikes with sexy pictures of flowing-haired women sprayed on to the tank. The portrait was reportedly based on a voluptuous Features reporter who used to like being shagged in the executive bogs down the corridor after the paper had been put to bed. My no-sex reply was the answer Dan had wanted to hear. But not the one that answered the real question. I knew exactly what Dan had really been asking – Dan's coded question had been: 'Were you involved in any shagging at the sex party? Did you get carried away and fuck one the guests at the sex club?' This was crucial in a job interview. A *News of the World* reporter was supposed to make his excuses and leave at all times – a key trait and a test of your moral fortitude. If you got caught with your pants down on a brothel job, it would be very embarrassing for the company.

If Dan was expecting me to squirm and show my shame, then it wasn't going to happen. Like him, I was a supercool blagger. The truth was, I hadn't made my excuses and left. I'd copped off with a busty nurse who'd been dragged along to the party by a freaky couple she knew. She wasn't exactly a Miss Whiplash-type, but in a dark, damp corner of a gothic dungeon, after a few bottles of Grolsch bought with the *Sunday Mirror's* flash money, one thing had led to another. Pressed against the crumbling brickwork, the sordid action (all straight-up – no kinky stuff) had not even stopped when she had unzipped my shiny shrunken-bin-bag-style kecks and found a tape recorder stuffed down my boxies. I never wrote about that part of the story in the super-soaraway *Sunday Mirror.* How could I, when I was sermonising against these sicko creeps for staging the sex parties in the first place? And I wasn't about to mention it now either, and fuck up my shot at the title. We moved on.

'Have you got good contacts?' Ray asked. Contacts are people that tip you off about stories in return for money.

'Yes,' I said. 'I've got a good royal contact who gives me good stuff about Camilla Parker Bowles.' At that time, Camilla was having a secret affair with Prince Charles. My tipster was an eccentric antiques dealer who lived in a posh village near Camilla's family home in Melksham, Wiltshire. She'd often tip me off when Charles was making a secret visit to Camilla's house for a midnight tryst. Me and the snappers, from the agency I worked for, spent hours in the bushes outside waiting for Charles to come out. Then as his official car roared off down the muddy track, we sprung a flashgun ambush. Freezing the countryside in a silver wash of brilliant light. For a moment, it looked like a scene from *Close Encounters of the Third Kind* had come to a dark field in the middle of the English countryside.

'I've also got a few hookers on the firm,' I boasted. My main vice contact was an alcoholic, drug-user called Gina, known in the trade as a 'tart with a heart'. She worked the dismal massage parlours of market towns in Avon, Somerset and Wiltshire. Getting hoofed day-in, day-out by stinking EU-subsidised farmers and the toothless peasant underclass – the depressing reality behind the countryside's chocolate box image in which I loved to poke around. Gina hadn't exactly given me any big stories yet, but she was always hinting that she was going to blow the lid on her big fish clients – coppers, judges, celebs, the town mayor etc. I couldn't see it myself – her face was pock-marked from years of boozing, skin flaking beneath her make-up. Her body had been battered all round the Gulf States during her glory years as a high-class call girl at the time of the oil crisis – most hookers claim to know Saudi princes personally. In these leaner times, she kept the fat tyres around her waist in with a bulging Lycra vest, reeking of talc and stained with baby oil. Her appearance was a human storyboard detailing years of abuse at the hands of men, including a disfigured jaw – courtesy of a pimp – that she hid by constantly brushing her hair on to her face. I always made my excuses after a debriefing from her. However, her promise of vice exclusives was enough for me to tolerate her rambling late-night phone calls. She knew how to work a reporter and during my time I would go through many Gina-style informants.

On a Sunday newspaper you live and die by your contacts. That's because you can't rely on news to fill the paper – leave that to the dailies. Sunday reporters work mainly on 'off-diary' stories. Some reporters are technically brilliant and can do 100 words-per-minute Teeline shorthand. They give good copy and cover press conferences accurately. For me, that was like watching paint stay wet. I had learned shorthand on my post-grad NCTJ course – but quickly gibbed it. I spent the early part of my career trying to remember what people had said or making it up. The only shorthand I possessed was the contemptuous nicknames I had for the subjects of my stories. Members of the public were known as tools, bell-ends and ball-bags. It was a simple device to dehumanise my prey. I had the perfect tabula rasa short-term memory for crunching up pop culture and spitting it out again – a blank. If a story had male and female subjects – for instance a couple involved in a 'shagging' story – I referred to the man as Jimmy Pisspot and the woman as Jenny Pisspot. These were the tools of my trade.

However, what I did possess was Factor X. A mythical quality possessed by an elite corps of hard news journalists. The ability to sniff out a story within seconds. Lock on to the person in the room who's got it and tease it out of them with a talk-round. I was a doorstep king. Factor X was the journalistic equivalent of The Force in *Star Wars*. Mainly it was about getting people to like you and to talk to you. Hard to identify but one journalist who's got Factor X in bundles is the legendary former *Daily Mirror* writer John Pilger. His articles, books and docos are dripping in Factor X. The only problem was I later identified the magic ingredient of Factor X – and it turned out to be the truth. The irony was that Factor X got me a job at the *News of the World*, but it was like a deal with the Devil. To actually succeed in tabloids from then on in, I would have to lie, squandering my Factor X on the way. The law of diminishing returns. Law of the Red-Top jungle – destroying the thing that had created me.

Like most things in newspapers, the job interview was short and sweet and on-the-seat-of-your-pants. Now and again, Ray jumped up from his spring-loaded seat and shouted out on to the floor. Things like: 'What the fuck's this? What's such-and-such saying about that story?' directed at a terrified reporter, or 'For fuck's sake, what the fuck is going on?' etc. Basically, Ray didn't have time for all this job interview bollocks. All that he wanted to know about a prospective reporter was whether he was:

1. No hassle – low maintenance.
   That I'm not going to bother anyone with daft talk of a chair to sit on on my first day. Or directions to the canteen. Or ask things like: 'Do I press 9 for an outside line?'
   And for the duration of my employment I'm not going to ask about holidays, contracts, car parking passes or pensions.

2. The Right Stuff.
   That I've got the resourcefulness of an SAS soldier trapped behind enemy lines. Coupled with the prison cunning of a gang member in a Detroit superjail.

3. Resilience.
   That I've got the fortitude of an American fighter pilot shot down over Hanoi who gets his leg broken by a mob of angry rice farmers and is then imprisoned in a semi-submerged rat cage for five years – in solitary. To endure privation without complaint.

4. On the Ball.
   That when Ray shouts out of his office at random: 'Get me Madonna's person on the line,' I'm not going to say, 'Have you got a number? Who is that? Do you want her agent or press officer?' You just do it. Fast.

5. Right Ideology.
   The fact that I'm sitting in an office at News Int. for a job interview proves that I've got the professional qualifications to do the job. But all professionals have to have the right attitude. In this case, it was subordination, deference and

complete realignment of my goals in line with those of Rupert Murdoch and his agents. I would never question any viewpoint or show any moral objection to any story whatsoever.

6. Hunger.
That I was as desperate to succeed. Ravenous, like a Cuban refugee drug dealer who'd just landed in 1980s Miami. The World Is Yours.

7. Fear.
Fear is the fuel that drives the tabloid news industry. In some newsrooms such as the *Sunday Mirror*'s, it's an undercurrent, a covert but menacing presence that keeps everyone running around, looking busy. But at the *Screws* it's a cardinal passion. Terror is as much a part of the corporate culture as footballer-shagging stories and the Fake Sheik. Fear is glorified. The more fear that managers could conjure up from the alchemy of corporate hierarchy, the better – fear of not getting a story, fear of my boss, fear of my colleagues, fear of a rival department, fear that when I get back from a week's holiday my swipe card will have been cancelled, fear that I can't talk too loud, fear that the all-important story confession will not have 'come out on tape,' fear that my indiscretions won't stay a secret, fear that I will be sued.

The great thing was, I was a friend of fear. I knew fear. Fear blackened the edges of my thoughts like a sheet of paper on fire. I was a child of Thatcher. Brought up in a recession. Steeled in a furnace of decimated lives, mass unemployment and deindustrialisation. My dad had been made redundant from an aluminium factory. My mum worked like a donkey as a part-time settler in a bookie's. My motivation wasn't even fear of failure – that was a luxury reserved for podgy grammar school kids. It was fear of not having a job. Full stop. Fear of poverty. As a child the only life lesson that was drilled into me was simple – get a fucking job. That's all that matters.

Work. Work. Work. Any job. It didn't matter which one. I never wanted to be a journalist – it was just a job.

8. Story-getting.
   That you can self-generate and deliver world exclusive stories week after week.

9. Story-getting..
   That you can self-generate and deliver fucking great world exclusive stories week after week

10. Story-getting..
    That you can self-generate and deliver big fuck-off mind-blowing world exclusive stories week after fucking week. After fucking week. Until you fuck up then it's down the road, no questions asked.

3

Pressure

Like most first days at work, my induction into life at the paper that sold 3.5 million copies every week was a high-pressure, uncomfortable experience. Traditionally, the working week at a Sunday newspaper begins on a Tuesday morning, at the relatively leisurely hour of 10 am. But at the *News of the World*, even back then, the atmosphere felt like a trading floor on Black Monday when the Asian markets had just opened up. As soon as I walked in, head well down, I could sense crisis building. Few of the reporters looked up – they were agitated and tetchy. Fraught with the kind of latent irascibility that I'd only ever come across doing stories about the long-term homeless and the ritually abused. I could tell, within seconds, that I had already become a burden. No breaks for the FNG. I didn't have a desk or a computer and when I asked a reporter called Helen Carter 'Where's good?' she nodded exasperatedly at the chair opposite. Carter was fiercely competitive and resented giving me the marginal advantage of work space. She ended up working for the *Guardian*. I remained a refugee for many months long before hot-desking became the feng shui of corporate cost-cutting.

I soon discovered the reason for the bad vibes when a pretty secretary called Tara suddenly stood up and shouted 'Conference'. Conference was the name of the weekly meeting between the writers and Features Editor Ray Levine. Each reporter was expected to pitch at least three story ideas 'for edition' – i.e. for that Sunday's paper. So if you're a celebrity or politician, whose life has been napalmed by the *Screws*, and have ever wondered where the beginning of the end began – it started here in conference, in a blank room overlooking two high-rise blocks of flats in Tower Hamlets.

Each story idea broadly had to have the following attributes. Firstly, it had to be totally exclusive. Then it had to be stand-upable within a week. That meant that all of the journalistic bits could be turned-around relatively quickly, including evidence-gathering, 'chats' with the main characters and getting pics. Most importantly, the story also had to clear the *News of the World*'s extremely high 'wow-factor' bar. No mean feat, considering the *Screws*' inglorious history of breaking big stories.

I looked around and felt the walls crowding in. The *News of the World* newsroom was adorned with intimidating illuminated light boxes showing off former front pages. Battle honours and scalps. 'Tory Boss Archer Pays Off Vice Girl' from 1987. Another displayed huge snatch pictures of Princess Diana and a shifty-looking Will Carling sharing a secret tryst. The effect of these adverts was like being screamed at by a regimental sergeant major letting me know exactly what's expected of me in conference. From 1910, there was a whole front page dedicated to the capture of Dr Crippen. Next to a six-foot-tall bus shelter-style hoarding with the headline: 'Confessions of Christine,' about the hooker at the centre of the Profumo scandal from 1963. 'Di's Cranky Phone Calls to Married Tycoon' – another headline framed in a smaller picture. Like natural light, no art or painting was allowed into the newsroom. Brainwashing tabloid propaganda was the only form of visual stimulation. On closer inspection, the strip-lights inside were littered with dead flies.

I followed a long line of depressed reporters past the rows of filing cabinets that I'd sneaked through on the way to my 'job interview'. Ray let us stew outside of the locked meeting room like a group of sixth formers waiting to sit an A-Level physics exam. Over the next few months I watched grown men turn white with fear at this point. One female reporter burst into tears. And that was even before the roastings kicked off.

A features writer called Dominic Mohan nodded a hello to me. Mohan had an Oasis-style bowl haircut. Before getting a job at the *News of the World*, he had been the youngest ever Editor of a national newspaper, when aged 21, he had taken over the *Sunday Sport*. Porn king David Sullivan had given him the top job based on Mohan's record of bagging big exclusives such as 'Monkey Lands Plane'. Mohan didn't seem to be arsed about the pressure of conference. Seconds earlier I'd watched him repeatedly replay a tape recording out loud on his office cassette machine. It contained the words 'electrical pylon' many times. It was either part of a taped interview, or a phone message that had been left by a 'nutter' over the weekend. 'Nutters' are readers that write illiterate letters to newspapers, or obsessively phone up about Elvis sightings and conspiracy theories. Mohan's looped taped recording of cranks had a surreal, comical effect in the black atmosphere before conference. He went on to become editor of the *Sun*.

I noticed that there were several veterans from the *Sunday Sport*. A sardonic, laid-back loner called Paul 'Mucky' McMullan took the piss out of my green woollen suit – even though he was much scruffier than me. Paul was a typical *NoW* reporter – an oddball-outsider defined by a kind of rootlessness found in army kids that moved around a lot during childhood. I don't know whether he was an army kid, but Mucky was completely straightforward about the absurdity of the job. He went on to become a phone hacking advocate and TV pundit made famous by his on-screen clashes about tabloid ethics with comedian Steve Coogan and Hacked Off film fop Hugh Grant.

To kill time, as I waited outside in the corridor, I looked back

into the newsroom through the slits in the blinds. Over the
no-man's-land of the back bench, I could make out the news
department digging in for the week. Their top boys were confident and relaxed. Jimmy 'the whisperer' Weatherup, talking with
his hand over mouth in case his colleagues could lip read. The
Ukrainians Greg Miskiw and Alex Marunchak. Greg later left his
wife and kids for a fitter, younger freelancer called Terenia Taras.
Alex set up a company to import vodka from the mother country
but later said that the business didn't take off. A *Today* refugee
called Ian Edmondson. Neville Thurlbeck and Clive Goodman
were deep in conversation. A tall, vivacious red-head interrupted
them and I could see the body-language of the men smarm into
servility at once.

'Who's that?' I asked McMullan.

'Rebekah.' No one ever used her surname. She had it all –
power, looks and she was still only my age. A real-life Lois Lane.
Marunchak would later describe the news team I was looking at
through the window as the best he'd ever seen at *News of the World*
– a gilded generation. All of them would later be arrested on
suspicion of phone hacking – including Greg's racy new bird.

Back to reality. Ray arrived for conference, grinning sadistically, his shark-like grin matching his pressed white shirt. About
ten reporters squashed in around a bleak pine table in a cold
room. Plastic jugs of tea and coffee were served by an African
woman. Ray put a custard cream between his teeth before looking
around for his first victim.

'OK who wants to start?' he boomed. No takers.

'OK, then let's kick off with you, Roger – what you got, Rog?'

Roger Insall was a professional paedophile-hunter. Short, perma-
tannned and a teddy boy's quiff toned-down for the office. The
middle-aged former-*People* reporter spent his working days posing
as a nonce in Sri Lanka, Thailand, Cambodia and Goa, entrapping
Big Fat Westerners who liked to have sex with pre-teen 'beach boys'.

'I've got a good dogging story,' Roger began, before going into
the details of his next sting. Roger the Dodger, as he was known,

was a one-man vice search engine, whose water-cooler conversations were cluster-bombed with references to orgies, swinging parties and tarts. He spoke non-stop about snuff movies, gunrunners and kiddie porn as though it was normal, in the same way a mother would talk about her kids' schools or one of the lads would go on about last night's footie. But his seedy fanaticism paid off – he repeatedly broke big exclusives and was credited with coming up with idea of the Fake Sheik.

As part of his cover story, Roger had successfully morphed into looking a bit like the degenerate predators he exposed. He was dripping with sleaze and gold trinkets. But tabloid journalism had not only taken a toll on his appearance – it seemed he'd paid a heavy price on the inside too. There was something dark in his soul, not in criminal way, but it was clear he'd seen too much of the demonic side of humanity and some of the residue had seeped in. Roger finished off with a couple of fillers, before Ray said, 'The dogging story sounds good – speak to me later.' Sensitive material was always dealt with one-to-one in Ray's office afterwards.

It wasn't long before it was my turn.

'OK, Halloween's coming up,' I said. 'What about a Halloween brothel story? There's a massage parlour in Bristol that's got a special offer for the 31st October. The girls dress up as witches. They decorate the rooms with turnips with candles in, that kind of thing . . .'

'No,' said Ray, cutting me off.

'Fuck,' I thought. That was a banker – a straightforward vice exposé. *News of the World* bread and butter. I'd scanned the small ads of the local papers to find that one – and if that particular massage parlour didn't work out I'd planned on bunging my hooker snout Gina a few quid to get one of her mates to mock it up, just to make sure of my debut piece.

'Next,' Ray said.

I hit him with my next three ideas, which I had saved up and secretly squirrelled away during my last weeks at the agency. With each 'no/next' the anxiety increased. I couldn't understand why – all of them were decent stories. I even put up a Royal belter about

Camilla that I'd got off my posh antiques dealer. I later realised that Ray knocked this one back because of politics – he was careful not to tread on Royal reporter Clive Goodman's toes. Further down the line I had to drop my Royal contacts altogether so as not to upset Clive. Like most *NoW* reporters, Clive was territorial. He believed that empire-building offered protection. Ten years later, Clive was the first reporter to be jailed over phone hacking after he listened to Prince William's advisor's messages. Conference was devastating – it turned out my ideas were good daily stories that would have waltzed into the *Sun* or the *Mirror*, but they just didn't have the depth of a decent Sunday tale. I knew I'd have to get it together fast or it was back to the regions in disgrace.

I didn't get a bollocking – even Ray would have looked bad kicking the puppy round the room on its first day out of the pet shop, despite the baying crowd of News hoodies egging him on. But he was certainly snarling at me a bit. Later, I walked past his open door. He was sat there in his office, his face half in shadow, like a crazed *Clockwork Orange* droog. Head tilted into his chest, so that his face was almost in the horizontal plane. Eyes glaring at me through his brows, mouth open. He looked like an electro-shocked Jack Nicholson in *One Flew Over the Cuckoo's Nest*. I could tell what he was thinking: 'What a fucking let-down. You talked a good game in the interview, giving it all the nuclear news Jedi stuff, but on the day of reckoning, you crumbled in the ring like a big girl.'

I was harder still on myself. I began to doubt my abilities. Was I really any good at this job? Or was I just another, 'I have recently' merchant. 'I have recently' merchants were the journeymen offspring of Britain's media-obsessed middle class, who bombarded news editors with CV cover letters that almost always began with the phrase 'I have recently . . .' Take your pick, as to what followed – 'finished my internship at the *Guardian*/come back from my gap year teaching windsurfing on the Nile/got a first in PPE at Oxbridge.' All of this meaningless over-achievement drew howls of derision from the talentless eccentrics who hacked out a living in the newsroom. Consequently, the 100g vellum cream-laid paperwork upon which the CVs had been obsequiously typed, got binned immediately. Such-like Fleet Street failures inevitably faced a life of humiliation and despair – they often ended up working for the BBC.

My conference fuck-up got me thinking – was I too just another overblown twerp who would end up running around White City in a North Face jacket with a furry hood on, a pair of combat trousers and bright blue Gazelle trainers? Was I just another beautiful person who couldn't face getting a proper job down the plastics factory? Or was I the hard news guerilla killer that I thought I was? Trained at the *News of the World*'s secret training camp in Libya. Behind Enemy Lines and Licensed to Thrill.

Dep.Feat.Ed. Dan lifted my spirits. 'Don't worry,' he said. 'You did all right today. Ray's a tough operator – but he isn't that bad compared to some of the editors I've worked for.' Dan was good at telling stories – his own was pretty good. He was 'discovered' by former *Sun* Editor Kelvin MacKenzie after his plane was delayed at a Midland's airport and Kelvin was flicking through the *Coventry Evening Telegraph* where he came across a showbiz exclusive written by Dan when he was a cub reporter. Dan was summoned down to the Smoke immediately to work for *Bizarre*.

Dan carried on with his story to cheer me up. 'One day, when I was on the *Sun*, my mate was so terrified of getting a bollocking off Kelvin that he pretended to faint in his office, hoping that Kelvin would show mercy and stop roasting him.'

'What happened?' I asked

'Kelvin carried on bollocking him as he dropped to the floor. Then he leaned down to get right into his face, wagging his finger at him and telling him that he'd fucked up. My mate was still laying there pretending to be unconscious.'

'Fuck's sake,' I laughed, buzzing off the anecdote. Everyone loved a bollocking story.

'What happened next?'

'Kelvin then stepped over his body and walked out into the newsroom, leaving my mate to be carried back to his desk. Still pretending to be out for the count.'

4

Stories

Over the next few months I learned that the key to getting through conference was to have a range of different stories. From then on, in the mix, I always put in one sex story, one feature idea and one showbiz exclusive.

Sex stories have several sub-classes. In short, they are simply excuses to get pictures of pretty girls into the paper. 'Curtain twitchers' are essentially minor sex-in-the-suburbs scandals. A good example of a bog-standard curtain twitcher is a story that I put up in conference headlined, 'BMW Beauty Also Available in Blue.' The list line is self-explanatory. 'An elegant receptionist who greets well-heeled customers and their excited little children as they arrive to look over their latest expensive BMW cars leads a secret life as a sordid porn queen.'

The story was no more than a vehicle to show pics of 36A-23-34 Verity Blain, 23, in 'disgusting, tawdry' spanking mags. Note the inherent hypocrisy of this sleight of hand. I assumed the reason behind the desire to show naughty pics was to thrill (i.e. give a semi-on) to the *News of the World*'s 3.64 million male readers. In 1997, 27 per cent of Britain's population read the paper – over half of them men, the majority being C2, D and E working-class lads in their mid thirties. The *NoW* was straightforward wank material for others – it was the most popular paper inside prisons. To expose what was essentially this girl's private life, a false justification always had to be shoe-horned into the story. In this case it was the risk that the receptionist might infect children coming to the showroom with her immorality. To counter the risk of the story being too down-market, I also made a reference to 'well-heeled' customers (respectable curtain twitchers). There was always another reason to inject posh or high-status people gratuitously into a story. As well as providing extra titillation to the cap-doffing peasant readers, newspapers were always trying to tap into a middle-market *Daily Mail* demographic – a lucrative golden fleece for advertisers.

'Shagging stories' mostly involve catching married celebrities out, who should not be shagging other people. Then of course there are kiss 'n' tells. Whatever type, there is no doubt that sex stories humiliate and demean women – that is their strategic function in a male-dominated society. However, some newspapers were much more no-nonsense in their desire to mess with women's heads and encourage sexual violence. They gorged themselves on what's known as 'rape stories'. The *News of the World* didn't use rape to titillate their readers, but another Sunday newspaper did – shamelessly. When I was an agency reporter, before I got a job on the *Screws*, on most Friday nights we received a call from an obscene degenerate on a Sunday newspaper who asked, 'Have you got any good rape stories?' The bosses of the agency refused to take his calls because he operated at such a low level.

But as a junior reporter, I was left to handle it. 'I'm doing a ring round for hard sex stories,' he went on. 'Any good rapes in court this week?' If the answer was yes, the questions that followed were appalling. 'Where did he give her one?' 'What's the girl like – is she fit?' 'What was she wearing at the time?' And of course, 'Was she asking for it?' I read out summaries of the court reports over the phone. I always imagined him at the end line, masturbating instead of taking notes.

Most of the reporters around the conference table had lots of pages ripped hastily from that day's *Sun*, *Daily Mirror* and *Daily Mail*. This was because they wanted to pitch 'follow-ups' of big stories in the news that week. I was always amazed by eagle-eyed reporters who could spot an obscure name in a story of a witness to some event. The idea would be to get a full chat and a new line out of them.

Other classic features included 'good reads'. For instance straightforward backgrounders on famous people. Then there are thematic stories. These are exclusive stunt stories that aim to ride the news zeitgeist that particular week. For instance, I remember a film called *Jerry Maguire* starring Tom Cruise was all over the papers. It was a rom-com drama about a sports agent.

This was a rare, easy steal in conference.

'On the back of *Jerry Maguire*,' I mused, 'why don't we find a real-life Jerry in Britain?'

Ray: 'Good idea.'

'I'll do a ring round of Britain's top ten football agents and scrabble together some of their anecdotes – money, pressure, sex etc.'

Ray: 'Love it.' Features Editors love these ideas because they are cheap, easy and non-libelous. But beware – reporters who routinely put 'furniture' up were considered coasters. I remember two, highly-paid, middle-aged feature writers who relied on 'set-pieces' to get them through conference. Ray mauled them.

'No. That's not going to work!'

Or 'For fuck's sake, have you checked cuts? That's been done . . . etc.' Woe betide anyone who put up a story that had already 'made'. Times were changing. With their dark blue suits and shiny shoes, they looked like early retirement coppers who hadn't solved a crime for a good long while. Looking at me with contempt – I had been brought in as a child labourer on McDonald's wages to see them off. I looked at them back. They were like Spitfire pilots with tombstones in their eyes. They weren't coming back from the dogfight and everyone knew it. On the other hand, I was coming back like the Red Baron with a fuselage full of stickers – lives destroyed. Including theirs. A few weeks later they had been 'disappeared'.

Sometimes, after conference, Ray would launch into a mass bollocking: 'That was fucking shit. Most of your ideas are fucking rubbish. I want three more ideas off each of you before lunch time. Ring round your contacts and get some good fucking stories. I don't know what the fuck is going on here – you're getting lazy. If this is the best you can do . . .' etc, etc.

I didn't get anything in the paper the first week. If I fucked up in the second week as well then I'd almost certainly get whacked. In *Star Wars*, before he strangles one of his admirals, Lord Vader tells the victim, 'You have failed me for the last time.' Ray Levine was less forgiving – you only had to fail him the first time, never mind a second. A few weeks later a young Welsh girl started one Tuesday. Before lunch time, on the second or third day, she had been liquidated. For being no more than a few minutes late, and 'not taking the job seriously enough'. She explained that she'd been up all night shagging a solicitor she'd met, understandably excited to be in London for the first time. She was bundled out of the office, her hair a mess, the contents of her handbag spilling out on the way. A stony-faced junior executive called Denna Allen kept shouting after her, 'Can you just leave the office now?' over and over again. I winced when a pretty girl was publicly humiliated. Maybe I didn't see that kind of thing so much because society, like their dads, tends to put little princesses on a pedestal. I suppose, in that way, in the looks stakes, the *Screws* was at least meritocratic. I watched many doughnut probationaries start. They were known as 'shifters' – young journalists from the *Sunderland Bugle* and the *Shropshire Freesheet* and so on, who'd been invited down to the *Screws* to do a few shifts, to see if they could cut it. Most of them turned out to be big round pieces of fried flour with a hole in the middle. Solid cats-up-trees-merchants but Factor X-less and very unstreetwise. Totally unprepared for life in the big, bad city. Consequently, most would mysteriously vanish after a few days never to be seen again. I was determined to be the sharp cookie in the cake tin and deffo not the doughnut.

Luckily, Ray had taken half a shine to me and wanted to keep me on the firm.

'You'll make a good *News of the World* reporter,' he said. 'Because no one will ever fucking believe that you are one.' This was true. I was an expert at 'getting into' Britain's new burgeoning under-class (despised by Murdoch) disguised as a smack-head or a 'scally' villain. To gain the trust of the local campesinos, I went around the pubs selling batteries and razors. Shortly afterwards I did a story exposing a teenage vampire cult in Dorset whose leader slit his wrists so that spellbound schoolgirls could drink his blood whilst performing naked rituals on gravestones. Afterwards, when I went to the local nick to hand over my 'dossier of evidence' – fuck-all really – the police didn't believe who I was, and thought that I was taking the piss. I stood behind the glass panel for a while and then just got off back to London. Ray also assumed that because I was from the lower orders that I'd be good on the doorstep on the estates. One day, when everyone in the office was given a Spice girls nickname for a laugh, I was dubbed 'council Spice'.

Consequently, at the end of my second week, Ray handed me a story on a plate, which made Paul McMullan jealous because it made me look like teacher's pet. It was only a medical miracle story, about a dying dad whose wife had saved his life by donating a kidney – which turned out against all the odds to be a perfect match. Easy-peasy, bish-bash-bosh. Did the chat with the happy couple. Got them to pose up for pics with their grinning bin-lids. Filed the copy. The big problem arose when I put in a call to the 'stunned' consultant surgeon who had performed the op. Problem was that he wasn't that stunned. It was as though it was an every-day occurrence to him. He said the odds of getting a compatible organ from a spouse were in fact not that mind-blowing – 1 in

36,000 to be precise. No big deal in the high-stakes world of organ transplants. 'Fuck! That's no good.' I said. The whole story rested on the fact that the match was an astronomical, lottery win-style occurrence. The headline needed to be: 'Wife in a Million Saved My Life'. Not 'Wife in a Few Thousand'. However, the problem was easily rectified. I took a knife to the surgeon's quotes and miraculously transplanted them from 'The odds are 1 in 36,000' to 'the odds are millions and millions to one against'. Thereby standing the whole story up. I reckoned that the surgeon was unlikely to complain as the story made him look good next to a nice picture of his grin. Bang! In the paper. Front of the book spread. Job saved for another week. This was the beginning of my descent down the slippery slope

5

Dark Arts

When I started at the *NoW*, it was like becoming a 'made man' in the mafia. I got access to a secret world that I never knew existed. Vice and secrecy were the stock-in-trade. The objective was simple – the destruction of people's lives with hitman precision. The mafia use trained button men to do their dirty work. Our secret weapon was the private detective.

Sixteen years later News International Exec Chairman and super scion James Murdoch may not have liked his company being compared to the mafia. And he denied to a Parliamentary committee ever knowing about the private detectives that his company employed to smear lawyers investigating phone hacking. But for me, working at the *Screws* was like watching a live version of *Goodfellas* streamed in real-time before my eyes in which everyone was getting leaned on. And 'enquiry agents' were the enforcers that would have made Sammy 'The Bull' Gravano wince. Not long after my first day, I was given a list of confidential numbers. One for a shed-worker gumshoe that could 'spin' phone numbers. Another for a 'blagger' – a professional impersonator/ mimic – who could deceive people into giving out valuable info on the phone. Another for an expert 'tracer' who can find the whereabouts of anyone in the world, by tracking their financial footprint. A 'sub-contractor' with a contact at the Driver and Vehicle Licensing Agency (DVLA), that could 'convert' car registrations. An ex-Customs officer, who had an insider in the passport office, who could slip out mug shots and bio data of anyone who had ever been abroad. A retired copper who could pull CROs, criminal records including confidential police intelligence reports. A mind-boggling array of 'secret squirrels' were just a phone call away.

Private detectives were like smart bombs. They enabled me to destroy people's lives with surgical impact without having to do lots of tedious legwork. Like the CIA calling in a drone strike, I didn't even have to leave the office. I had no idea papers used these 'inquiry agents', as they were called, despite having sold stories to the nationals for two years previously.

I found out by accident about one week into the job when I was desperately trying to come up with a story. As an agency reporter, I'd done quite a lot of background on the Fred and Rose West murders at the 'House of Horrors' in Gloucester. In November 1995 Rose West was sentenced to life imprisonment, so I was trying to get a new line on the story. I'd got to a former victim called Sharron Compton, who claimed that she'd been raped by Fred in a satanic ritual – complete with red satin robes and all that. Sharron had a few issues – she was hard work and morbidly fascinated with the sense of control that being at the centre of a story gave her. In addition, I'd spoken to another 'one-that-got-away,' a fucked-up lesbian who claimed that the case opened up a can of worms. Through scary, piercing eyes she hinted that the multiple murders were linked to an underground network of necrophiliacs who traded in dead bodies out of the back door of mortuaries. All far-fetched, gruesome stuff – but the depths of the Wests' depravity knew no bounds so I had to check it out. The witnesses had given me the possible second names of other people that I needed to track down in Bournemouth and

Wiltshire, in the hope of corroborating their stories, and giving me more info. I needed to find numbers for one of them quickly so I could do a quick 'phoner' with them and arrange a sit-down interview if it was worth following up.

Usually in newspaper offices, at that time, there was a cupboard with dozens of chunky phone directories in them. Phone books were the first places to start. I asked the Features secretary Tara. She looked surprised and showed me to a little shelf with a couple of out-of-date blue BT books on them. The Yellow Pages were ripped to shreds, so it was clear that no one really relied upon them.

I phoned 192 directory enquiries, but I didn't have a full name, and the number I wanted was probably ex-d anyway. In those pre-internet days, when 'a tablet' referred to an ecstasy pill and not an iPad, there was only one way to track people down – by hitting the streets. Firstly, I phoned the local papers in Wiltshire and Hampshire, to see if they had a number or address of the people I was looking for. I never liked doing this because it risked tipping off the local journos, who would often double-bubble you to their contacts on the *Sun* and the *Sunday Mirror* and so on. Plus a lot of local reporters were useless doughnut time-wasters anyway. It looked like I'd have to hit the road. Go to the local libraries in person, wade through the electoral registers to find a proper address. Often the info was out of date, so then I'd have to pull a birth or marriage certificate from the local register office. All very tedious, time-consuming and expensive. I'd put the stories up to Ray in conference on Tuesday – I'd have to deliver by Friday, so I didn't really have two days to fuck about with, knocking on doors all over the countryside. Just then Ray walked briskly over and looked at the phone book as though it was a curiosity from a more genteel era.

'Take this number down,' he said. 'His name is Steve Whittamore. He's a PI.'

On the other end of the line was a jovial, avuncular voice with a dry wit. Steve lived in a sunny part of Hampshire on the coast.

He had a gentle but mischievous sense of humour that was a refreshing ray of light in the tricky atmosphere at the *News of the World*. We hit it off immediately. I gave Steve the surname of the person I was trying to trace.

'Do you know where they live?' Steve asked. I gave him the name of the approximate cities and towns where I thought they might be.

'All I know,' I said, 'is that one of them is in Wiltshire and she's a woman in her mid thirties and she's probably married.'

Within half an hour he was back on with an ex-directory phone number.

'Do you want anything else?' he asked.

'What like?' I said

'Well, I've got her address, and the names and ages of the woman and everyone who lives at that house with her.'

In 30 minutes, he'd traced a target that it would have taken me two days to find in a previous life – saving me a 200-mile round trip to Wiltshire and a ball-aching day of banging doors looking for people who like to have sex with dead bodies.

Steve was basically at the centre of a spider's web of secret inquiry agents. Each one had a crafty speciality. For instance, in Salisbury, Steve knew an investigator whose talent was relieving mobile phone companies, including British Telecom, of their data. The sub-contractors could have dealt direct with us, but because Steve was such an amenable and trustworthy person, they all bounced off him. He was a front-of-house broker for Britain's network of shady data pirates. I began to use Steve on almost every story that I worked on and found out the full reach of his services.

On the next story I used Steve to do some tracing. He didn't even need a proper name to find people. Flaky newspaper tipsters, who frequently overheard stories in the gym or at work, would often give me the wrong names of targets, or at least dodgy phonetic spellings. No matter. Steve routinely found these long-shots using a combination of intuition and experience. A wide Area Search cost £60 a throw. If I gave him an old address of a target, he could do a 'trace on' to a new or current address, and then back again to almost every previous address they had lived at since they were 17, the age at which they generally appear as adults on electoral rolls. This historical data was a goldmine. If I was digging up dirt on a celebrity, I could find old girlfriends, ex-wives and secret love-children. Alternatively, if I was working on a murder case, I could quickly find out where the parents of the victim lived, along with current addresses for brothers and sisters, so that they could be 'death knocked' literally before the body got cold. By the time the pack turned up, the *News of the World* had the 'buy-up' in a hotel eating prawn sandwiches, watching Sky News and dreaming about the holiday in Spain bought with our blood money.

Steve owed his sorcery to the Square Mile in the City. He told me that he'd learned his trade whilst working as a financial investigator in the '70s and '80s. He would track people down that owed money to the wealthy businesses that made up his client base. Some of this could be done perfectly legally by accessing files at Companies House, which holds the names, addresses, and DOBs, of every limited company director in the UK.

In addition, Steve could trace people who'd deliberately hidden their identities, changed their names or gone on the run. Once I found a supergrass, who was in hiding on the police's secret witness protection programme, with a £100,000 contract on his head. Within an hour of making a call to an inquiry agent, I'd tracked the dead-man-walking down to his safe house, something two of Britain's biggest drug barons had been trying to do for years in order to iron him out.

Steve didn't just use the electoral role. He often confirmed someone was living at an address by saying: 'There's a gas bill going into that address under such-and-such's name.' He could find out who was paying for what utilities, and a whole range of credit info. If a person had a County Court Judgement (CCJ) against their name, then that might give you an idea of whether they were 'pond life' or not. The *News of the World* viewed the world in black and white – scumbags (the great unwashed mass of poor people and criminals) and posh people (middle class and above, high status and celebs).

A couple of months later I tried to buy a mobile phone for my girlfriend at Christmas, but I failed on the credit check. I kicked off in the shop, losing my temper, and seething things like: 'Do you know who I am – I'm a *News of the World* reporter?' etc. to the not-very-arsed staff. Cringe-worthy explosions of wrath were becoming normal. Not only in me, I noticed, but also in my control-freak colleagues. My new-found status, along with my belief that I could do anything by sheer force of will, was making me quick to anger. Anyway, when I calmed down, I asked Steve to spin my own address – and he found three CCJs against my name from three £400-odd-quid student loans I'd taken out to fund my 2:1 in Accountancy and Finance from Lancashire Poly. Thus proving to myself, that in the eyes of the *NoW*, I was in fact a scumbag.

Spinning numbers was also one of the most effective tricks in Steve's spell book. Like magic, the process could conjure up proof that made it possible to run stories. After a couple of months I started doing consumer investigations. I found myself in a Manchester backstreet with a giant purple 'Tinky-Winky' under my arm. In the other, I was holding two red 'Po's by the 'TV aerial' circles on their heads. Move over Woodward and Bernstein.

Eh-oh! Evil toy-trader Surinder Greual was the mastermind behind the scandal of the killer Teletubbies. Greedy Greual was just one of the many two-bit 'villains' that I 'exposed' in the *News of the World*. His crime? Grinning Greual sold cheap, counterfeit toys on market stalls. Or, by the time his story had gone through the scamulator, he flooded Britain with fake Teletubbies that could 'kill or maim a child in seconds'. Of course, this claim was a gross exaggeration. However, by the time I'd finished with him, he'd gone from being Del Boy on the street corner to a threat to national security. In many ways, a Tellytubby turnover was a perfect, bog-standard *News of the World* 'investigation'. The *NoW* may be famous for its big, set-piece exposés such as bungs to the Pakistani cricket team or the Fake Sheik–Sarah Ferguson sting. But the vast majority of people who were targeted by me and my fellow journalists were straw men. Petty criminals and rogue traders who we could trick, before hyping up their wrongdoing beyond recognition.

The reason was simple – they were often poor, powerless and confused, and rarely had the resources to fight back. Backstreet Asians and ethnic minorities were easier marks because they were often working in the black economy, illegal immigrants who were unlikely to complain when they were splashed all over the *News of the World*. A time-honoured trick of the trade.

I could never understand the huge amount of resources that would go in to exposing a low-life that even Trading Standards wouldn't bother with. Hundreds, sometimes thousands, of pounds were spent on inquiry agents to find out every detail. Surveillance photographers plotted up on them, 'followers' tailed them through the streets and £150-a-day video bags caught them red-handed peddling their tin-pot wares.

The problem on this one was that Greual never dealt direct with his customers. He did deals over the phone and directed his customers to pick up his fake Tellytubbies at shady warehouses at which he was never present. He rarely used his real name and he kept his home address secret. Although I had his mobile number, I had to make sure it was linked to him. I gave the number to either Steve or another 'phones man' called Skinner. The agent then 'span it' and 'converted' it to a name and address. A mobile reverse trace cost about £75. Bingo! The phone number came up as belonging to Greual. Therefore, we could prove that Greual had given us his real name, and take a snatch pic of him coming out of his house.

Once we had given a number to Steve Whittamore, he then passed it on to one of his sub-contractors, such as a long-haired Hell's Angel on the Sussex coast. The Hell's Angel was a blagger who used a scripted spiel to con British Telecom workers into handing out addresses attached to numbers as well as ex-directory numbers. He charged Steve around £40 for this service on top of which Steve loaded up his fee of £35. Coincidently, Skinner also offered a similar service but he was connected to a rival gang of bikers called the Outlaws.

6

Bully

I was standing in the tiny living room of a Victorian terraced house in a solidly working-class part of Liverpool. The decor was comforting, like going back in time to the 1950s and '60s – lots of doilies, porcelain figurines and brass ornaments. The kind of kitsch antiques shops sell in the Royal Borough of Kensington and Chelsea for an 'I saw you coming' amount of dough. But this was for real. Familiar smells of cooking wafted in from the back kitchen, however I couldn't see behind the curtain to see if anyone was in there. The atmosphere reminded me of my nan's house and those of my uncles and aunties. These were my type of people. But I wasn't here to get sentimental. I was here to put on a 'performance'.

I was here to act out a subtle kind of blackmail on one of the football Premiership's biggest stars, England and Liverpool ace Steve McManaman. If I could crack it, this was a big story because McManaman was a big name at the time. Not only was he a star striker at Anfield, but off the pitch he had gained notoriety as a 'Spice Boy' who revelled in being a bit of a lad, drinking a little too much and modelling Armani suits. Unusually, I wasn't here to lean on a football player for shagging a Page 3 girl. I scanned the room again. In between the clocks and mirrors, I was looking for evidence of get well cards on the mantelpiece or pills on the small round table by the window. Was there any medical equipment on show in here, such as portable infusion pumps, bedpans or disposable gloves – the detritus of chemo-therapy? I was here to lean on Steve McManaman because his mum had cancer. And I wanted him to talk to the *News of the World* about it, whether he liked it or not.

When I look back on this bizarre scene, I feel ashamed at how callous I'd become. However, I've got to tell this story as it is a good example of the routine bullying that I dished out week-in, week-out. Regularly intruding into the saddest and most private parts of people's lives, often when they were at their weakest and without any justification. Gratuitous persecution for no good reason, as many of the stories didn't even make it into the paper. Intimidation was a good way of making sure I got maximum rewards from fishing expeditions.

The story had started the week before, when a tip came in from an anonymous ring-in that Steve McManaman's mum was dying of cancer. Once a tip like this comes in, the sole objective is to get an 'emotional' sit-down chat with the star in question, saying how hard it is to deal with the cancer, with pics of him and his mum together. This type of celebrity tale is known as a 'my cancer hell' story. If she gets better, then it can easily be flipped around into a 'medical miracle' story. The hideous truth is this – neither I nor the *News of the World* really cared about Steve Mac's mum or any other cancer victims – the prize is just a chat with the footy player at the end of the day. End of Story. That may sound harsh, but I'd be lying if I said anything else. The interview was just a vehicle to get a cheap, non-libellous celebrity story into the paper. The mad thing was: I no longer thought that there was anything wrong with this. As the months went by, I was becoming increasingly desensitised to the suffering of others.

First of all, I called a footy contact who knew Steve McManaman to get some background, to sound them out on the QT. I asked whether he had heard on the grapevine that his mum had got cancer, and if so, what were the chances of McManaman doing a chat about it? 'Fuck off,' my mate said straight off the bat, 'If she has got cancer, he's keeping it quiet and no one knows. And anyway, Stevie is fiercely protective of his ma, so he won't talk to you. You've got no chance.' It was clear that McManaman wouldn't want to speak about such a sensitive aspect of his private life.

However, this was a common problem in my line of work and there were several established *News of the World* protocols for dealing with it. Basically, the process amounted to a subtle form of blackmail to change McManaman's mind. In short the *News of the World* would say to the player that the paper is going to run a story anyway, with or without the player's or his mum's say so – a straightforward cancer story announcing to the world that Steve's mum is in a bad way. The intended effect was to shock and awe his mum, who probably wanted to suffer in private, which in turn would put Steve under pressure to enter into negotiations with us. Of course, this is a despicable strong-arm practice, but so common that I didn't even think twice about it.

To increase the chances of the blackmail working, it was better to be armed with real medical evidence. Not a problem – I had been commissioning inquiry agents to illegally pull confidential medical records for a month or two, as I grew more confident about going ever deeper and darker into the lives of others. However, on this occasion the job was given to another reporter. To ring up an enquiry agent to pull McManaman's mum's medical records. First of all, the agent found out her full name (Irene), age (48) address, social security number and then an NHS number. Looking the address up in the *A to Z*, I remember being surprised that a Premiership star's mum still lived in a two-up, two-down in Bootle. Steve McManaman could have afforded to buy the whole street with a month's wages. In fact, his best mate Robbie Fowler went on to become the richest player in British football by doing just that – by buying up whole areas of terraced houses in run-down areas all over the UK. Coincidentally, at around the same time, I'd tried to turn Robbie over for going on the piss a couple of nights before his first England call-up. I ended up blagging my way into a party in his hotel room during the early hours. Secretly, I'd boshed-off some sneaky shots of him, sitting on the bed with a bevvy of beauties draped all around. But the flash on the disposable hadn't gone off, so the pics didn't come out and I lost the story.

Back on McManaman's mum, the story moved on to the next stage of the process, which was heavily dependent on 'blagging'. The inquiry agent then phoned up her GP and tried to blag the receptionist. The blaggers usually posed as NHS officials from regional hospitals who were trying to update records. One blagger that we used, who later went on to work for the Fake Sheik, was a woman in her thirties called Marjorie. She was a busty, tactile, dirty blonde who loved SAS soldiers and reading about the Troubles in Northern Ireland. According to Fleet Street folklore, Marjorie was also the illegitimate daughter of Moors Murderer Ian Brady. Though clearly untrue, this image gave her a dark edge, perfect for her job. From her luxury dockland's pad, Marjorie blagged hospital nurses and the back office staff with a reassuring estuary accent

Unfortunately, on the McManaman case, the inquiry agents largely drew a blank. The failure didn't necessarily mean that the mum didn't have cancer, and that it was a duff tip, because medical records are notoriously incomplete and the bureaucracy was painfully slow, especially so in the days before computerised files.

After trying to blag several of the local hospitals and hospices, the enquiry agents still hadn't got the specifics I needed – the type of cancer, date of diagnosis, treatment etc. So, I then put a surveillance photographer on the house, in the hope that we could get a picture of the mum showing signs of illness – if she was having chemo, for instance, her hair might have fallen out. Or hopefully, she might get driven to a local Macmillan Centre on which we could focus our inquiries.

When faced with this situation, many newspapers would simply drop the story. Not the *News of the World*. In fact, the opposite is true – it was time to re-double resources and blag harder. I decided to front Stevie and his mum up and blag it myself.

I drove up to Liverpool. On the way up, the local photographer who was watching the house said that he could act as a go-between. Billy Griffiths revealed that he knew Steve McManaman person-ally because he was regular match photographer at Anfield, and had taken pics of him several times. Instead of banging on his door cold, Billy said he could arrange for us to go around and see him. That might be a more sensitive way of handling the story, I thought. I get a foot in the door, Steve McManaman doesn't get a nasty surprise and his mum doesn't get 'monstered'. 'Monstering' is newspaper jargon for ambushing a target and aggressively bombarding them with questions.

Sure enough, Stevie agreed to talk to us. For anyone else, this might have been an embarrassing situation, but I had skin like a crocodile. Of course, I feigned humility and empathy. My patter, delivered with phony humility, went something like this:

'Steve, we know it's a bad time for you and your mum. And we really, really, really don't want to give you any more grief than you've already got on your plate. But there's two ways of handling this. Either we do a straightforward, up-and-down news story [covert message: If your mum's fucked already, then this might tip her over edge further] or you can do a tribute story to her. Do a nice bedside chat with us, that kind of thing. You can have control of the story and copy approval: "How I'm helping mum to fight cancer . . . How she inspired me etc." We'll even throw in a few grand's worth of donations to a cancer charity of your choice.'

Steve was gracious when I put the 'allegations' to him, but frus-tratingly he denied it straight away. I tried to front it out, blagging that we had definitive proof in the hope of backing him into a corner.

'Listen, I know it's a sensitive time for you and believe me, I didn't want to do this, but my bosses in London insisted. It's down to them – if it was down to me, I wouldn't have come, out of respect for you and your mum. But the bottom line is that I know that your mum definitely has got cancer – we've got a very good source and I've seen the paperwork . . .'

I was getting very good at faking the right human emotions and responses. Later in my career, when I turned into a proper reporter, I met a professional contract killer dubbed The Rock Star, who had thought about killing me twice after I exposed his drug-dealing partner and put him in jail. Over a Fiorentina in Pizza Express on Millbank, he told me his history – how he had helped to kill his own brother at the age of two, carried out his first hit at 14 before clocking up more than ten further targeted killings. The Rock Star told me that he no longer felt human emotions, but that he was a good mimic of feelings because it made getting through day-to-day life easier. He knew when to laugh and joke and put on a sad face when grieving. I realised that I had undergone a similar process while working at the *News of the World*.

But Steve remained completely calm and firm. 'It's not true,' he said. 'You've got your facts wrong.' It was unusual for targets to be so robust, and I smelled a rat, as it was often quite easy to get people to fold under questioning with a dose of passive-aggressive intimidation. I immediately got on to what was going on. I suspected that Billy and Stevie were conspiring to play me. It was obviously in Billy's interests, even though he was an *NoW* free-lancer, to keep in with Steve, and Billy had probably tipped him the wink that we didn't have any real proof.

What happened then was a very absurd and humiliating charade – humiliating for his mum, that is.

Stevie said: 'Well if you don't believe me, you can ask my mum yourself.' Sure enough, a frail but well-dressed lady appeared from a curtain near the back kitchen. She was smiling. I could tell that she was shy, but she was pulling off some good, forced cheer.

Steve said: 'Look at her – she looks the picture of health.' And sure enough, as though she was reading from a script, Irene told me that she didn't have cancer. It reminded me of when Jewish women in the camps had to rub pin-pricks of blood into their cheeks to make themselves look healthy so that the camp doctor wouldn't select them for extermination. In this case, to my disgrace, I was playing the role of the feared inspector.

To hide my embarrassment, I said: 'The cancer rumour was probably just somebody winding me up, rival fans spreading gossip, to have a go at Steve.' She looked at me, relieved that I'd bought it. But there's no way that she was getting off the hook that easily.

'So you haven't had any tests or that kind of thing?' I pushed.

She looked hesitant.

'Or you haven't had a cancer scare, and then it's gone into remission?'

I could see that she was wobbling, and she looked desperately at her son for guidance.

'Listen, my mum hasn't got cancer, OK,' Steve intervened. 'My mum's OK and you can see there's nothing wrong with her.'

By sticking to a limited rebuttal, they could truthfully say that she hadn't got cancer at that moment, and obscure any more niggly questions about previous or future attacks. It was obvious that Steve had put on this show to prove to me that I was talking bollocks. Quite rightly, in order to protect his mum. Steve had double-bubbled me. I had gone up to blag him and he was blagging me, in another of those bizarre and merry dances.

What could I do but apologise profusely and get off, head bowed? Outside, I felt a strange mixture of fear and confusion. Fear that I'd have to tell Ray that the story had fallen down, with all the usual long silences, the odd 'For fuck's sake' followed by 'What else have you got?' But also I felt a sense of humiliation that I had degraded Steve McManaman and his mother.

We couldn't use the story without an admission. A couple of years later Steve's mum died of breast cancer aged 50. Not long after I'd gone to front her, she'd become bed-ridden with pain. She'd been fighting the disease for six years.

Back then, I didn't feel any real sense of shame or sorrow. Today I can only apologise to Steve McManaman and his family for my behaviour. I take full responsibility. However, at the time it felt like I had been brainwashed. Later, I remember reading about how the US army conditioned new recruits in Vietnam to dehumanise the enemy. Most trainees were appalled at the idea of killing people and their officers knew it. The commanders knew that young men had to be coached to accept death as routine. Consequently, the first job new soldiers were given on arrival was burying dead enemy soldiers. Soon, they were encouraged to boot in the heads of dead VC and throw their bodies off cliffs. A gruesome but effective ritual in order to desensitise normal people so that they would disrespect and be cruel to other normal people. I could understand that. In my case the enemy were people like Steve McManaman and his mum.

Without a conscience, I was able to carry on doing stories in which medical records were pulled and sometimes they worked out. However, doctor's notes were expensive to get – around £500 if successfully obtained and a story based on their contents went in the papers. So the service was mostly confined to high-value celebrity stories. To prove that starlets had had an abortion. To prove that they had got AIDS or other diseases. Eating disorders. Sexually Transmitted Diseases. Alcoholism. Depression. Drug abuse. Medical records were doubly useful, because if the star didn't want to talk about their specific affliction, it was common practice to blackmail them into giving me another completely unrelated story to use instead.

7

Official Files

Steve could find out a plethora of information held by the government on a person – social security files, National Insurance numbers, Inland Revenue tax codes, information which could then be used in a variety of blags to get wage slips, benefit payments and immigration status documents to build up a dossier on a target. He had a civil servant on the payroll. In addition there were blagging manuals that contained psychological profiles of benefits staff as being 'subservient to the rules, rather lacking in personal character' and 'utterly paranoid about bogus callers'.

The script advised: 'The way to con this type of person is to convince them that you are just as prim and proper as they are. Don't even bother calling them under the pretext that you are a cockney or an idiot, because you won't last five seconds.'

Here are the other data-rich files targeted by private-detectives:

PO Boxes
Good value on vice stories to find out who was behind the small ads that traded in pervy mags, hard core porn, swingers, sex clubs

and high-class cat houses in the pre-internet age. I once exposed a load of cranky neo-Nazis in Manchester by identifying them through their PO box. I then blagged the password to open the box and stole the contents. I often stole mail from ordinary houses as well. If I was doing a door knock or a watch (surveillance of a house), and no one was in, I'd sneak up the path and swipe their letters as a matter of routine – just to make sure I had the right address – and have a nose at their correspondence.

Bank Accounts
I asked inquiry agents to look into the accounts of several famous people but to be honest it was often boring and inconclusive.

Criminal Records
Always hard to pull, as the police were continually clamping down on it, building in more security traces or moving around the moles that the papers relied upon to non-sensitive posts. Despite having a civilian worker at South London's Wandsworth police station on the payroll, Steve's service was hit and miss. In order to log on to the Police National Computer, his insider had to create phony reports from the public to justify each pillage.

Two ex-coppers, who had been booted off the force for having shadowy links, joined forces with a bent immigration lawyer and could sometimes get police data. Later, when I worked at the *Sunday Mirror*, two journalists were hassling me to pull the criminal record of a boyfriend of *EastEnders* star Jessie Wallace. I phoned them up and they sent over a dossier, which they claimed was a 'criminal record'. However, much of the data seemed to be in the public domain already.

Often gangsters were the best people to go to for criminal records. The reason was simple – they were always paying off bent civilian workers at police HQs to get info for them so that they could stay one step ahead of getting nicked. A feared underworld enforcer once sold me the Merseyside Police Threat Assessment of Liverpool captain Steven Gerrard for a £1000 in cash.

Extract from blagger training manual

One day I asked Ray if there was anyone else in the office who could pull criminal records. He told me to go and see one of the reporters on News called Neville Thurlbeck. Thurlbeck was nick-named 'low level Neville' because he was prepared to go where others wouldn't to get the story. To get horizontal even. He gained notoriety in 1998 after naked pictures of him were published on the internet showing him getting a rub down off a swinger masseuse that he was supposed to be exposing. Later, when the paper was forced to publish the pictures with his privates blacked out, Neville's defence was: 'I am NOT ashamed of these pictures. As the Chief Crime Reporter at the *News of the World*, I have to operate at the very sharpest end of journalism to bring our readers the stories of crime, vice and deceit amongst the great and the good or the lowest of the low.'

A couple of years later he was charged with and eventually cleared of police corruption related to the way he was able to get criminal records. Today he is on bail following arrest over suspi-cions of phone hacking. As well as being a highly respected *NoW* journo – he served as News Editor and Chief Reporter – Neville was a typical eccentric outsider. He cultivated a 1940/50s retro-faux-country gentleman's look, complete with tweed jacket and brogues. His hair was slicked back like he'd just walked off the set of *Casablanca*. He often wrote under his granddad's name Jack Tunstall. Like many senior *Screws* reporters, he was cash-rich – £90,000-a-year salaries were de rigueur – and he spent his day off on Monday doing the schedule A accounts of his portfolio of buy-to-let properties that were rapidly becoming the staple invest-ment of salaried Blair-boomers.

Quite a few of the reporters had this weird olde-worlde nonsense going on, a sharp contrast with the bland functionality of Fortress Wapping. The Royal reporter Clive Goodman retro'd himself back to the Great Depression days with aplomb, often sporting a long mac and an Al Capone-style felt fedora. He went too far and actually used to arrive to work in some kind of sombre, dark-coloured English classic car. I think they were trying to recreate some golden age of Fleet Street. But to be honest they just looked like a pair of tools. I never had the money or time to buy a new suit. For years, I was still wearing a cheap, dog-tooth sports jacket that I had bought as a skint agency reporter. My boss at the agency always used to say that I looked like a bag of shit tied together around the middle with string. The rest of my ward-robe consisted of a two-sizes-too-big Gieves and Hawkes blazer, which was either counterfeit or stolen, that one of the lads had sold me before I left Liverpool.

In 2003, around six years after I first started using Steve Whittamore, his house was raided by the Office of the Information Commissioner as part of Operation Motorman, an investigation to crack down on illegal information. In 2005 he was found guilty of obtaining and disclosing information under the Data Protection Act after passing on files from the police national database. The sentence was a two-year conditional discharge. The Information Commissioner found a sample of *News of the World* searches: 228 transactions from 23 reporters. His invoices mirrored headlines: 'Bonking headmaster', 'Dirty vicar', '*Street* stars split' and 'Miss World bonks sailor' were just a few. He grossed £1.6 million in the period 1995–2003.

I never stopped to think about whether any of this was illegal. To tell you the truth, I didn't care. There was definitely a feeling that we, the *News of the World*, were above the law, and that we could do anything we wanted. Who was going to turn us over? No one. Why? Because that was our job. We turned people over. Not the other way round. Anyway, the police looked upon us as the good guys, or so we believed.

Then there was the fear. The fear of failure far outweighed the fear of getting into trouble with the law. I was so fanatically devoted to the *News of the World* that I would have gone to prison for it. It was a kind of brainwashing. I wasn't the only one – Neville Thurlbeck was prepared to go to prison when he was facing allegations of bribing police in 2000. During the trial, the court heard how Neville secretly pulled his CROs. He gave a copper called Dick Farmer info on criminals the *News of the World* had exposed. In order to do that, Neville had to register as an informant under the codename 'George'. In return, Farmer gave him criminal record info from the PNC. The judge found nothing improper and said it was a 'symbiotic' relationship.

Having access to private detectives had a simple effect – it gave me an immense feeling of personal power. At the time, I wasn't really aware of it because, being a reporter and living a life of distraction, I never had time to reflect on my condition. But the power kind of seeped into me, and expressed itself in a blundering arrogance.

A few years earlier I'd been a jobless pothead sitting on the couch at home in my boxers with the central heating turned up. Now I had been granted an instantaneous power to find dirt on anyone – and destroy their life.

For the first time in my life people feared me: everyone from politicians to celebs to footie players. Three years earlier I couldn't get into a nightclub. Now the most powerful people in the land are taking my calls and sweating on the other end during the long silences and the buttering-ups. Falling over themselves to keep me on side. Then I'm monstering them on the doorstep, sermonising to them about their degenerate behaviour. I was the tabloid evangelist.

This had knock-on effects. Reporters and editors began to build personal fiefdoms, based on their access to inquiry agents. The types of personality that the *NoW* attracted were greedy for power and status, and once they realised PIs were an instant fix, the phenomenon created a kind of arms race to see who could get the ones that would break the law further and faster. A new generation of Princes and Princesses of Darkness started to stalk the corridors of News International.

The other dangerous effect was incremental illegality. Once one criminal act had been committed, it was no big deal to go a bit further, and do one that was a little bigger. Once I was able to spin a number I wanted more. Could I get an itemised phone bill attached to that number so I could find out who the person was calling? Once a reporter could get the phone bills, could she or he hack into their voice messages? Once they'd listened to a soap stars' phone message, was it such a big deal to do a Milly Dowler? Once they'd hacked the voicemails was it such a big deal to tap into live conversations? Could they bug rooms? Well, if they can tap the phone and bug the bedroom, then it's not such a big deal to hack the computer on top of the kitchen table, is it? Driven by fierce internal competition, this is how Fleet Street sleepwalked into the phone hacking scandal. Steve Turner, of the British Association of Journalists later concluded: 'Bullying and greed are at the heart of the phone hacking and blagging scandal engulfing Fleet Street tabloids. Reporters and writers have been bullied into breaking the law for fear of being sacked if they didn't cooperate.'

8

Blags

My next big assignment swooped in one Friday night when I was crashed out on a stinking mattress in my grimy, linoed-up Holloway shithole. I was only earning £400-a week, which in London, didn't go very far. I'd moved into my mate's bedsit flat off the A1. Gav was an aspiring writer and filmaker The February chills had exhausted me during an outdoor surveillance job all week, so I was looking forward to recuperating. The bonus was that my flatmate Gav was out, so luckily I could have the proper mattress. But fuck – the extremely loud ring on my Nokia suddenly went off.

Ray: 'Where the fuck are you?'

'In bed,' I replied.

Ray: 'Well, listen, get dressed and get down to Caspers Bar. It's in Hanover Square. Ring me on the way and I'll bring you up to speed.'

No rest for the professionally wicked. Within minutes I'd hit the streets and I was swerving my way through the headlights of Friday night traffic on the way to the nearest tube. Finishing getting dressed on the move, my Nokia jammed in between my tilted head and shoulder with Ray filling me in.

It turned out that England and Glasgow Rangers ace Gazza was on the piss inside Caspers Bar, while – SHOCK! HORROR! – he should have been at home with his pregnant wife Shazza, who heartrendingly was about to give birth. That was the story. No big deal to me. I couldn't give a fuck what Gazza did. But apparently millions of our punters would like to know this and the *News of the World* newsroom had gone into a most severe DEFCON 1. Forces were being marshalled all over the place.

The problem was this. Ray had already sent in half-a-dozen reporters to shadow Gazza. However, they'd been rumbled by the overweight Geordie and his smart-arsed Scottish teammate Ally McCoist. Then Ray had sent in a few of the sexy-looking girl reporters. They'd also showed-out. As had loads of doughnut photographers. Ray was throwing bodies at it left, right and centre, but it was a forlorn hope. I was the last throw of the dice.

When I arrived, in my scruffy grey Berghaus fleece, the problem had gotten considerably worse. A fully-blown media circus had landed. Around 20 reporters from four or five rival newspapers were disguised as Friday night office workers, and were also desperately trying to lock on to Gazza. We no longer had the story to ourselves. So now, not only had I to follow the overpaid bell-end, get a story out of him, but also I had to simultaneously shake off the competition.

I stood back from the crowd and took stock. Like an army officer sizing up the enemy before an attack, I tried to figure out what resources I could bring to bear to maximise success. I quickly concluded that there was only one God-given grace that offered any hope of a solution. I'd been doing it all my life and now was the chance to show the world what I was made of. This was my pièce de résistance.

Blagging – derived from the French word 'blaguer', meaning to prank – is the act of using clever talk and deception to obtain information or access. It has been the bedrock of my 'career'. If the philosopher Thomas Aquinas had studied tabloid journalism in his treatise *On Being and Essence*, he would have surely found blagging to be the essence of my profession. If you hadn't already got on to it, tabloids are basically about blagging secrets that someone doesn't want you to know, or blagging into places that someone doesn't want you to go.

I had learned all I needed to know about my future calling when I was 16. In 1984 I 'blagged' my way into Wembley to watch the sell-out Charity Shield clash between Liverpool and Everton. I couldn't get a ticket, so first of all I found out what firm did the catering at Wembley, an American outfit called ARA. I also found out that the same company had a concession at the International Garden Festival in Liverpool. Promptly I 'appropriated' some of the liveried overalls from the show's kitchens when the chef wasn't looking and then used them to bunk into the VIP box at Wembley disguised as a kitchen porter. I managed to get within a few yards of the Royal Family by pretending to sweep up whilst carrying an empty box of crisps.

A few years later I winged a £400 student loan, photocopied a counterfeit press pass that my mate had bought from a Thai brothel and blagged it to the frontline of the Yugoslavian civil war. These were my rights of passage into Fleet Street. A far cry from the recruits into the Fourth Estate today, who prepare themselves for a life of distraction by obtaining degrees from Oxford and Cambridge, and doing work experience from the age of 13.

Culturally, I'd been immersed in a milieu of blagging during my formative years. My teens coincided with the emergence of the rooting tooting 'scallywag' youth culture in which blagging was considered a virtue by a generation of terrace urchins obsessed with exotic sportswear and good music. In the 1990s blagging seeped into mainstream pop culture through 'laddism'. Streetwise short cuts to success were celebrated. Noel Gallagher 'blagged' Beatles songs. Underachieving barrow boy-types blagged highly paid jobs in the City. Young British Artists blagged the establishment and entered the high-end art market. Blagging was the zeitgeist. Fortunately for me, I was one of the best blaggers of my generation. So it was only a matter of time before the *NoW*, a blue-chip company that ranked 'blagging' highly in the corporate skill set, would pluck me from obscurity.

And now, as I faced Gazza across the crowded bar, was my chance to step up. To give the News International shareholders some Return On Investment. 'Let's do it to them before they do it us.' The motto I always whispered to myself before going into action. I waited for the exact moment until Gazza swilled the bottom of his last pint into his gob, and was about to leave the pick-up joint. I quickly ran outside. Three cabs were stacked up on the rank. I paid two to move off the runway straight away. Then jumped in the remaining one. Just as Gazza got to the top of the stairs, I slammed the door in his face and told the driver to go.

Now, obviously I knew that Gazza would be desperate for a cab, to get away from the pack and the paps that were now swarming around him. Bang on script, as the driver shifted into gear, he started knocking on the window frantically saying 'Let me in, let me in,' and crying like a big girl. The driver slammed on the brakes as Ally McCoist put a hand out in front. Playing it cool, I wasn't going to let Gazza in straight away – in case he tippled that he was being set up.

'What the fuck do you think you're doing?' I shouted at Gazza through the glass. 'This is my cab.'

As if on cue, he sighed: 'Please, mate. Help us out. I'm getting followed by all paparazzi and I need a taxi.' His daft mates were acting the goat behind him going, 'Do you know who he is? It's Gazza, let him in.'

All the time the pack was closing in, lighting up the rank with flashes. But it wasn't time yet – I let him sweat, letting the blag soak in, all the while risking that he'd walk away or someone from the assembled press corps would recognise me.

'Well I can't help you, mate.' I replied. 'You'll have to wait for the next one. Get out of the way.'

Gazza: 'For fuck's sake, mate – give us a break. Let us in and we'll pay for the cab to wherever you've got to go.'

Bingo! He was now begging me to get into the cab.

'Come on, mate,' intervened Ally McCoist. 'His wife's just given birth – he's wetting the baby's head.'

I kind of pulled a sympathetic face and looked around as if to say: 'Yes I see your point – you're surrounded by all these nasty press men.'

Finally I relented: 'Go on then, mate. If it was anyone else I wouldn't do it. But seeing as it's you' etc.

I opened the door and Gazza and four teammates piled in as though it was the last chopper out of Saigon. The carry-on out of them was unbelievable – you'd have thought I had rescued them from being chained to a radiator in Beirut for three years, I was their savior – they thanked me profusely. Invited me out on the piss. Back to the hotel and all that. Later, I watched Gazza fall off the toilet, and collapse with his trousers around his ankles, whilst being sick.

At one point, Gazza and I had become so close that he burst into tears and opened up his heart. Another player started crying that his gaffer didn't like him. These footballers – what a bunch of fannies. It turned into a *Jerry Springer*-type scene with all these players breaking down and telling me how hard their life was. All the time the tape recorder whirring. All the time I'm nodding and saying that I feel sorry for them.

During the party, I slipped out into the foyer to check in with Ray.

'For fuck's sake – that's fucking excellent,' said Ray about the caper. 'I knew I could I rely on you.'

That night I got a hotel room and watched Gazza being carried into his. And at breakfast I was next to them on their table.

The headline on Sunday was: 'Gazza Walks Out as Shazza Has His Babba.'

When I got back to the office I got a hero-gram from Rebekah herself. We'd already been getting on well but this sealed the bond. I was from Liverpool and she was from Cheshire, just down the road. We were both the same age. Both had the drive and ambition of extremists. She was all over me, rejoicing in one of the funniest Fleet Street to-dos she'd seen in a long while. Of course, in the manner of a courtier, I said that it was all in a day's work for a fool like myself. Rebekah had taken it upon herself to groom Shazza as a personal contact. They had become best mates. The canny Deputy Editor had figured out that Gazza was a conduit to speak to the lumpen peasantry that largely made up our readership: toothless Geordies in football shirts, criminals and the underclass, the people she believed inhabited the estates that besieged Wapping. If Rebekah could wrap his wife up, then that would be a goldmine of stories. Rebekah made Shazza feel like the only footballer's wife in the world. She was also made up with me because by wrapping Gazza up in the cab, we had perfectly complemented each other like yin and yang. Rebekah was grooming me to become one of her special little soldiers that every court-in-waiting needs before the final ascent. It wasn't long before her tasty-looking secretary was bringing over mugs of tea (cue hateful, wide-eyed glances from my colleagues) telling me that Rebekah thought I was the golden boy. I returned the compliment by inviting the secretary out for a drink, abusing my new patronage and making a mess of her in the bogs in the Kentucky Fried Chicken near Liverpool Street Station, before she jumped back on the train to Essex. That was my unofficial reward.

The professional skills of a reporter were always the main factor in standing up a story. But in order to maximise our chances in addition we had almost unlimited support to fall back on. Tools and techniques such as surveillance photographers who routinely spent weeks outside of a target's house in blacked-out vans, shitting in bin bags like the SAS. A video-bag man, who looked like John Thaw off *The Sweeney*, clad in a shiny '70s bomber and polar neck. His steel flight case housed a box of tricks to rig up reporters and their hotel rooms with state-of-the-art pin-hole cameras. A rock-hard if slightly crazed ex-copper, known as a 'follower', who tailed cars around London on a motorbike. An *NoW* staff man with an orange tan and a long mac on, on permanent standby in the records' office pulling births, deaths and marriages. And a harem of honey-trap girls – 'glamour' models, *Penthouse* pin-ups and ex-hookers – used to lure daft blokes into public humiliation.

Much of the time the *NoW*'s resources were better than the police and security services. The reason was simple – almost unlimited budgets. I knew this because I occasionally worked with the same sub-contractors that worked for MI5 and Customs and Excise. They told me how they were forced to use obsolete, government-made equipment. If Gerry Brown, a former *NoW* hack turned video-bag renter, wanted the latest recording device, he simply jumped on a flight to Singapore to buy it. Gerry Brown had exposed Jeffery Archer's hush money hooker scandal back in the day. The consensus was that MI5 were fat grammar school kids, just playing at it.

Despite these resources I always liked to do my dirty work myself. I started blagging people direct, instead of paying private detectives to do it, to save the *News of the World* money. I cannot remember an executive ever sending a memo to warn me that using PIs on some searches was illegal. But every few months, he did send me a three-line circular in a reusable buff envelope complaining that my private detective bills were spiralling out of control. From now on, every inquiry had to be approved by him, personally.

As a loyal functionary, and in order to prevent further suffering to News International shareholders, I started to blag criminal records by myself. Necessity being the mother of invention, I stumbled upon a useful trick whilst doing a paedophile story one day about a sex offender who moonlighted as a security guard at a children's attraction. Whilst sitting on my bed in a Wirral hotel room, I phoned HM Prison Service central records office. I didn't pretended to be a prison officer but the civil servant on the other end of the line presumably thought I was. The man was very help-ful and gave me a full CRO of the paedophile that I was looking into. Under the dim glow of the bedside lamp, as I scribbled down the type and date of offence, a mixture of pride and impatience overwhelmed me. So much so that I could barely wait till the call was ended. I was so eager to get off the phone and tell Ray how well I'd served him.

Irrational devotion was a common theme. For me, a childlike need to suck up to Ray and be stroked by him was always more important than the story itself. Praise from him was the only emotion that penetrated my exo-skeleton.

Another technique I used was called 'swarming'. 'Swarming' is a method used by the CIA to undermine foreign governments. Secret agents whip up crowds to repeatedly 'flashmob' the authorities. The coordinated attacks have the effect of panicking those in charge, as has been the case in Serbia, Ukraine, Iran and Libya.

I regularly used a simplified version of swarming to panic people into giving me confessions. Some people are just too hard faced to admit to doing something wrong. Take building society boss Helen Watson. The petite brunette had pulled off one of the oldest cons in the book. She told everyone that she had cancer, and ripped off her mates. Her colleagues at the Bristol & West building society broke down in tears, had a whip round and bunged her a £10,000 fund-raiser to make her death more comfortable. Miraculously, Helen got better and used the money to start up a small business.

My tipster told me that the police had investigated her for fraud but I drew a blank when I tried to pull her criminal record – obviously she wasn't convicted. That often happened when suspects were let off with a caution. Someone pulled her medical records. Encouragingly, they made no mention of her cancer but that didn't prove that she was a con artist. The only way to stand up a story like this is to wheedle a confession out of her on tape. Easier said than done.

When I fronted her up, at first Watson wouldn't let me into her plush Georgian flat in the upmarket district of Clifton, Bristol. A string of 'no comment's followed. She knew how to play the game. The weakness with people like Watson, though, is that they are ruled by fear and greed. This was fortunate as I was also ruled by fear and greed and knew which buttons to press. Through her letterbox I shouted that we would pay her for her story (greed) and that she might as well talk to me as the story was going to break massively and soon there would be a pack of ruthless journos like me on her doorstep (fear). She lived in a nice area so I knew she wouldn't want to attract heat from her neighbours.

Eventually I was let inside but Watson was still poker-faced and giving nothing away. Then I offered her more money and told her that she could turn the story around to her advantage, use it to say sorry before using the publicity to catapult her to fame. It's amazing how many people believe this. I told her that she could have full control of the story and that we wouldn't write anything bad about her. The point of this is to bombard the target with a kind of verbal shock therapy. The CIA call it 'coercive interrogation'. It's about provoking a hurricane in the mind. Then there comes an interval, a sort of suspended animation, which an experienced interrogator, like me, gets on to – the point at which targets are most likely to make concessions against their will.

It was at this crucial point that I broke off negotiations and pretended to make a call to my office to get £10,000 in cash sent down to her immediately. Instead I was secretly calling my mates outside. Earlier I'd arranged to pay four or five photographers and reporters to pretend to be a press pack who'd suddenly arrived from London to monster her. They started banging on the door and 'hosing down' the property with their flashguns. They began to swarm her house shouting that the story was going to be on all the front pages, that the Prime Minister had even jogged in and was jumping up and down, threatening to make a statement on the scandal in the house, and that the sky was about to fall in any minute.

I turned to Helen and said: 'This is getting serious. Who do you want to talk to? Me or them? Compared to that scum I'm a nice feller.' I pulled a big Tony Blair-style grin of reassurance across my face. 'If you tell me the whole story then we'll tell the pack that you've done an exclusive deal with us and they'll back off.' She folded instantly and gave me the full confession. Of course, and quite rightly so, we hung her out to dry that Sunday and she never got a penny.

9

Spoofing

I was sat in a noisy, steamy greasy spoon near Whitechapel tube in East London disguised as a street dealer. Five months into the job and it's a freezing cold February. The Bengali waiter placed down two teas on the table. Sat opposite me was a blond-haired, blue-eyed race warrior called Mark Nodder who wholesaled Ecstasy tablets to fund his fascist Combat 18 offshoot. Nodder handed over a sample of his deadly wares. A *Screws* snapper had hidden himself in a street-market close by, waiting for Nodder to come out, to 'snatch' him covertly on a long-lens.

According to Nodder's back-story, the Führer-worshipping white supremacist was obsessed with guns, loved attacking black people and chilled out listening to SS martial music. I wasn't scared though, despite Nodder boasting of his knife fights and links to Irish UVF terrorists. For me it was all in a day's work. I was an investigative reporter for Britain's premier campaigning newspaper. Crusading for truth and justice was my duty. The small talk relaxed Nodder and we even shared a joke or two, strained though it was, before he launched into a racist tirade.

On the following Sunday, my courage was rewarded with a full-page exposé of Nodder's abhorrent views. The headline screamed: 'What a Nazi Bit of Work. *News of the World* Exposes Thug Who Peddles Drugs to Fund Evil Race War.'

True to format, there was a grainy, covertly-taken photograph of Nodder, wearing shades and carrying a brief case, walking unawares out of the café into a bustling street. The caption said it all: 'Twisted.' The evidence was damning. An adjacent photograph showed a far-right magazine called *Wannsee* that Nodder admitted to publishing 'to spread his message of hate'. The next picture was the money shot – a handful of 'E' tablets that Nodder had sold me, enough to get him nicked and jailed. In all, it was a perfect *Screws* story replete with the vital ingredients – drugs, Nazis, hidden worlds – that was sure to liven up a punter's dreary Sunday.

I'd written the story strong. The intro roared: 'Britain's most evil racist thug has found a new way to discriminate against blacks – through the killer drugs he peddles to raise cash for his Nazi-style hate campaign.' The gist was that Nodder was supplying an inferior, cheaper and even deadlier type of 'E' for sale to black people.

The sick bigot explained: 'They're cut to **** and if you have enough, they'll kill you. But who gives a ****? One less n***er the better.'

The next paragraph proved that Nodder wasn't simply a lone nutter, cranking up the fear factor. The extent of the threat was self-evident: 'Twisted Nodder, in his 30s, commands a group of 200 white supremacists bent on stirring up racial violence right across Britain.'

As was customary, the payoff was a commitment by the paper, that had already put hundreds of villains behind bars, to bring Nodder to justice: 'Our dossier on Nodder and his vile pals is being passed to Scotland Yard.'

There was only one problem – there was no 'dossier'. Neither was there a Nodder. Nor any of his 200 vile pals. There was no

Wannsee newspaper. There wasn't even a taped conversation of the meeting and his allegedly offensive rant.

The reason was simple – the whole story was a complete fabrication from start to finish. Millions of readers had been totally duped. The page 30 exclusive was no more than a fairy tale, or rather a nightmare, depending on your viewpoint.

It's what's known in the trade as a 'stunt-up'. Not one word or picture is true. I made it all up. Nodder wasn't a neo-Nazi. In real life, he was my flat mate Gav, to whom I had promised £400 to play the role for a day. The quotes didn't come from Nodder – they came from my imagination. *The Wannsee* magazine had a grand circulation of two – I paid Gav to knock it up on his Commodore 64 computer and print it out in our bedsit on a rainy February day. We both read it, proud of our ingenuity.

If you have ever believed that the news you read is true, be very careful. There is a long tradition of 'spoofing' on Fleet Street, which goes back hundreds of years and permeates both tabloids and posh papers. The disgraceful practice also extends to television. Fabrication is a complex issue. The example above is spoofing in its simplest form – a 'rogue' reporter like myself making up stories primarily to make himself look good, however obscene that sounds. But I wasn't the only one – there was an ingrained culture of story fabrication at the *News of the World*. I knew several reporters who systematically spoofed stories, or at least parts of them, when the pressure was on and the goods had to be delivered up to the gods. The bottom line was this: the pressure and expectation to deliver world-class belters week-in, week-out was too much.

However, the wider context is also important too. In a general sense, made-up stories appear in the papers nearly every day. Common examples include staged showbiz paparazzi pics, orchestrated by editors, celebrities and their agents. Bullshit Hollywood interviews. Government propaganda by the armed forces, secret services, police and some other official departments. (For example the lie about weapons of mass destruction that paved the way for the Iraq War)

The American commander General David Petraeus describes Afghanistan as a 'war of perception, conducted continuously using the news media.' At the MOD's psychological warfare facility in Chicksands, Bedfordshire, the warriors are trained in 'information dominance'. Political spin. According to Ralph McGehee, one of the CIA's pioneers in 'black propaganda', known today as 'news management', modern wars invariably begin with a 'master illusion'. Deliberate share-ramping in the City pages. Commercial misinformation. Smears planted by PR gunslingers to undermine enemies and competitors (a hugely profitable but secret industry).

Unlike the phony neo-Nazi, strategic media lies are more complicated so may not be identifiable as outright frauds straightaway. They are a more subtle form of lying that depends on what renowned media boffin Noam Chomsky calls the 'manufacture of consent' – an insidious form of collusion and self-editing between powerful interests that wish to trick the Great Unwashed en masse. It's the reason why Britain's concentrated media reports the same old issues in the same way time and again, strangling all dissent. At the height of the Cold War, Soviet journalists used to marvel that the same effect could be achieved in Russia only by sending journalists to the gulag.

In the Mark Nodder Nazi stunt-up, both Gavin and I had gone to great efforts to get all the details right. To make the pictures convincing enough to get past my boss Ray Levine and the rival News department. News would have relished the prospect of exposing a Features reporter for a fraud, if they could have spotted a clue to a story's lack of credibility, so this was important.

Consequently, preparations began a few days before. Gav got his hair cut short and bleached to disguise himself, so that no one would recognise his real identity in the paper and make a connection to me. Dutifully, he sourced clothes from a charity shop that had no connection to him, and mirror shades. Shades always looked a bit silly, and sent suspicious signals to a streetwise news executive, especially when worn in winter. But it was a risk we had to take to keep Gav's facial show-out to a minimum.

For the main prop, I always had a few Ecstasy tablets hanging around in my top draw at work – along with wraps of coke, chunky blocks of cannabis resin, speed and poppers. Not that I was a cheesy quaver. It's just that, as reporters, we were legally allowed to buy small amounts of gear because of a loophole in the Misuse of Drugs Act. We were always doing drug investigations to demonise Ecstasy in the wake of teenager Leah Betts' death, so the samples just built up. Under the law, I was supposed to send the drugs off to a Home Office-approved lab for analysis and safe-keeping. But no one seemed too arsed about the law and several reporters had mini Black Museums of narcotics in their pencil trays, which they'd show off and I suspect occasionally dabble in.

For the fictitious far-right free sheet, Gavin had chosen a mast-head name with a believable historical context. It had to have a sinister dimension, the 'right feel' if you will. The Wannsee Directive – named after a Berlin suburb where SS leaders met during the Second World War – was a secret set of instructions given to Nazi functionaries in 1942 to prepare and plan for the Final Solution. Gavin's girlfriend was Jewish. He lived in a North London suburb and had a wide circle of Jewish pals. In addition, he was a life-long socialist whose father had been a commie before him. At school, he used to write essays about assassinating Margaret Thatcher, which drew great approval during the bitter recession of the early 1980s. We were both left-leaning, armchair anti-fascists, so we saw the anti-Nazi theme of our stunt-up as an all-round win-win. I got a story that kept me in a job for one more week. Gav got a 400-quid bung. And we both relished the opportunity to demonise the far right and take the piss out of them in a fantastical manner. We also buzzed off the fact that we were getting one over on my tyrannical bosses, especially Gav. He was a lifelong Liverpool fan and trade unionist who instinctively hated Rupert Murdoch, still more so after Hillsborough.

It never crossed my mind that I was trivialising the Holocaust. Or trading off that memory. Or insulting the victims – which I was. Or that I risked giving the far-right a propaganda victory, if they ever found out the story was a fantasy. Neo-Nazis are always claiming that the establishment 'Jewish-run' media is making up stories about them. In my corrupt mind, I never thought that I was falsely inflaming race divisions that didn't really exist. What a fucking knob-head I was. But there you go.

Today, I read the cutting of this story with a deep sense of shame. I feel depressed, deceitful and dirty. Something inside feels broken and awkward, like a person in therapy might feel. But at that time I felt nothing – I'd become desensitised and selfish to a murderous degree. The philosopher-emperor Marcus Aurelius said that lying damages the soul – a portion of mine definitely shrivelled up into nothing that day.

However, like the Yorkshire Ripper, once I'd done my first one, it was easy to keep on going. Stunt-ups soon became another trick of the trade to deploy when I was having a dry patch. The next one wasn't so much of a stunt-up – where identities and props are faked – but was what's known as a 'flyer'. A flyer is a story in which a small key fact is exaggerated to such an astronomical degree that the story no longer has a rational basis in truth.

One week I had nothing for conference when I spotted a story in one of the dailies about Oasis axe-man Noel Gallagher doing a charity single for War Child to raise funds for Bosnian orphans. I hot-footed it into conference waving the ripped-out *Bizarre* exclusive like a shield that would save me from the wrath of Ray.

Ray: 'OK, what you got?'

I winged it with the flyer.

'There's a showbiz story in today's papers,' I said, offering up the page, 'about £4 grand-a-week bad boy snorter Noel Gallagher secretly having a heart of gold. What's not known is that behind their hell-raising facades, Liam and Noel give loads to charity.'

I could see Ray's eyes glazing over at the mention of do-gooders and helping old ladies across the road. This was the *News of the World* not *People's Friend*.

Ray: 'How much have they given away?'

Me: 'Loads. Fucking loads. I'll find out from my Oasis contacts.'

I could carry this off because I was considered to be a minor authority on Oasis. The reasons were: Number 1: I was considered to be working class.

Number 2: I was from the north.

Number 3: I had done loads of mad-for-it exclusives in the past – first an interview with their doleite brother Paul Gallagher, a Liam Gallagher kiss 'n' tell, etc., and many doorsteps resulting in Liam threatening me in person to stay away from his mum's old house in Longsight, Manchester.

In truth, I had no idea how much Oasis had given to charity, if anything at all. Their arsy press officer Johnny Hopkins wasn't playing ball either. However, by the end of the week, by the time the story had gone through the scamulator, the headline was, 'Wonder Wallet.' Incredibly, in the story Noel and Liam had donated a 'staggering' one million to charity including £250,000 to ban nuclear testing, £300,000 to assorted unnamed good causes and £225,000 in foreign aid. All complete bollocks, by the way. Flyers like this work because they're harmless and Oasis aren't going to complain that we've over-egged their generosity. It's a subtle 'manufacture of consent' that underlies most showbiz journalism and one that would play a central role in the explosion of celebrity culture that was to come.

Stunt-ups always left me feeling hollow inside. The lies chipped away at my self-worth. I felt like a shadow man, as though my life was simply a rehearsal for a proper life that would come later. Shrinks call them 'dissociative events' when a person experiences a situation and perceives themselves as outside. Is that why so many *NoW* reporters were outsiders? Were they the only type of people who could cope?

This life, it would seem, could be frittered away on untruths and bodily needs. A permanent sense of cloudiness hung around at the front of my mind, pressing down on the back of my eyes. I felt a faint net of tension across the top half of my torso, like an invisible, sinewy cage. Once I'd had a brilliant memory that could recall the periodic table of elements, whole soliloquies from *Henry*

IV Part One and the reasons for the Franco-Prussian War, a minor feat I'd carried out without the aid of a private education or a tutor. My emotional intelligence had been as sensitive as a Geiger counter – the smell of a chemical could rewind me back into the chemistry lab at school in a breath. I could pick up on people's moods and feelings like a whale can hear sounds underwater from hundreds of miles away. Now the world was a faint, transient mush that made no impression on me. Like a senile pensioner, I could no longer remember what I had done 30 minutes ago.

I was staying at the Moat House Hotel in Liverpool that Sunday night. I was now living in limbo virtually full time – deliberately staying on the road to avoid my flea-ridden flat, and to avoid the day-to-day responsibilities outside of the tabloid bubble. Domestic responsibilities such as shopping seemed like enormous tasks. When my girlfriend turned up at my flat I couldn't wait to get rid of her. I was turning into a very dark version of Alan Partridge.

I got talking to two girls at the hotel bar. One was an agitated blonde who had a black eye after being thrown out of a nightclub – I could tell almost at once that she hadn't been to finishing school in Switzerland. The other one was a fat slapper in a short black dress. I invited them back to my room for a drink. I was a lonely guy. I remember waking up to a hissing and splashing sound. I turned over, and through my hangover haze, saw the big fat girl squatting in between the twin beds and urinating over the warped, ciggie-burned floor tiles. I was completely blown away at how long her relief went on for – it was like watching a police horse at the match piss in the street. It was a grim scene and some-how symbolised the existential problems that I was going through.

10

Stunt-Ups

From then on, my stunt-ups roughly followed two types: theme-based and prop-based. Ideas for theme-based frauds were inspired by that week's news agenda. It could be a big sporting event like the UEFA European Championships, and I would make up a story to cash in on the public interest.

Prop-based fake stories depended on my ability to source genuine criminal merchandise such as real guns, counterfeit official documents and drugs which I could then attach a 'body' to, and fabricate a false investigation.

Ironically, what started out as a quick fix to get me out of a hole occasionally turned into a surreal production line in which the fake stories took more money and more effort to construct than the real thing. The theatrics and the drama became increasingly elaborate, and I began to take a perverse pride in the attention to detail. I used to call it the 'studio system', churning out fictional drama efficiently. It was like being a cross between Nick Leeson and the deluded Colonel Nicholson (Alec Guinness) in *The Bridge on the River Kwai*.

'What do you want this week?' my mate Phil asked. Calligraphybuff Phil was an unemployed, part-time TA soldier with an A-Level in art.

'I'd like you to paint the symbol E96 on this tablet,' I asked, handing him another Ecstasy from my collection.

'No sweat,' he replied. 'I've got some really thin brushes and I'll use a magnifying glass. Should be OK.'

Carefully, Phil painted on the colorful logo of the Euro 96 football tournament on the tablet. He repeated the process on a sheet of LSD trips that I had bought and given to him.

Headline: 'Evil Ecstasy Dealers Score at Euro 96: They're Flogging Fake Tickets Too.'

Best made-up quote: 'Menacing Roy McManus, a 40-year-old Glaswegian, selling his vile wares in Liverpool and Manchester, gloated: "Business is good. Football and drugs. What more can you ask for? The E's are bang on at 5 pound each. What about £90 a sheet for the trips."'

Evil Roy McManus was of course as real as Mary Poppins. He was a friend of a friend who was glad of a £100 bung to play the part and take his cue from me.

I recruited my best mate Samy on to the firm and he became a secret full-time fixer on *NoW* stunt-ups. By day, he was a general manager cum prop-finder. By night, he was a black cab driver who had easy access to a ready made pool of unemployed foot soldiers who would have walk-on parts in the productions. Most of them were glad to do it for two reasons. It was easy money without having to break the law – some of them were petty criminals glad of some hassle-free graft. In addition, there was the usual sense of criminal camaraderie combined with an undercurrent of resistance. A lot of people in Liverpool still hated News International following the Hillsborough disaster in 1989 when the *NoW*'s sister paper the *Sun* had falsely accused Liverpool fans of urinating on and stealing from the dead.

I disguised McManus using a joke-shop wig and a baseball cap and then 'beauty-paraded' him down the street so that a *News of the World* photographer could get a snatch of him. The snappers were never part of the deception. Sometimes the picture editor Ian would call me to thank me for 'dragging' the target out into the open so that his snappers could get a good shot of him. He said I was 'always very helpful'.

The beauty about stunt-ups, as opposed to real stories, was that they were 100% controllable and not affected by the million-and-one variables that made doing real journalism a nightmare. If the Features desk asked for something extra, their desire would be met immediately. All of the prep took days, but the stories were useful in boosting my reputation as someone who could deliver on demand without fail. I remember Denna Allen, the new Deputy Features Editor rang me up.

'Yes, I like this Euro 96 story,' she crowed. 'But can we link McManus directly to the football? For instance, would he sell us any tickets to a game?'

'Oh!' I said faux thoughtfully, 'I don't know about that, he's a drug dealer not a ticket tout but I'll give it a whirl.' My can-do attitude got brownie points. As soon as I had finished the call, I phoned Samy to source me a real ticket for a Euro Championship game, which he did from a real tout. This was then given to our in-house graphic designer Phil, who crudely doctored it to make it look like a fake ticket. Which I then told Denna had been sold to me by McManus. Denna Allen was really thankful – she could then go into conference the following morning with a new line on a story that was working. Denna rang me: 'You've really done well on this all week. I really appreciate your hard work.' Like a serial self-harmer, I was incrementally salami-slicing my reputation in order to please her. Later that day an agency photographer from the News team in Manchester was sent round to take a picture of the phony counterfeit ticket. The snapper was immediately suspicious that the whole thing was a stunt-up. But I knew he wouldn't grass me up because I knew him and his boss. They weren't happy but again it was a case of we've got no choice but to go along with it.

Samy: 'I can get some fake car documents there – blank driving licences, phony insurance cover notes, and counterfeit tax discs.'

Me: 'Ace – we can build a story around that? Let me think. Yes, I've got it. What about a petty villain who supplies fake car docs to banned drunk drivers to get them back on the road?'

Samy: 'OK, sounds do-able.'

Me: 'Can you get me a body to front it?'

Samy: 'Yes, one of the lads on the taxis will do it for a oner?'

Me: 'OK. We'll call him Paul Humphreys. We'll set it in, erm . . . let's say Sheffield. We haven't used that as a location yet.'

I always used a different city in each stunt-up in order not to arouse suspicion.

Headline: 'Licensed to Kill. NoW Investigation.'

Intro: 'Car sprayer Paul Humphreys looks like a harmless grease monkey in overalls and baseball cap – but he shamelessly deals in death putting convicted killer drivers back on the road with fake licences.

'Evil Humphreys rakes in thousands selling forged documents to banned drunks and crazed joyriders. Some have never even passed a test.'

Best made-up quote: '"I flog a service,"' he boasts. "Everyone drinks and drives. It's no big deal. At the end of the day if you get caught it's just rotten luck. It's not like I'm helping people who've done something really bad."'

I was astonished that no one ever found out. All of the stunt-ups had tell-tale similarities. In each photograph the target always wore a baseball cap. The copy contained drama-heightening phrases like 'glancing from side-to-side the shifty villain offered to etc . . .'. Or alternatively, 'Looking over his shoulder, etc . . .' They contained far too many, long-running flowery quotes – on average a 30-paragraph story contained 12 paras of reported speech. This was immediately suss because villains are notoriously tight-lipped during 'handovers' – the meetings at which contraband is physically exchanged – and in reality for technical reasons very few real conversations came out clearly on tape.

I was also surprised that Ray didn't pick up on the unusual

admin footprint left by my fake stories. They were extraordinarily cheap compared to real investigations. I was very conscious of not ripping off the company financially. Strangely, I thought that financial fraud was a greater moral crime than deceiving the readers, probably as a result of my fanatical devotion to the News International deity. But mostly, I was so deliriously happy to deliver up the stories to Ray, and see his face light up, that I didn't think for one moment about the costs of stunting-up. Consequently, I only ever put through small tip fees in relation to the shows. On other occasions, I paid them for ghost stories – a common practice on newspapers. Paying them money for projects they hadn't worked. Those were paid directly from News International contributors to stunt-up fixers such as my flat mate Gav and taxi driver Samy. That covered their production fees for the fabricated stories and sundry expenses such as payments for props and actors. As the productions were becoming more elaborate, I often paid out of my own pocket.

One day I stunted-up a story about a phony underworld armourer who sold homemade bullets. A few weeks later, the fixer on the story said that he could go one better. He could supply a whole range of highly illegal guns, weapons and explosives.

'Great!' I said.

'OK,' he said. 'Meet me in Liverpool tomorrow. I will take you around all the lads. You can buy whatever guns and stuff you need.'

'OK,' I replied. 'Once we've bought the props we'll relocate to Manchester. I will get a body to pose up as the seller. And bingo! That's done.'

The next day we went around Liverpool buying up whatever weapons we could find. First of all, we went to a backstreet garage in a district called Walton where the mechanic took us around the back. He rummaged in a bin and pulled out a sawn-off shotgun wrapped in a towel. Without prompting, he loaded it and fired off two cartridges at a rusty metal bin in the back alley. Boom! Boom!

'Fuck's sake!' I said, genuinely surprised. 'What the fucking hell are you doing? You're going to bring it on top for all of us.' I was looking around for neighbours who might be wondering what three shady looking fellers were doing in their back yards with a gun.

'Don't worry,' he said calmly. 'There's always people shooting around here – no one's arsed.' He was right. At that time, there was a fierce gang war raging in Liverpool between armed drug dealers that drew routine armed police patrols on to the streets for the first time on mainland UK. No one raised an eyebrow. I bought the gun and 40 rounds of ammo for £150 and put them in the boot of my hire car.

Our next stop was a drug dealer who sold me a Colt .45 pistol. Then we went to a lad who was in the army. Under his bed, he had a 'hand-launched phosphorous rocket', a thunder flash stun grenade and a case of British forces standard issue nine mm bullets. For good measure, we bought a couple of 18-inch US military coshes and balaclavas from another supplier based in Manchester. We put them all in a 'swag bag'.

Headline: 'This Evil Thug Will Sell You Anything from a Rubber Truncheon to a Rocket.

NoW Investigation into Stolen Weapons.'

Picture caption: 'Sinister. Molloy and part of his armoury.'

Intro: 'Drug gangs are being supplied with stolen Ministry of Defence weapons to enforce their reign of terror on the streets.'

'The *News of the World* has infiltrated the network of a major underworld dealer.

Over the past few weeks we've been able to buy an armoury of hardware including a phosphorous rocket complete with launcher.

'Almost all of the items have tell-tale markings. They are normally destined for Northern Ireland or NATO firing ranges.'

Best made-up quote: 'They are high-projectile flares. There's enough pyrotechnics in there to destroy whatever you need. If you fired one at a man there'd be nothing left but ashes.'

Payoff: 'Our dossier is now available to both detectives and military police.'

As with most newspaper investigations, the police weren't really interested in following them up. The reasons are varied, ranging from lethargy to genuine legal issues. For example, newspaper-gathered evidence of crime is rarely of a high-enough standard to wash with detectives and the CPS. Newspapers use provocation to entrap targets, collect evidence in a non-structured way and are highly selective on the damning quotes they use from taped conversations.

However, on this occasion, I was forced to contact Greater Manchester Police because I needed to dispose of the guns and flares safely. Being in possession of unlicensed firearms is a strict liability – that means it's totally bang-on and you can't get out of it by giving the excuse, 'I'm a journalist and I bought them as part of story in the public interest.' They were sloshing around in the boot of my car. Two officers came down from Greater Manchester Police on the train, picked up the swag bag and we never heard anything again.

My descent into spoofing didn't happen overnight. It was an incremental fall from grace, driven by a combination of inner demons and external moral problems

The first problem was that I never had any morals – I didn't even know what morals were until I was 39 years of age when, on the tail end of a long-running nervous breakdown, I walked into a bookshop in Aix-en-Provence in the South of France and bought a book on philosophy. It was a revelation to learn that there were six virtues to keep at hand, namely Truth, Patience, Kindness, Courage, Prudence and the mother of them all Justice. To me, this was truly fucking mind-blowing. And why no one had ever told me, I couldn't work out. As a kid, I'd had a vague sense that it was important to be kind, hard-working and humble and I came from a loving family who randomly reinforced these virtues. But that was the extent of my classical education.

11

Contagion

I was sitting in a surveillance van with an experienced staff photographer called Alistair. It was a gloomy November day in swish West London. Ray had phoned me a couple of hours before, instructing me to link up with Alistair. 'He's got a good story,' said Ray. 'Something about cannabis and Princess Di.' Say no more – I'm there.

Alistair was an angry former cruise holiday snapper with a black sense of humour. He could be vindictive if you got on the wrong side of him. Unfashionably flashy, on his day off he drove an Arnie-style jeep with chrome roll bars that matched his mirror shades. Took the job seriously though. The white Renault surveillance van, that he used for snatching celebs and villains, was kitted out with state-of-the-art fittings, walkie-talkies and swivel chairs. On mind-numbingly boring 'watches', Alistair passed the time by painting his Nikon telescopics in Airfix camouflage, so that if and when he had to hide in the bushes he wouldn't be seen.

Today we were looking at bushes, rather than creeping around them. In the gardens at Kensington Palace in West London. For once, we weren't trying to get a pap picture of Princess Diana.

Alistair had got a tip that 'guerilla gardeners' were using Di's back-yard to grow cannabis. As soon as he told me, I thought it was a bit moody. I suspected that it was a stunt-up but I carried on drinking my plastic cup of tea, and looking at the rhododendrons, waiting for the dopey horticulturalists to turn up.

Lo and behold, shortly after we got there, as if on cue, a sneaky villain straight from central casting started crawling out of the bushes into the car park, holding a bouquet of skunk leaves and wearing suspiciously familiar mirror shades. Not only that, he was glancing from side to side, like he was looking for Germans in *The Great Escape*. Are you joking or what?

Give him his due, Alistair did his best to feign astonishment, jumping out of his seat and simultaneously bosh-bosh-boshing with his Nikon through the blacked-out windows. The piss-taking gardener slithered on his belly right past the van, before he stood up just like that and melted into the crowd of tourists.

'There's one. Look at that. Got him red-handed,' Alistair beamed. 'That was fucking lucky, wasn't it?'

'Deffo,' I said, trying not to laugh.

The story was clearly a stunt-up. Only this time it wasn't me doing it, but another journalist. I was suddenly faced with a subtle dilemma. Do I go along with it? Or do I take the moral high-ground and front him? If I go with the flow, then it's a risk, because it's a stunt-up that for once isn't under my control. And it was such a blatant spoof that everyone back at the office would get on to it as totally phony. Alistair had clearly none of the production values that made my own stunt-ups so believable. Shameless. What a fucking amateur, I thought.

By raising the issue, I'd have to play the goody-two-shoes super straight reporter, who would never dream of telling fibs. That would have a tactical advantage of double-bubbling everyone away from my previous stunt-ups. But I couldn't grass him up – that would be unforgivable. I decided to test the water and see where it went.

'Fuck off,' I said. 'Are you mad or what?'

At first, he tried to bluff it: 'What are you on about? That's a great story – good tip, worked out, what are you trying to say?'

Then he did his best to hide his embarrassment. He was shame-faced because he was spoofing and because it was such a poor effort.

'What are you talking about?' he asked, trying it on again.

'You fucking know what I'm talking about – that pile of bollocks that's just happened. I've seen some fucking spoofs – but that takes the biscuit.'

After realising that he couldn't blag a blagger, Alistair went on the offensive: 'Listen, you can talk, some of them stories that you've been getting away with recently looked a bit skewwhiff.'

I was fucking outraged. How dare he? The cheeky twat. Him trying to pour shit over my stories. I fronted it out and parried the attack, my face not giving anything away.

'Those stories are all straight up,' I said.

He smiled knowingly. 'Listen, I just thought you'd be up for it, that's all. You're right, it's a moody story. The cannabis man in the Barbour jacket is just a mate of mine.'

For a moment I held his fate in my hands, and he didn't know whether I was going to bell Ray and call in an airstrike on his career. Quickly, he launched into a talk round, a compelling mix of self-pity and bravado. First, he played wounded because he knew that I held his life in his hands – if I bubbled him to the Picture Desk then he'd get the sack immediately. But he knew how to play a reporter.

'Listen, if you don't want this story, then I can give it to another reporter. There's plenty on News who'd like an easy by-line.'

To back up his claim and make me see it as a competition, he then mentioned the name of a very senior reporter on the paper, who went on to be a big shot at another Sunday newspaper. Alistair claimed they regularly worked on spoofs together. It was the first time that I had first-hand testimony about a culture of fabrication at the *News of the World*. Another photographer later backed this up. Two other names were also mentioned and a series of spoof stories were cited as evidence. Wow – I would never have guessed. One was a great tale about a modern-day grave-robber and another one was about a big-time money forger. Strangely, it felt like a relief. I no longer felt so ashamed inside, so alone, so dirty. I also felt jealous that if I were to knock Alistair back, I might be giving away a free story to a rival reporter. Alistair knew what buttons to press.

'OK.' I said. 'I'll write it up and make it sing. But next time, just tell me beforehand, OK?'

'Nice one,' said Alistair, clearly relieved. 'What shall we call cannabis man?'

'What about Will Brereton?' I said, naming the cannabis man after a kid I knew at school.

'Spot on!' he said. 'We'll fuck off home for the rest of the day – I won't tell the Picture Desk what I've got until the close of play.'

Headline: 'Dopes Grow Cannabis in Di's Back Garden. *NoW* investigation.'

Strapline: 'Hash gang reap fortune at royals' Kensington joint.'

Picture caption: 'Taking his leaf – grower Will creeps off.'

Intro: 'Evil drug barons are growing cannabis in Princess Diana's backyard at Kensington Palace.

Best made-up quotes: 'It's ideal,' he bragged. 'The soil's good and the undergrowth protects plants from the wind and rain.'

The files of the British Association of Journalists trade union tell a story of fabrication right across the industry. A senior executive forcing reporters to make up stories about young women as a pretext to get pretty pics of models into the paper. An exec who threatened to sack staff if they didn't falsify drug dealing stories dubbed 'special assignments'. Another boss who bullied staff into stunting-up at four national newspapers, as well as fabricating his own. Bullying was common to all cases.

One of the reasons I and others were able to get away with lying was that part of the *News of the World* was one big lie. Some of the corporate culture was healthy and natural, but a lot of it was constructed on lies that were kept in place by the sheer force of will of the News International commissariat. One example of this was that editors actually believed the *News of the World* was a serious paper. Execs were convinced that members of the public thought the paper was a credible organ. Most people thought it was a scandal sheet full of nonsense and dirty vicars and took the piss out it. Another example was that they were very serious about some very unserious people. The powerful *NoW* elite had a very simple view of working-class people in as much as they thought they loved soap operas. They would run *Corrie* and *EastEnders* storylines – weddings, fights etc – as though they were real. One day Stuart Kuttner came up to my desk to print something off and he said: 'Do you ever watch *The Bill?*' He then went off on one saying it was the greatest thing on telly and beautifully made and how it was clever, and that its clear line on cops and robbers was an education. I was like: 'It's only a TV show, mate, calm down.' But that's what they were like – their lives and beliefs were full of bollocks. When you see so much bullshit everyday, everything becomes relative and I thought: 'Well if that's all bullshit, one new piece of bullshit won't do any harm.' That was my attitude. Not right, but that's an accurate account of how I felt. It reminded me of a story I'd read about soldiers during the Vietnam war. Disillusioned infantry were forced to go out on patrol even though it was dangerous and futile. But in order to tick the boxes, they simply walked out the gate, walked 200 yards down the road and stayed the night in the comfort of the local village. They radioed in to say that they were in the middle of the jungle and fabricated body-counts. I understood that mindset.

Another one of the reasons that enabled me to get away with spoofing was that there was a phenomenon, common to many tabloid newsrooms, that I called 'suspended disbelief'. Like most switched-on people, reporters and editors have good bullshit-detectors – in fact they are trained observers and professional human lie-detectors. However, often when faced with a pile of bollocks, editors will turn a blind eye or let it wash over them for

the sake of expediency – they have 96 pages to fill every week. No
one wants to challenge anything as it interferes with business and
they don't know where it will lead.

Some editors deliberately spoof. Former *Sun* editor Kelvin
MacKenzie was notorious for his tongue-in-cheek, take-the-piss
spoofs. 'Some stories are too good to check,' he said.

On a couple of occasions I was rumbled for spoofing. One day
I stunted-up a scare story about counterfeit alcoholic drinks. I
was getting sloppy – to make the 'props' I simply poured antifreeze into bottles of orange juice. I drove an actor – dubbed Neil
Williams – along the M62 from Liverpool to Leeds so that I could
'drag him out' for a snatch.

Headline: 'Alcopop Poisoner Peddles Death.'

Strapline: 'Fake hooch is made of antifreeze.'

Intro: 'Evil bootlegger Neil Williams is risking kids lives at
Britain's music festivals – peddling lethal fake alcopops.'

Best made-up quote: 'I'll be making up two or three loads soon
– but most of that will be going with me to the Glastonbury
Festival.'

The only problem was, when I checked in with the office, Ray
Levine asked me to take the hooch to get tested, so that we could
get an official line in there. I took the bottles to the public analyst's
laboratory at Liverpool University. The £300-per-hour chemist
went ballistic. During tests, the white-coated boffin discovered
that they contained 22 per cent ethylene glycol that could cause
serious damage to the respiratory system and kidneys. Alarmingly,
he declared them a risk to public health. And sent out a national
warning to police, customs and trading standards.

'Fucking hell,' I said. 'What did you do that for?'

'Got no choice,' he crowed. 'It's the law – strict procedure.' I
didn't want coppers or snoops sniffing around my house of cards.
The exchange was awkward. The public analyst started asking me
questions and I could tell he was on to me. 'Fuck him,' I thought.
Grabbed the samples and raced off.

*   *   *

I suppose I never lost sight of the fact that tabloid journalism was simply a business. At the end of the day the *News of the World* was a vehicle designed to carry revenue-generating adverts. My copy was simply a device to draw the reader's eye in, in the hope that then they would briefly brush their gaze over an ad for a new video from Currys, or a turkey roast from Iceland, on the opposite page.

Up until the 1920s and '30s, newspapers were a heady mix of spoofs, speculation and guttersnipes. Ironically, this allowed many reporters to ferociously attack the establishment. The great Irish muckraker Claud Cockburn summed up their mischievous dissent when he said, 'Never believe anything until it's officially denied.'

But following the growth of mass consumer markets, newspapers had to smarten themselves up in order to appear respectable to advertisers. Dissenting voices were quietened in order to appease corporations. Instead of self-generated lies, spoofs were now provided for them by PR firms. The tobacco industry paid feminists to smoke so that cigarettes became 'torches of freedom'. Communist menaces were fabricated in banana republics like Guatemala to pre-empt regime change. Reporters were encouraged not to lie for themselves, but only if the lies benefitted commercial or powerful interests. Sigmund Freud's nephew Edward Bernays invented the profession of public relations to rationalise this process. In 1928, Bernays said PR was as 'an invisible government which is the true ruling power in our country' thanks to 'the intelligent manipulation of the masses'. His secret weapons were 'false realities' which then became stories. The objective was to spread commercial propaganda. The lies were made elaborate in order to fool consumers into buying sponsors' products. Now, I was just the latest in a long line of spoofers.

12

Close Shave

A few months later, I had another close shave when I 'exposed' a
prostitute protection racket in a Liverpool red light district. The
local delinquents used to throw bricks at kerb-crawlers to deter
them until the working girls gave them a cut of their wages, after
which they'd obviously quieten down. I paid my mate's niece to
pose as a brass in a skimpy top and short skirt, and her younger
brothers to play the part of the racketeer hoodies.

The story made a decent page lead. But on Tuesday, the shadowy Ukrainian Associate News Editor Greg Miskiw waltzed over
with a fax from a Liverpool solicitor. The fax stated that the kid's
mother had blown her top after seeing the pics of her daughter in
the paper, and that she'd found out that I had orchestrated the
story and paid the kids – all massive and sackable transgressions
of the PCC code. Oh dear! She was now suing us and threatening
to blow the lid on stunt-ups. I imagined the solicitor sitting there
in his snake-skin shoes rubbing his hands. Don't ever have a
Scouse compo lawyer lock on to you. They are vicious, meddling,
greedy bastards who single-handedly invented Britain's out-of-
control compensation culture.

Then the vice squad from the Toxteth section of Merseyside Police called up. The officer also said that the story sounded like a load of bollocks to him and that he'd never heard of such a nonsense protection racket in all of his 15 years of busting johns, hookers and clippers on the mean streets of Liverpool's red light area.

'Fuck.' I thought. 'Word is getting around fast.'

I quickly got on the phone to my stunt-up fixer Samy: 'Do us a favour. I want you to go around and see the ma of those kids and shut her up – double-quick, mate. It's coming on top badly etc . . .'

Samy: 'OK, no sweat. She's a single mum – she's probably trying it on for a few quid.'

Me: 'Exactly. Give her three-ton and talk her round. Get her to phone that meddling Scouse brief and close him down before he gets on one.'

Samy: 'OK, mate – I'll sort it.' And he did. We paid her off. Persuaded her that telling tales was the equivalent of 'grassing', which is still a serious taboo in many working-class communities up north. End of story.

I suppose that one of the reasons that I told lies was that I never really wanted to be a reporter. Consequently, I never had any sense of journalistic heritage. Many decent reporters have often wanted to be journos since they were kids. Devouring newspapers and editing school rags while I was out smashing up phone boxes and picking magic mushrooms. They revered newspapers as though they were Shakespeare plays.

Me, I couldn't give a fuck. I had an A in English at O-Level and that was about it. I was driven by fear of not having a job – any job. In our house, tabloid papers didn't happen. Everybody was busy working all the hours God sent and we instinctively knew they were full of total bollocks anyway – Princess fucking Diana and Freddie Starr and *Coronation Street*. Got better things to do. At weekends we used to swap our *Mail on Sunday* for next door's *News of World*. As a horny, spunk-soaked teenager I was secretly titillated by the naughty stories in the problem pages of young lads shagging older women. To me, that's all that the papers were – wank.

I only ever read and respected one journalist – that is the eminent John Pilger, often described as the greatest living news-man in the world. When I first became a national newspaper reporter, I used to go home at night and devour his writing. I was blown away at how he tackled massive stories such as the miners' strike, the Liverpool dockers' dispute and the Israeli-Palestine conflict. Using simple tabloid language, that he had learned on a strict, adjective-free training course in his native Oz as a cadet reporter. Before honing his style as feature writer on the *Daily Mirror* for 23 years, to reveal the truth about complex, agenda-driven stories. Straw men were not on his radar. Pilger attacked real power which took real courage.

The contrast came when I went to work the next day at the agency, steeled with a new determination to be John Pilger. But I may as well have had an ambition to be a spaceman. I wrote about Camilla Parker Bowles shagging Prince Charles, Mr Blobby, lottery winners, Myra Hindley's day out to Cornwall with her lesbian mate, transvestite bus drivers, real life – 'I was attacked by a swarm of bees' or 'My wife ran off with a Turkish waiter'. In the end I thought: 'What's the fucking point?' What's the difference between the shite I write and outright lies. Nothing much.

Long before I'd got to the *News of the World*, I'd started stunt-ing-up daft stories for the agency. I got a dog owner to dye her Dulux dog pink, saying that she did it after watching the *Flintstones* movie. I also got my flatmate in Bristol – a Phd student – to say that he was maniacal fan of *The Flintstones*. He dressed up like a caveman and said that he'd been to see the film 100 times. A couple of poor students pretended to say that it was love at first sight after meeting in the queue to buy lottery tickets. It made a *Sun* splash. Another couple said they broke up because one loved Oasis and the other Blur. When *Batman* was popular I persuaded a man to say that he'd invented a Bat Torch which was going to make him millions. Countless phony vox pops and case studies.

I used to pay a party stripper girl to say that she did themed kiss-o-grams on whoever was in the paper that week. For instance when Major James Hewitt was demonised for being a cad, she said that she was doing booming business in Hewitt-o-grams. During Comic Relief I'd paid her to pose up in a bra made of big Red Noses that motorists put on their cars. Sounds daft but stories like that sold like hot cakes. To get the job at the agency I pledged to the owner that I'd contribute more to his fixed costs than any other reporter on his books. And I did. When I left to go to the *Screws*, he told me that I'd made more money than anyone he'd ever employed. It paid to fabricate stories.

I understood right from the outset that there were no ethics in journalism – it was a business. Stunt-ups like these are the life-blood of many agencies and freelancers. And again they require a weird manufacture of consent between all the parties, often shored up by the media's need to plug a product such as a film or a record.

By the time I got to the *News of the World* I was already on the slippery slope. The increased pressure was now a stronger motivator of course. I was also acutely aware that *News of the World* investigations weren't really anything of the sort – they were often no more than excuses to turn over petty criminals whose crimes were then blown out of all proportion in order to promulgate scare stories that spread unnecessary fear and division amongst readers.

My next stunt-up was headlined 'Crooked Tutor's Lessons in Fraud: He Sells Illegal Aliens False Birth Certificates.'

I paid a hard-up mini-cab driver called Peter to pose as a teacher called Kenneth Muirhead, 49, from Balsall Heath, Birmingham. The counterfeit IDs that he allegedly sold were blank birth certificates that had been sold to my fixer Samy the day before by a petty criminal in Liverpool.

I also did a similar one based around a counterfeiter who traded in funny money and stolen American Express travellers cheques. Samy had sourced the fake £20 notes on the black market while I commissioned our in-house designer Phil to mock up a few travellers cheques with untraceable serial numbers. For this outrage, I recruited an old mate of mine to play the part of an underworld forger. Bungy was a reformed alcoholic whom I'd met whilst working on a building site in London during the summer when I was a student. He desperately needed the money. When the fraudulent story was published, I was nearly rumbled once again. Three different people smelled a rat. Firstly, a drug dealer recognised Bungy and phoned me up. In a very subtle way, he tried to blackmail me, implying that he knew the story was false and that he was going to tell my boss. Samy was dispatched to straighten him out and talk him around. Secondly, a genuine forger phoned me from jail. The villain, from Stepney Green, East London, laughed at the story and said that it was clearly moody. He sent me a visiting order and I went in to see him to talk him around. I took up the invitation in order to placate him. In the visiting room, the old lag tried to go easy on me. I could tell that he knew that I was a conspirator, but he said: 'You've been had. Whoever the guy in the picture is, he's not proper and those travellers cheques are complete nonsense.' Finally, the next day the head of security at American Express called. He wanted to see the cheques. I fobbed him off.

The irony was this – I never had to spoof. Even without fake stories, I had a phenomenal hit rate for legit big stories. In the annual byline count, overseen by the editor Phil Hall, to determine who was going to get bollocked and binned, I came third or fourth. Ray later described me as 'prolific' in a statement to an industrial tribunal. In between spoofs, I was breaking genuine dynamite exclusives. It was true to say that the beast was never satisfied. My need to lie was born out of an irrational fear of unemployment. A cancerous complex heaped upon a whole generation of youth by Margaret Thatcher whose monetarist shock therapy heralded a natural rate of unemployment designed to terrify the pupils of post-war comprehensives. In my case, she succeeded.

In addition, I had low self-esteem, which probably dated back to my lacklustre O-Level results and my failure to live up to the hopes of my aspirational C2 ma and pa. When you're a tabloid journalist, your self-worth is directly linked to whether you get a story in the papers. You've heard the phrase, 'You're only as good as your last story'? It's not even that. You're only as good as your *next* story. Tabloid journalism is like a stock exchange of self-esteem. One day you're soaring. Your story is working out and it goes in the papers. The next your esteem turns southwards like a run on the pound that falls off the screen – because your story falls down and Ray is shouting down the phone, 'Are you taking the piss? What the fucking hell you do for a living? For fuck's sake . . .' etc, etc, etc.

I desired the esteem boost at any cost – and to avert the attacks. So like a crack-head who boots in the door of the bedsit downstairs to get some rock money, I did a stunt-up every time I needed a quick fix.

13

Kiss 'N' Tell

When the high from the stunt-ups wore off, and I felt I could no longer live up to the expectations of my boss – I turned to drugs.

I racked out the stripes on top of a cistern in a small cubicle just outside the staff canteen at Wapping. Even before I snorted, the comforting odour of the powder gave me a tingle-on. Smelling like fresh, wet brick. The yellow stickiness indicated that the gram was right off the block. High-quality gear that I'd robbed from my girlfriend's bathroom cupboard – she scored off a high-roller who served up to Oasis and Pulp. She was into that – hanging around with bands. I leaned in to do the nasty. Excellent! The chemically nectar rolled satisfyingly into the back of my nose, through the nasopharynx passageway into my throat.

I opened the door. The cheesy vapours from the kitchens poisoned the clarity, smothering the pleasant taste of the gear. Taking cocaine in Wapping, a death camp of the soul, is a deadening, gut-wrenching experience.

My flirtation with cocaine did not last longer than a few months. Snorting was never going to get out of hand – I was too ridden with the vices of a different nature, such as of ambition, to allow any other cravings to become top dog.

Like most people I took cocaine for two reasons – to stop thinking and to anaesthetise perceived pain. Today, I realise that the most powerful asset any human has is the ability to think, to basically whittle down your thoughts to find out the truth in any given situation. On the few occasions that I had time to reflect, and reason burst through, it was a terrifying and stressful experience. Immediately, I concluded that tabloid journalism was killing me. But then I was too terrified to leave. So in order to stop me ever thinking this again, I took cocaine. A vicious circle.

I also found it difficult to relax. After living a life of complete distraction, time off when there was nothing to do made me anxious. I stayed in the office till ten of a night, and came in on Sunday and Monday. When there was no more work to do, I kept up the stress levels by taking cocaine.

Cocaine also blocks out the pain. The blackness of being a hack was converted to mere blankness. The brain-box political editor at the *Sunday Mirror*, where I later worked, suffered a nervous breakdown at deadline one Saturday afternoon. He was found squatting on top of the office bogs with a crack pipe, in a stupor drug-users refer to as 'sledging'.

Drugs were rife. A former high-flyer at News International told me this: 'What the hacking scandal overlooked is this: it's the culture of News International to have drink and drugs problems.'

Nervous breakdowns due to stress are also common. This goes to the very top. Alcoholism even in the case of a former editor. The more stress the worse the problem. The high-flyer added: 'The editor once told me in his office that I would be shocked at the number of people on Class A drugs and with alcohol programmes at the paper that he knew about. We were doing a piece about the wide use of cocaine in society. He said there was a well-masked problem at the paper which he was aware of. A current senior executive offered me a line of coke at my job interview when I began my career. His behaviour was marked by extreme mood swings as a result of cocaine use and made working for him extremely stressful and unpredictable. But that type of personality is encouraged – he is now at the very, very top of the pyramid. The stress was comparable with a constant fearfulness, the only thing I can compare it with in my life now, away from newspapers, is the feeling that one of my children may be hurt. Not a healthy place.'

Celebrities take cocaine for the same reasons. Fame is an unnatural state of being, driven by a person's irrational craving for praise. When the fame wears off, the victims turn to coke, for the same reasons I did. As a tabloid reporter, my job was to track celebrities to find out these moments of artificial love, when the celebrity felt vulnerable, when the mask slipped momentarily and they turned to cocaine. My goal was to home in and expose the celebrity for immoral behaviour. The hypocrisy was not lost on me.

Kiss 'n' tell stories are an excellent way of getting relatively cheap sex and drugs stories into the paper. It's double-bubble – the papers gets two immoralities attached to a big name for the price of one – the 'shagging' story and the coke shame. Great!

Kiss 'n' tell stories follow a loose formula. The Wapping workshops churned them out like a factory. The raw material was 'the bird', as she was known. The birds were generally sub-divided into two types – models, often girl-next-door Page 3 types. Or 'slags' – strippers, hookers, groupies, wannabe WAGs, party-on types. The Page 3 girls would often get slightly better treatment so as not to damage the Page 3 brand of the *NoW*'s sister paper, the *Sun*. The slags got stuck in a hotel, babysat, 'water boarded' with prawn sandwiches and warm wine, until they'd done the chat and been coerced into putting in a taped call to the target of the kiss 'n' tell. Often a famous footballer/*EastEnder*/politician that she claimed to have had sex with. The purpose of the taped call was to provide proof, to back up the claims that she had made in the interview. I'd put down my micro-cassette tape next to hotel phone, plonk the girl on the side of the bed, and put my TP3 earpiece into her external auditory canal, a device which recorded both sides of a conversation.

Before the call, the girl would be coached and a rough script scribbled into my notebook. I also used prompt cards to guide her in real time through the conversation. The girls acted normal and flirted with the man, dropping in questions like: 'Remember that lovely night we spent together?' To which the guy would often reply: 'Yes – can we do it again?' Bingo – proof that they were together.

Then I'd hold up the next line.

Girl: 'I can't wait to see you. You were so good in bed – remember how you fucked me? Etc.'

Or: 'Wow I was really caned off that coke you gave me.'

At some point the man, on the other end, would start to get a bit suss about all the leading questions, saying things like, 'What are you on about? Why are you saying things like that?' But by then it was too late – he'd already hanged himself on tape.

Some of the more experienced soap stars and footie players, who had been turned over regularly by kiss 'n' tells would start to get to know the drill, get on to it and stay silent or slam the phone down. But more often these girls could lure them into phone sex – spicing it up with lines like, 'This time I want you to snort a line off my arse, etc.' He goes, 'Yes yes I will.' Bingo! Game over. That's all the proof that was needed to stand up the double-page spread about the 'Soccer Ace Who Scored Between the Sheets' etc.

At first, in order to cheat her of her story, the girl got promised a ten grand 'contract' that wasn't worth the gibberish that it was written in, a holiday in Spain and a boost with her career in modelling. We'd tell her that the *News of the World* was going to build her as a big name. However, once she had done the full chat, and the story was in the bag, she got dropped the minute the story came out – and also stuck with the £700 hotel bill. I often left the hotel by the back door, into the car park and back to London in readiness to repeat the process the following week.

And when she phoned up on Tuesday for her money she was getting threatened with all sorts that would go in the paper if she didn't go away. Getting well and truly fucked off. If she was lucky, if we needed to keep her onside for legal reasons, in case the target PCC'd or sued us, then we might show mercy by renegotiating. After being asked in court why a dominatrix hooker who turned Max Mosley was paid only half of the £25,000 she was offered, a later editor of the *News of the World* called Colin Myler said 'every fee is renegotiated'. Instead of the big-time studio modeling contracts, the wannabe Page 3 was humiliatingly offered a 'Dear Jane' photo strip which saved the paper having to pay an underwear model.

On the face of it, a kiss 'n' tell seems a more expedient way of getting a sleaze story into the paper. The alternative is to catch the celebrity red-handed. Of course, I have done this many times – but it's like trying to catch an international drug lord with a couple of kilos of cocaine under his arm. You have to be very patient. I have spent weeks following celebs around. It costs the papers thousands of pounds to wire up hotel rooms and toilets with secret video cameras, on the off chance that the target is going to have sex and a snort. Then, when the pressure's on and the bills start mounting, the legal side often begins to stray across the line. How can you be sure that there is definitely going to be a secret date between a footballer and his mistress? Listen to their phone messages, of course, to pin down places and times. How can the paper be sure to get the evidence on tape? Illegally bug the room. And when none of these things work, it's time for a bit of entrapment. Entice the celeb in an orchestrated honey-trap by paying a tart to deliberately seduce him. Sometimes, papers do all these things at once.

In theory, a kiss 'n' tell is a short cut all around this hassle. The truth is kiss 'n' tells are enormously draining and emotional experiences. The process requires: stamina; patience; head-burning-out levels of concentration; guile to outmanoeuvre the prey; and sharp organisational skills to take care of the 100 simultaneous jobs going on all around. Being hothoused in a hotel with a girl who you've got to control is extremely dramatic, entailing a whole range of unforeseen twists and turns that always left me thinking: 'What kind of a fucking life is this?'

Shirley Ann Lye was Fleet Street's Queen of the kiss 'n' tell. To the untrained eye, she came across as a painfully skinny, haggard-ish woman in late middle age. She was frail, slightly stooped and buck-toothed. But as soon as she opened her mouth, it was like being hair-dryered by Alex Ferguson. Like a cockney dockworker, the expletives 'fack' and 'cant' rampaged out of her spittle-tangled gob into sentence after sentence. Hard as nails, foul-mouthed and mean to the point of indecency. Going out for drink with her was like going on tour with The Who, involving a trail of trashed hotel rooms, smashed glass, falling-over-drunk violence, deviant behaviour and abusive clashes.

During the rapacious golden age of 1980s tabloid excess, she'd made a fortune selling big buy ups to *Sun* Editor Kelvin MacKenzie. Enough to buy a smart terrace in swishy Barnes with her incongruously mild-mannered partner who did 'something in the city'. Her graft was simple. Once upon a time she'd been a model before drifting into being an agent. But she quickly real-ised her stable of Page 3 girls could make stacks more money from selling their stories of nights out with celebs than from photo shoots. She became a kind of mini-Max Clifford. By the time I arrived at the *News of the World*, she had worn out a long line of reporters and a few of them would only deal with her in short bursts because sometimes she was a fucking nightmare.

One day a reporter called Phil Taylor came over to me desk: 'This woman's got a good story – give her a ring.' I got the feeling he was glad to offload her. As I was always desperately hungry for stories, I took up the baton.

'Who the fack are you?' she screamed. 'I want a proper facking reporter – not some facking arsehole who just landed from up norf. Those facking bastards pay you fack all to run round like a cant . . .'

I charmed her round and eventually she said: 'Get down to facking Wine Press on Fleet Street – I've got a good story for you.'

The Wine Press was a fucking nightmare. An old-style hack-haunt that should have died out with the print unions. A place where previous generations of journalists spent their days and nights on the piss. Today's journalists like me didn't drink much – it was a sign of weakness, strictly for bullshitters and time-wasters. Too much pressure. For my generation, brainwashed by the corporate propaganda of the workaholic yuppie, lunch was an uncomfortable, rushed affair. I ate cheese sandwiches and portions of chips stealthily at my desk, answering the phone and replying to messages, terrified that Ray or one of the other editors would look over accusingly and think that I was skiving.

The decline of the long lunch was just one of many barriers that sprung up to isolate reporters from the general public. Not only were the nation's greatest communicators banished to sterile gated communities like Wapping, or into the gleaming citadels of Canary Wharf like Trinity Mirror, but they also seldom had human contact with people outside of newspapers. The Wine Press may not have been cool but I could see its purpose.

There were ex-coppers flogging titbits from inside the Yard. (My motto was: stay clear – there's nothing as useless as an ex-copper. Too slow. Too tedious.) Wizened-faced, odd-bod ex-hacks. Mad women who made a living by linking up lawyers with journos and poncing off the stories they traded. Drunken barristers. The Wine Press was a *Star Wars* bar of has-beens and hangers-on. A stock exchange for sleazy stories.

Shirley always had good stories. But there was a strict ritual of getting to the pot of gold at the end of the rainbow. She'd tap-dance around the houses, and then bleed you and the newspaper dry, for every single penny she could get – down to the free soap from the bathroom in the hotel that she was comped on jobs. First of all, she got me to put my card behind the bar. Then it was an early hours crawl around some very expensive wine bars – Motcombs of Belgravia and the Ebury Wine Bar. Then we were joined by Antonia Moore, a former Miss Whiplash, who also demanded free drinks and 'cars' everywhere. The next day Shirley Ann Lye forced me to pay for a £350 cooked breakfast for one of her contacts saying that it helped one of her dodgy clients remember a story. The problem was Managing Editor Stuart Kuttner was such a 'cant' that he would red-line through most of these expense claims for 'entertainment'. I ended up subsidising the News International shareholders once again.

'I've got a girl onside,' Shirley whispered. 'She's getting on a bit now. But a few years ago she was a bit of a goer – she was fucking Michael Douglas and Jim Davidson.'

'Mad one!' I muttered. I couldn't think of a weirder scene. Michael Douglas, the Hollywood superstar son of screen legend Kirk Douglas, who went on to marry Catherine ZetaJones, after making his bones in *Wall Street* and *Basic Instinct*. And Jim Davidson, the East End comic noted for his casual racism and 'nick, nick' imitation of a police siren.

'Was she shagging them at the same time?' I asked.

'No, you facking wanker – on-and-off over a few years. She had affairs with each of 'em, separately.'

'OK, that sounds good,' I said. 'Two kiss 'n' tells for the price of one. We'll do a spread on Douglas first and then one on Jim Davidson.'

The next day both Shirley and I went down to Worthing, a depressing seaside town in West Sussex. Sideways rain battered against my brand new but hopelessly underpowered Peugeot 103. The skies were grey. 'Come, come nuclear war,' it was that kind of place.

At 17, Jenny Strachan had been a Page 3 girl with London at her feet. Rich men falling over themselves. Showered with gifts from wealthy Arabs. Dripping with invites to celeb parties and film premieres. Just over ten years later, she was a heavy drinking single mum, who lived in a rundown semi near the seafront, with a cold bog at the top of the stairs and a sun-bleached plastic swing in the garden. She was hanging on in quiet desperation. Struggling to keep the grease off her slope. Bewildered that real life had hit her.

Today was a big day. The *News of the World* roadshow had rolled into town. The one chance to relive her glory days. To get back in the limelight. To recapture the power of her sexuality. To make some big dough – and a possible ticket out of here.

It was always very sad – these old kiss 'n' tell birds like Jenny often believed that selling a tawdry story was much more than it was – that it could be the beginning of something big, leading on to books, films, TV and that all-important presenting job in the media. Of course, I did not disabuse them of this idea. Like a pyramid salesman in a church hall, I always talked this line up to whip up the hysteria.

When we arrived at the house, there was a delivery boy from the local offy arguing at the front door. He wouldn't hand over her weekly case of booze until her bill was settled – as usual I paid. There were several empty bottles of plonk piled up in a milk rack by the doorstep and around the drain at the side of the house. This was the first rule of a buy-up. Keep them happy. Keep them plied with drink. She got someone to look after her seven-year-old kid Aaron and we went to a local hotel. That's the second rule – get them to a hotel so that you can control their movements and their thoughts. Getting them off the plot keeps them away from rival newspapers, their family and their friends – hideous two-bit meddlers who often try and talk the birds out of it. Fuck them.

The hotel was big, draughty and empty. Late winter and feeling a bit like *The Shining*. Shirley Ann Lye had tagged along, salivating over the prospect of a free hotel room, steak and chips and all the house white she could guzzle. There was definitely something unattractive about an old person who hadn't yet worked out that it was unwise to crave pleasure so avariciously.

Over my cook-chill lasagna, I started to tease the story out of Jenny. When did she meet Michael Douglas? When did you first have sex? Was he good in bed? In return I got scant details. Then the games began. 'How much?' she wanted to know. I phoned my boss. Back to the pub lunch. Like a pair of Venezuelan drug dealers, we bartered – she went high, I went low. Faxes went back and forth to Wapping with contracts and amendments. Every half an hour, I slipped off to the bog to change my tape – she kept getting suspicious at this. Twenty grand was her price. No way. I launched into the standard crib-sheet patter used to barter down greedy girls.

'C'mon,' I winced. 'Michael fucking Douglas? May be famous love – but he's always been a shagger. So you're not the first. That seriously undermines the value of your story . . .' etc.

She was still acting the goat.

'Listen it's a fifteen-year-old story – you were having it off with him when you were 17 – now you're 32. That makes it fucking ancient in newspaper terms – nowhere near twenty grand. Sorry.'

Then she claimed the usual fake-prudish roll-back on the pictures, a common state with glamour models who want to reinvent themselves and be taken seriously.

My response was: 'We can do the pictures tastefully but at the end of the day if you're not going to do the underwear pics, then that fucks it up a bit. I know you've got kids – but the readers want to see photographs of sexy women, simple as that. That means a negligee or a basque, stockings, the full tackle.' Even if kiss 'n' tell girls refuse to do kit-off pics, then inevitably it happens when they get to the photographic studio. The booze comes out, the house music is pumping through the speakers, the stylist is buttering them up.

Shirley explains to Jenny that the days of big newspaper dough are over – budgets are tight etc, with falling circulations, hard times, so she's best to go for the deal on the table.

By the time I'd gone through the rigmarole, I'd knocked her down to between 5,000 and 10,000. All do-able. But even after I'd given her an on-publication contract, she wasn't happy. She still wasn't going in-depth about the sex and she threatened to pull out. This was all standard. I knew the drill. I could wait.

Then we went to the room to do the full chat. More wine. More prawn sandwiches. More chintz – I've seen more florid soft-furnishings than is healthy for one lifetime. Whenever I checked into a hotel room, I went through an obsessive-compulsive routine. All the leaflets, menus, directories, stationery and remote-control holders were immediately swept off the tables into the bin. I needed clean surfaces to lay out my tools – notebook, pens, contacts book, paperwork, phones – like a dentist-torturer might lay out his drills before a coercive interrogation.

I sat on the bed and plonked her on a hard-backed chair in the middle of the room. She was still playing hard to get. Now she's saying that she doesn't want to do the story in case it hurts Michael. All the usual bollocks. The last-minute worries. Foolishly, like most daft girls, she still thinks she and Michael have a got a chance – that he's going to land his Gulfstream at Biggin Hill private airport and whisk her away to Beverly Hills. I'm looking at her. Under the glare of the wall lights, she's got a millimetre of foundation on, to cover up the craters in her face and the veins in her nose. Her breath stinks of alcohol. She is slurring and her brain is in an oscillating relationship with her mouth, swinging between emotions whilst mumbling angry words to herself. She reminded me of my hooker contact Gina. I mould my blag around her pretensions, explaining that doing a *News of the World* story is the best chance she has got to get back with Michael. It's a chance to send an open love letter to him. To the world even, declaring that you still love him. Eyes on the prize. Eyes on the prize. She's still coming out with all the bollocks. 'But don't worry,' I tell myself, 'this is in the bag.' Little by little, step by step. Tape still whirring. 'Why do you love him so much?' Bollocks. Bollocks. Bollocks. 'Was he good in bed?' Not quite the killer lines yet. She then starts crying. I comfort her. She puts her arm around me. Then cuddles me. I stay straight. But her hands begin to wander. Next minute she drops on to her knees and starts to take her clothes off.

'Erm . . . no,' I say.

'C'mon, we can do the story later.'

She tries to take my trousers down. I jump up.

'Why don't you want me?'

This scenario is a minefield – but also a very common one in tabloid newspapers. It's like a form of Stockholm Syndrome in which the captive falls for her captor. The underlying politics between us was a weird form of control and cunning. As well as being drunk, and friskily yearning to relive her glory days, she was also trying to win back control of the story from me. She wanted to turn the tables on her interrogator. A more sinister turn was also at play. Jenny was trying to compromise me. At this stage in the game, she had a good idea that I was trying to turn her over. That once I'd got the chat and pics, it was slash and burn and I'd be off to Goodwood for the 3.15. Bump her for the five grand and that's that.

She wants a hold on me, so in the event that it does go nuclear, she can phone Ray and say: 'Pay me otherwise I will go to a rival paper and tell them about your scandalous reporter.'

In addition, I suppose she also wanted me to bat for her, thinking that if she could get me onside, I'd whack her money up.

I'm no great shakes looks-wise, but I've had loads of these seedy seductions hit on me from WAGs, models and actresses. Some of them deliberately did it near the end of the story cycle, when they suddenly got cold feet and wanted to use it as leverage to pull out. When I came back to the office, Ray always used to say: 'Well, did you fuck her then?'

But I had to be double careful with Jenny here. There's a delicate layer of sexual politics that also shrouds the situation like gossamer. If I knock her back, I've got to do it gently, because a woman scorned and humiliated may explode and walk out – and I'll lose the story. My mind was tap-dancing furiously

'Why won't you let me give you a blow job?' she carried on. 'Shirley says you like blow jobs?'

'No. Well, yes. Doesn't everyone? Er . . . But I'm a *News of the World* reporter. I'm a professional. It's not that I don't want to. It's not that I don't find you attractive. It's just that I can't do that when I'm on a job.' I was also conscious that my recorder was on and I didn't want to catch any of this mad chat on tape. I know a few reporters who have got into trouble for sleeping with kiss 'n' tell girls, including one who had sex with a Liam Gallagher buy-up and went on to become a deputy editor of big red-top.

There is a rational explanation for Jenny's behaviour – kiss 'n' tell girls like her can't be held responsible for their own actions. Slags like Jenny have been used and abused by men for a large part of their adult lives. Living examples of the depravity of men – and especially celebrities whose desires have got to be fed by sexual cannon fodder like Jenny. The hidden trail of jetsam that powerful egos leave in their wake – and then the *News of the World* comes along and wants to exploit them further. Often, the only way they know how to deal with men is through sex, especially in difficult situations, where there are issues of control at stake. That's their default setting as a method for dealing with men who want something off them. Often, these kinds of girls have been bullied and coerced for years, and when that happens again they use sex to cope with it, to control those who are doing it. Makes for a very fucked-up situation during a kiss 'n' tell

The constant delaying tactics on kiss 'n' tells also stem from their baggage. Kiss 'n' tell girls often flip-flop whilst doing a story because it's too much pressure on their emotionally fragile frames. The act of selling a story is seen as selling a part of themselves, a process that is intensely private for them. They become resentful and lash out. Become uncooperative. 'I've sold my body over the years in real terms and in kind – and now you want me sell part of my soul.' That kind of thing.

At the time, I couldn't give a fuck about all this. I just wanted the story. More large glasses of wine were poured into her. Instead of the polite talk, now it was time to put her under manners.

'For fuck's sake, you're wasting my time here', I bullied her. 'Who the fuck do you think you are?' I shouted. 'Fucking tell me this story now. I'm warning you, right, I've got enough now to run it, with or without your fucking say so. If you fuck me about any more that's what's going to happen – we'll print the story and you'll get fuck all.' More wine. More abuse. More threats.

Suddenly, Jenny sprang up like a ninja. 'You cheeky bastard.' She dived across the bed towards me, sending the table full of bottles and empties crashing to the floor. She was still holding her glass of wine. But I could see her bringing it up horizontal, holding the stem like a knife handle. Thrusting it towards my face. I parried slightly and ducked. The glass smashing against the wall. Her hand was bleeding but she recovered quickly.

'You smarmy little cunt,' Jenny shouted. Shirley Ann Lye just stood by and laughed.

Most of these kiss 'n' tell women are as hard as nails, often from poor backgrounds where they've had to fight tooth and nail. Jenny tried to stab me with the razor-sharp stem again, but I doubled back, vaulting the bed to get out of her range. A cascade of bottles and glasses shattered against the walls and floors behind me as I bobbed and weaved. Foolishly, she then came at me with her feet and fists, but soon lost her balance, falling over into the half-eaten room service which sloshed all over the chintz. Seeing my outro, I stepped over her, opened the door and got off down the corridor.

But like a Messerschmitt ME109, it wasn't long before she was on my tail, armed with a fresh wine bottle. Down the fire escape, through the lobby and into the hotel bar. She flew down seconds later blazing a trail of expletives and threatening to 'smash this bottle over your fucking head – how dare you? I'll break your fucking neck . . .' etc. To be honest, I lost my nerve. I began to panic. The manager-cum-barman didn't know what to do. Neither did I. This was fucking embarrassing. What do you do?

For no more than its shock value, I shouted to the manager to call the police as she pursued me around the lounge and restaurant. I knew that would calm her down – and it did. Then she was on the phone to her old man. Oh no! Here comes trouble. I steeled myself for the local hard man to come bouncing through the double doors like John Wayne to rescue her. I thought of the options? Do I knock him out? Good for self-defence but bad for business. Since I had been handed down my Section 47 for avenging the rape of my girlfriend, I had always been wary of fighting – in case I got the sack. My brush with the magistracy had knocked the stuffing out of me. I often turned the other cheek. On the mean streets of London most of the time, my boxer's face and accent were enough to buy me some time before things got spicy. The other options were to get off out the back door. Or front it out. I decided to front it out. In the end, her boyfriend turned out to be a reasonable feller, a pilot who flew light passenger planes to the Continent. He obviously understood that his partner had problems and I got the impression he'd been on the ropes a few times himself. He calmed her down. She had a drink. He took her home.

The next day Jenny didn't remember what had gone on. Sure enough, she was as good as gold. Did the chat. Eventually, she started to talk. For me, the interview was always an anti-climax. Most of their stories were boring – it was like listening to some-one read out the phone book. I was only ever interested in the little details that gave glimpses into the lives of these girls behind the scenes – how they lived when they weren't out partying.

Jenny said: 'We ended up back at his apartment. He seemed shocked when I asked if I could have a bath. But I wasn't trying to be sexy – I just wanted a soak because I lived in a grotty bedsit and never got the chance.'

She lived a double life. By day she was a teenager living on the poverty line in a stinking hovel strewn with dirty underwear and unwashed dishes. By night she was a teenage sex siren clad in the latest designer gear in the hottest clubs.

I whisked her up to London to do the studio pics. Bang – in the paper.

Headline: 'Love Rat Michael's Night of Lust with Film Beauty. Kiss and Tell Exclusive.'

Picture caption: 'Steamed up: Michael made love to me in the bath.'

Sad Jenny: 'Still in love.'

Intro: 'Glamour girl Jenny Strachan last night broke her silence on her steamy affair with movie idol Michael Douglas – and revealed how he first seduced her in the bathtub.'

Best quote: 'Although I stripped off for a living and appeared in a soft porn movie I wasn't into that kinky stuff and walked away. He was very adventurous and was the only man ever to satisfy me. After drying ourselves we got on to the bed and explored each other's bodies.'

Payoff: 'I realised that this was the man I loved. Now his wife's divorcing him maybe there's hope. I've spent hundreds of pounds trying to get in touch. But you only get that kind of ending in the movies.'

I went on to do many big name kiss 'n' tells and they all followed a similar pattern. I did girls who'd slept with Wayne Rooney, Jarvis Cocker, Liam Gallagher and Jonathan Aitken. I turned some of my old mates over to get the Liam one. What did I care? Friends were no longer useful. I had joined a cult, and began to cut all ties with my previous life. And the story was a valuable prize to boot – no one had done hellraiser Liam before. It all started when three enterprising students, who I'd known for years, came to me for help when they found out I was a rising star on the *Screws*. They'd set up a small indie dance label, and one day asked me to help with publicity for their latest act, a little-known singer from Hull called Berri. She'd already gone Top 20 with her debut single, but needed one more push into the big time. However, instead of bigging her up, I plastered Berri all over the paper for her one claim to fame: getting shagged by Liam Gallagher in the bogs of a hotel. Berri was left genuinely lovelorn after Liam never called her back, like he'd promised to, as he'd bent her over the cistern and whispered sweet nothings in her ear. It was always good to end one of these stories with a comical payoff. That one was: 'For heartbroken Berri the truth had finally dawned – Gallagher just used her for a convenience.' How we laughed!

Headline : 'Oasis Rat Liam Loo-ved and Left Me.'

Picture Caption : 'Ladies Man Liam . . . passionate sex in hotel loo.'

No one ever heard of Berri again, her career in tatters after being publicly humiliated. And my mates realised that I'd just used them as a convenience as well. But what do you expect when you come to the *Screws* asking for publicity? A dance with the devil, no less. 'Like Berri, you're going to get fucked.'

I carried on doing more kiss 'n' tells. Footie players, soap stars and movie types all went through the sausage factory. These were the good times – no privacy laws, or super-injunctions, before phone hacking when we could get away with anything we wanted. Even men started doing kiss 'n' tells on famous women they'd bedded. Boyfriends turned over girls such as model Sophie Anderton and *EastEnders*' Samantha Janus. And finally, now I'm doing the ultimate on myself. I'm blowing the lid on me – in this book. Pop culture eating itself. Mad, innit?

14

Conman

Peter Trowell was a corpulent former con who specialised in tipping underworld stories with a precariously 'investigative' edge. His MO was simple. Peter used entrapment to manipulate targets so that the stories escaped the slur of 'fabrication' by slivers of evidence so thin that the in-house lawyers asked, 'Fucking hell – this is not one of his is it?' every time his name came up during legals. An incredible bullshitter-cum-fantasist, the thirty-something businessman had started working for Her Majesty's Press when he was a guest at one her prisons a few years earlier. Trowell had started out on his career in journalism in estimable fashion – by ringing the *News of the World* in 1994 from Ford Open Prison – where he was serving time for video piracy – and ratting out a fellow con who had been caught running a multi-million pound fraud.

Trowell was an ideal *News of the World* contact for several reasons:

1. He was a professional conman.
2. He was a shameless and persistent liar. If you stopped him on his way to buy a pint of milk he would tell you that he was off to the opera.

3. He had a massive ego – like the majority of fraudsters he was convinced that he was cleverer than most. People were there to be 'played' for his benefit – including the journalists he worked with. Everyone was fair game. Astonishingly, this streak of dangerous arrogance gave him the ability to plough through stories at breakneck speed, not caring for the consequences.
4. He had a cavalier attitude towards the truth – and a complete disregard for legal constraints such as libel laws and PCC.

For all these reasons and more, Trowell became a prized asset, one whose career flourished under my watch. In short, Peter made a living by turning over the lags he'd been padded up with in jail, one after the other. Many of them were still inside. Which was great, because at the time, the tabloids were screaming out for prison scandals that 'proved' the government was soft on crime. The first story we did together was what's known as a 'cushy jails' story.

Many prisoners in open nicks are cons who are coming to the end of long sentences. In order to rehabilitate them back into society, they are often given work placements in local firms to get them used to life on the outside, which sounds perfectly reasonable. Not to us, it wasn't – this was just a good opportunity for *NOTW* to turn them over and manipulate them for our own ends. What if we could intercept some of these 'outworkers' as they exited the prison gates and lure them into falsely constructed compromising situations to heap shame on the prison service, the justice system and the Home Secretary? In addition, what if we could grossly exaggerate the threat posed to the public by these monsters who swaggered through the streets in civilian clothes and were not identifiable as cons? 'Great story,' said Ray when I put it up in conference. 'Let's do it.'

It was easy. The lags at HMP Ford Open Prison, near Littlehampton in West Sussex, were low-hanging fruit. Of course, we didn't tell them we were reporters. Our cover story was that Peter had a VO (visiting order) to see one of his old cellmates.

Instead of waiting by the gates, Peter pretended to bump into the resettlement workers in an alleyway as they came out of prison at rush hour in the morning. We caught some with small talk, leading them on to boast on tape about how good their jobs were, before secretly trailing them to their offices and workshops. Firstly, we followed convicted murderer John McCourt – doing time for sadistically bludgeoning his father to death – to his placement at the Body Shop, of all places. Bingo! There's the headline straightway. Another lag called Francis Quinn walked to his job through the town centre. Though it had been 20 years since he had committed murder, and he was reformed in the eyes of the prison professionals, we made a big deal of the fact that his route took him though a park where children played, as though he was eyeing them up to kill them, which he wasn't. The exaggeration of risks is a common theme in tabloid stories, as it spreads fear and prejudice among readers, making them easier to govern. Tactically, the overblown threats can also be used as justification for stories that are not in the public interest. For example, Rebekah Brooks' 'For Sarah' anti-paedophile campaign whipped up hysteria that was seen by many as disproportionate to the problem.

However, when I checked in with the desk to update them of my early success, one of the execs said: 'That's good – but we haven't proved that the place is fucking Butlins yet, have we? They're not all sunbathing or going down the pub, are they?' Oh yes, they are – if you want that. I told Peter what was required to 'make it work' and he was only too happy to oblige. After all, if the story didn't 'make' then he wouldn't get paid. The vast majority of stories on tabloids are payment-on-publication and therefore there's a lot of internal pressure on freelancers to 'make them work at all costs'.

As we were watching the alleyway, to see which lags would come out next, Peter locked on to a convicted wife-killer called John Featherstone. We found out that his cushy number was to fix boat engines for the Chichester Canal Society. Later we pretended to bump into him at the marina where he worked. In order to get the pics, Peter bought him three pints of lager from a nearby pub and pushed them into his hands, along with packets of crisps, cigarettes and cigars. All the while the snappers were boshing him off from the other side of the boating lake. I wrote the story as though Featherstone himself went to the pub every afternoon and made no mention that we'd bought him the booze and staged the whole thing.

All in, the story had taken less than a couple of hours, which left it wide open for an early dart back to our luxury hotel – Arundel Castle. As usual, Peter cleaned out the mini-bar on arrival, loaded up the room service with a couple of hundred pounds' worth of booze and fine dining on the sly, in my name, and then fucked off.

Headline: 'Killer's Let Out to Work at the Body Shop. Butlins Nick Lags Unleashed on the Public.'

Picture caption: 'Cheers – Evil Featherstone enjoys his pint in the sun as children play nearby.'

Not long after publication the Executive Editor, an elderly former Royal Naval officer known as Cap'n Bob, plonked a massive complaint on my desk. The prison governor had fired off a big letter to the PCC. 'Can you do me a full memo on this, please?' Cap'n Bob asked.

'For fuck's sake,' I mumbled under my breath. Writing memos is the bane of a red-top reporter's life. No one wants to be bogged down in last week's fish 'n' chip paper when there's huge pressure to come up with stories for this week. Filled with the usual pre-memo dread, I picked it up – it read like a death sentence. The governor had blown the lid on all of our devious tricks. Of course, I went through it line by line and rebutted everything. Contrary to popular belief, complaints to the PCC were taken very seriously. Not because we cared about the targets, whose life we had unjustifiably destroyed, but because you risked incurring increased wrath from above. I always tried desperately to wriggle out of everything. Never cough to nothing. Never give anything away. Never tell it straight when it can be waffled and obfuscated. The art of rebuttal was simple. Inevitably, complainants made small errors in their memos. Home in on these to undermine the greater thrust of the attack. A trick that I had picked up from reading about New Labour's Rapid Rebuttal Unit at Millbank.

Often my memo lies didn't pass muster and we lost the complaint and the PCC instructed the *NoW* to publish an apology. Oh dear! I had the ignominy of not only having the biggest ever apology in the history of the *News of World* – my record was only surpassed years later by ads taken out by Rupert Murdoch himself re: phone hacking – but also the highest number.

My record-breaking PCC apology came in the aftermath of the Canary Wharf bomb in 1996. A 23-year-old African office cleaner called Barbara Osei was horrifically injured after her face was cut to shreds by flying glass. As she lay recovering in her hospital bed, with all pipes and tubes sticking out of her, I posed as a relative and sneaked on to the ward with a bunch of flowers. She was about to go into an emergency three-hour operation to save her eyesight. Instead of comforting words, I pulled out a disposable camera and bosh-bosh-boshed her off. Even in her semi-comatose state, high on morphine and still reeling with pain, Barbara could sense something was terribly wrong. The flashes were distressing and my aggressive posture was intimidating her. Reflecting back on this now is like looking back on someone else's life – I can't believe I did it. Barbara struggled, her bandages bloodied, to save her dignity, shifting helplessly in the bed and feeling for the panic button. But I carried on hosing her down with the flash. 'Calm down, Barbara!' I whispered, as I checked no one was coming to her aid and toed the door shut. I was nervous but my cruelty was strangely emboldened by her babyish vulnerability. What could she do? Fuck all. 'Don't worry. I'm a friend,' I said pathetically, as I stepped round the side of the bed to get a better angle. I was hoping that she would think I was some kind of doctor, taking pics of her injuries for medical reasons. Barbara started to scream. The weak nature of her voice rattled me. I dropped the flowers on the bedside chair and walked purposefully away down the corridor, to the lift. Apologising for shocking behaviour seems self-indulgent. But I do accept what I did was wrong and I'm ashamed of it.

In the fresh air, I was ecstatic with delight – proud of my cunning and my bottle. I could barely wait to ring this one in:

Ray: 'Hi, how's it going?'

Me: 'Got it – it's in the bag. Got a pic of the Canary Wharf bomb victim.'

Ray: 'Great – well done, Graham.'

Praise was like hearing that I'd got an A in an exam.

Me: 'No problem.' Humility was my watchword.

I can't remember exactly what else I'd told Ray. To cover my back, I think I told him that Barbara had actually cooperated and given me permission to take the pictures.

Ray: 'Did she say anything else – did she talk about her ordeal?'

This threw me – he was asking me a straightforward question but to me it was as though he was trying to catch me out, hinting that I hadn't gone far enough. It was as though I'd failed and getting the pics wasn't enough.

'Yes,' I lied. 'She gave me a little chat.' I made up a few anodyne quotes and filed them across. It was a high-risk play. But I was relying on two get-outs to cover my arse.

1. That Barbara was so pumped full of pharmaceuticals and trauma that she wouldn't remember what she'd done or said. In the unlikely event of a complaint, it would come down to her word against mine.
2. That she was a poor, powerless African immigrant, confused by the horrific events that had befallen her and that she wouldn't dare go up against the *News of the World*. I guessed that she was barely literate – so who was going to write her fucking memo?

Her fucking maxillofacial surgeons, that's who. Two of top doctors that were caring for her went into shock-and-awe when they saw the article in the paper. A pair of them got on their high horse and fired off a letter saying it was strictly forbidden to take pics in a hospital whether we had her permission or not. I wriggled and squirmed double-hard. I was confident that if I could get to Barbara I could talk her round. I went to see her again I kissed arse with her, her brother and her employers. Paid them some money. She said that it was all OK and that she wasn't really worried about the docs. Phew! I had done this loads of times before with complaints – headed them off at the pass with some fancy footwork.

But the docs weren't having any of it. When they heard I was trying to divide and rule, and confuse the girl further, they went ballistic. I couldn't give a fuck – who were these meddling fucking Teddy boys anyway? They went over Barbara's head and put pressure on the PCC to take a stand. Cap'n Bob was on the phone, sweating. People respected him and said he was a nice feller. But he spoke in a faux-posh accent, clearly designed to lend his racket respectability. He reminded me of one of those cad antiques show presenters on daytime telly. All this old naval stuff lent an air of trustworthiness to the whole charade.

Even so, I upped the ante. One night I drove 300 miles from a job up north to Barbara's dingy tower block in East London. I woke her up and got her out of bed. This time I leant on her, coercing and bullying her into signing a scribbly hand-written (by me) 'statement'. It was a get-out-of-jail-free card stating that she had given me permission to do all the bad things to her in the hospital and she didn't want to make a complaint against us and that she considered the payments I'd got her as sufficient compo.

Before I left her flat I flipped it, saying that I was going to lose my job if she didn't straighten the doctors out. Pathetically, I asked her for pity. Barbara was vulnerable and lonely and living in a shithole, but I left her in no uncertain terms that I'd be fucking livid if she didn't sort all this shit out. After all, she was a fucking cleaner. As the silver metal doors closed on the piss-stinking lift, I could see the ridges of scar tissue on her arms and face – the remnants of the 300 stitches that had sewn her back together. I was pleased – it was a good night's work.

But the doctors still kept firing off letters and Cap'n Bob wasn't happy with my statement scrawled out on a ratty piece of paper. This time I tried to dig the dirt on her. Find out her immigration status to see if she was illegal. Was she working cash-in-hand and claiming benefits? I made inquiries to see if she was involved in petty crime? I drew a blank. In the end none of it worked and Cap'n Bob caved in. The *NoW* published a massive apology.

Later, when I fell out with Rebekah Brooks, she called me into a meeting in her office. Like the sneak she was, she pulled out my complaints file from under her desk as though she was pulling out a gun to finish me off. The stacks of paper looked like a copy of Hansard – with some heavy-duty European Directives thrown in for good measure – it was that thick. For effect, she was throwing reams and reams of letters and memos on the tabletop and saying things: 'This is not good – look at all these complaints you've got. This is not a good record.' I just stared at them. I may have been a perennial reoffender, but handing out legal memos at the *News of the World* was like handing out speeding tickets at the Indie 500, as Martin Sheen said in *Apocalpyse Now*. All I could say in response was that it was because of the relentless pressure to come up with stories. But by that time I didn't care – I was a defeated man. I was shaking with some kind of post-traumatic stress disorder. The game was up. My world had collapsed.

15

Sex Kid

Spring in full bloom. Sunny April day. Strolling into town, along a glistening cobbled street, with my new girlfriend – a 12-year-old schoolie called Susan. I was supposed to be making small talk, getting her relaxed for our first date together. But what do you say to an anorexic tweenie – I knew nothing about kids? Especially ones with issues. I was an anti-family corporate drone who ate prawn sandwiches at my desk all day. Maybe we could visit the medieval castle, its scrofulous walls casting a dark shadow over the Middle England market town where Susan plied her trade. Shiftily, my face reddened, acutely conscious of how on-top we looked, as we made a bee-line through the tourists and the shoppers.

Rake-thin and dirt-poor, Susan was the post-Thatcherite offspring of Britain's new underclass. Nibbling her nails to cover up the cloud of submission that enveloped her whole life. A Victorian match-girl zoomed forward into the dirty shopping malls and retail parks of the old heartlands. Susan was a child prostitute. Her clothes were the trademark rags of Milton Friedman's residual pool of labour – off-the-market bubble jacket, JD sweatshirt and paper-thin trackies. Topped off with greasy, stale, moussed-up hair. A complexion bleached white by never-ending urban winter. Pimpled-up by junk food.

'I need the cash to get my ears pierced,' she said. A little satellite of her friends tailed us at a respectful courting distance. Not watching out for her, but egging her on to go into the baby changing room in a nearby shopping mall. A girl with her blonde hair, pulled tightly back on her face, shouted: 'Go with him now and do it, she wants as much money as she can get.' Laughing, they wanted a cut of the £15 that Susan claimed she regularly charged for sex.

'I'll meet you in the cubicle,' Susan whispered. Raised on a diet of crisps and ice pops until she was old enough to neck Ecstasy tablets. 'You can lock it inside.'

'OK, that's good,' I said, brazening up now. Getting into the zone. To the meat and bones of the story. As usual, tape whirring away in my inside pocket like an extra bodily organ. I couldn't really give a fuck what anyone thought now – I had a job to do.

'How much is it, to . . . er . . . do it . . . with you?' I asked.

'It's £15,' she replied.

'D'you mean sex?' I said emphatically for the tape.

'Yes,' she confirmed. 'But I will do whatever you want. And I want paying up front.'

When the story was published on the following Sunday, the fifth paragraph read:

'Even an experienced *News of the World* investigator was moved when Susan pathetically offered her young body to him in broad daylight for a paltry £15.' This was a lie.

Or, rather, I was moved – but to relief and excitement. When Susan muttered her offer for sex, in exchange for pocket money, I was buzzing. Getting the offer on tape is the crucial part of the story. Journalistically, very important. But legally like gold dust, because the story won't get in the paper, if that offer isn't on tape. In her words. Clear as a bell. End of story. So, I wasn't really saddened by Susan's plight. Simply focused on getting her to say the right things. Ticking boxes and getting through the day.

Now I was free to crack on with a bit of colour. Push her harder for more shocking revelations. Always a risk. But even if she backed off now it didn't matter, because I had the main part of the story in the bag. To me, Susan was just low-hanging fruit. I left the melodrama to the sub-editors.

I stalled her with small talk, in a bid to get more out of her. Before making my excuses and leaving. No way I was going into the cubicle with her – out of sight of witnesses, including the *News of World* surveillance photographer who was shadowing us like a Rolex robber in Mayfair. Imagine that – after the story comes out, you get accused of shagging a 12-year-old-girl on the job. For fuck's sake! The things that go through your mind. A dark world of twist. Once you enter, it fucks you up just thinking about these things. No wonder Roger the Dodger's head was wrecked. Doing this day in. Day out.

'I'm a bit nervous,' I said. 'Have you done this before?' An old one, but it always gets a reaction for the tape.

'I've lost count the number of times I've done it. I'm not happy about it. It's just something that happens.'

Susan's was one of the easiest stories that I've ever done. Even more so than a stunt-up. It's very easy for a professional liar like me to manipulate a 12-year-old girl into saying anything that I want. How do I know that she's telling the truth? How do I know that she really is a child prostitute? She could be telling me a pack of lies. I don't care. I could get her to confess to anything. Selectively choose the quotes that stand up the story. Discard the one's which make her look less serious. This is my trade.

How do I know that she's hasn't been groomed by the tipster to big-up the story? Am I bovvered? Her pram-faced mate was still hanging around. I'm a glory hunter not a Pulitzer Prize winner. One of the tipsters was a 16-year-old paperboy, who claimed to have seen Susan going into the cubicle, night after night, with strange men. But how do I know he hasn't just cooked the whole thing up? Groomed the girl on what to say. In order to rip a few quid out of the *News of the World*. The correct journalistic approach would have been to put

surveillance on Susan for a few days. Plot a van up on the taxi rank.
Watch the cubicle where she allegedly solicited punters.

Caught them red-handed. Independent corroboration. But the
expediency of modern journalism won't allow time for that. This
story had to go in the paper fast. We had the confession on tape.
That's that.

I asked Susan where she lived, agreeing to walk her home – so
I could find out her address. Spin it through Steve Whittamore.
Find out her second name. Identify her parents. Once that was
done, I was off.

After I'd cut her loose, I phoned the senior tipster on the story
– the one who'd delivered up the paperboy. His name was Paul
Samrai and he worked part-time in his dad's newsagent's, opposite Sainsbury's. After his shift selling sweets to school kids, he
moved next door to the chippy, also owned by his dad.

I found him behind the counter.

'Sorted!' I told him. 'Your child prostitute tip worked out.'

Paul: 'Thanks, mate. Fucking well done, mate.'

Samrai looked like a typical newsagent. A Punjabi Sikh with
bed-head hair from a crucifying 5 am start to get the papers in.
Blue Berghaus fleece, scruffy jeans. Smoked like a chimney
because his fags were free. Just after midday, but already slightly
manic from booze. The warrior yeomen from the Jalunda plains
had a soft spot for that homegrown burn-throat whisky they
drank. But Paul's poison was straightforward British lager. Paul
had alcohol issues.

However, there were hidden mysteries to him. And if you
looked closely enough, they gave you clues as to a previous life.
Glimmering around his furtive eyes, super pricey designer glasses.
Not for sale on these shores. Incongruously red £200-a-pair hand-
made socks. Fine-stitched leather shoes, more at home in chambers than on the patchy lino behind a sweet counter. And a cash-
mere overcoat with shoulder pads that suggested he'd been out of
circulation for a while.

'I knew you'd stand it up,' he projected in near-enough received pronunciation over the mag stands. 'I knew you'd get her.' Paul was beaming, knowing that for a spread he'd get a tip fee of around £3500. Paul was extremely clever and manipulative. He would go on to become one of the country's highest paid freelance journalists.

The following week, I flew off to New York for a mini-break with my new girlfriend. A hard-as-nails fifty-grand-a-year fashion buyer for a high-street supplier. Her own tasteful terrace in Watford with a spiral staircase and a brand new company Beamer outside on a permit. We weren't suited. We'd only got together after I nearly got into a fight with Pulp bassist Steve Mackey at a backstage Oasis party in Manchester a few weeks before.

Angela was a Pulp groupie who hung around with a pony-tailed cocaine dealer-to-the stars. Later, the dealer became mildly controversial in his own right, after Noel Gallagher slagged him off at an awards ceremony for being an old man with a ponytail who sucked the life out of the music industry. Anyway, one night we were all talking in a hotel bar. I started acting the goat. Chatting this half-tasty redhead up. Next minute the Pulp man came over. I was pissed. He was all right, to be fair. Bit of a student ponce. A fanny-head fringe, hanging over a miserable Morrissey pout. But I started spouting off about my claim to fame – that I was the reporter who'd just turned his band-mate Jarvis Cocker in a £30,000 kiss 'n' tell in involving a busty make-up artist.

Steve Mackey started crying about tabloid scum, saying that the story had nearly given Jarvis a nervous breakdown. I played up even more, 'That's a good result for us,' before the coke-dealer bundled them out. Anyway, a few weeks later I called Angela. She was looking for someone to settle down and have a baby with after years of partying hard. I was like, 'Fuck all that', but I had my eye on getting out of my Holloway bedsit and slipping between her Egyptian cotton sheets. How shitty is that? But that's how I viewed everything then – I was the centre of the universe and it was all about what could I do to get myself any advantage. The venality and selfishness that I nurtured in my professional life was now guiding my private life. I told her that I was on much more money than I really was.

Anyway, we were doing the whole Cool Britannia thing. Shacked up in a Manhattan boutique hotel, where the lobby smells of fresh lilies and expensive coffee. I was hanging around the retro cappuccino machine, in the teak-hemp-furnished breakfast bar. Nodding away to 'Free John Gotti' by the Fun Lovin' Criminals on MTV. Suddenly a gay concierge in a grey Paul Smith suit smiled at me. 'Mr Johnson, there's a call for you from the Clay Ravine somewhere.'

Ray: 'Where the fuck are you?'

Me: 'I'm in New York with my new bird.'

I gathered that Clay hadn't dialled me up himself otherwise he'd know – he must have got Tara to track me down.

Ray: 'For fuck's sake – are you on holiday?'

Me: 'I told you I was going away.' Butterflies, my breath nipping itself in. 'Last week.' No wonder he'd forgotten – I'd buried it in a busy conversation. Asking for holidays at the *News of the World* was like asking for a pay rise. I'd been there 18 months and this was my first official break. Asking for holidays felt shameful, a double-barrelled admission of betrayal and weakness. At Christmas, I was so exhausted that when my previous girlfriend turned up at my flat, dressed in a naughty Xmas costume, I couldn't do anything because I was so tired. In order to get a few days off, I'd lied to Ray that my dad had had a heart attack. He was back in Liverpool, fit as a fiddle. I was telling so many lies to everyone that I couldn't remember what was true. One day the Editor Phil Hall took me out for lunch, and asked how my dad was. 'He's sound,' I said. 'He's into cycling. He rides 20 miles a day on his hand-built Pete Matthews . . .'

'Wow – that's a quick recovery,' Phil said.

For fuck's sake, I'd forgotten about my dad's phony heart attack and now he's asking me about it.

'Yes it is, Phil,' I spoofed. 'It is a great recovery. After a scare like that, he's got bang into fitness.' Red-faced, moving on.

Anyway, fast-forwarding back to New York. Ray was obviously seething.

'For fuck's sake,' he continued. 'What a fucking week to go away.'

'Why? What's wrong?'

'The Chief Constable of Warwickshire has gone fucking ballistic over the child prostitute story. Saying that it was a load of bollocks and that you stitched the girl up.'

'Fuck off, Ray, I had her bang to rights on tape.'

'Have you got the tape with you? Can you do me a transcript and a full memo?'

'No – course not. I'm on holiday. I'm not in the habit of taking my tapes with me on holiday.

'It's in my desk, if you need to listen to it.'

I knew he wouldn't go for that – who wants to go scrabbling around in my desk, listening to tapes of all mad stuff? I was just hoping that he wouldn't courier it to the Big Apple. So that I'd have to spend the rest of my holiday doing up a big fuck-off memo for him and Cap'n Bob, when I should be out having a drink with Westies or something. Of a day, Angela had been 'working'. Out taking sneaky pictures of £2000-a-piece designer dresses on Fifth Avenue. That's what fashion buyers do – they're no better than *NoW* reporters. They make a copy of a designer dress in a shop, by covertly snapping it or sketching it. Send the design off to an Indian sweatshop. And get 20,000 made up for the UK high street. I couldn't believe it. Anyway, of a day, while she was out doing that, I'd taken to walking all over New York to all the worst bits – Brooklyn, Queens, Harlem. Fuck the Empire State and holding hands in Central Park. I preferred to take a look around Little Italy and the West Side.

'OK, wait until you get back,' Ray said. 'But don't fucking take all day about it, because we've had a letter off the girl's social worker as well. Saying that the parents have gone fucking mental and that the girl wasn't really on the game.'

"Who gives a fuck?' I replied. 'They're bound to say that, aren't they? The police are going mad because we make them look silly by exposing a child prostitute under their noses. Same goes for those social workers, fucking socialist worker students, whatever.'

'I know,' Ray agreed. 'But I just don't want any shit off them. OK. Well, have a nice time.'

'OK, ta. See you next week.'

'Oh, just before you go, one more thing.'

Here we go, I thought, the old Columbo bollocks.

'I want to ask you a question,' said Ray, 'and I want a straight answer.'

'OK. What is it?'

'Did you fuck her?'

'Did I fuck who?'

'The 12-year-old prostitute, that's fucking who.'

'What?' I exploded. 'Are you fucking mad?'

The colour drained from my face. I felt weak and worried.

'No I'm not mad. This is important. Did you fuck the child prostitute in Warwick or not?

If we're going to fight this, I need to know that there aren't any skeletons that are going to come back and bite us in the arse.'

'No, of course I didn't shag her. For fuck's sake, what do you think I am, a nonce?'

'I've got to ask you, that's all.'

'Fucking hell – you've knocked me for six there. I'm being accused of being a paedophile and having sex with 12-year-olds when I'm supposed to be enjoying a mini-break in New York with my bird.'

'No one's accusing you.'

'Well, you are, aren't you?'

'I'm not accusing you. I'm asking.'

'Well, the answer is fucking no.'

I got paranoid. Even telling the truth. What value had the truth in my world? Where only lies and blags had currency.

'Why?' I asked. 'Are the busies saying that I shagged her?'

'No, course not, but I've got to be sure.'

'Fucking hell, you're freaking me out. One minute you're saying to me "have a nice time," the next you're saying that I'm noncing off underage schoolies on the job.'

'Don't worry about it. See you later.'

Phone down.

Everyone was getting jittery about vice stories. Rumours were flying around the *News of the World* about how one investigator had raped a 14-year-old prostitute on a job, after buying her drugs in exchange for a story. On another job, an agency freelancer had gone on a brothel job for Features and said that he'd made his excuses and left. The prostitute had a different recollection. On the Tuesday, after publication, she rang in saying that the reporter in question hadn't been entirely virtuous. Saying that he hadn't made his excuses but had paid her and then gone on to have anal sex. When confronted, the reporter denied it. But he was caught out by a million-to-one chance. Astonishingly, the hooker had been secretly working for our rival department, News, on a completely separate long-running job. A different team of *News Of the World* investigators had wired up her massage room with secret video cameras in order to catch a celebrity who was meant to be visiting the girl. How mad is that? Of all the brothels in all the land, the agency reporter chose to go into one that was already *NoW* property.

'Not possible,' said the *Screws* executive who was talking to her.

'Well, if you don't believe me then,' the prostitute said, 'here is the fucking videotape, showing the reporter shagging me up the arse.' And it was true – she had it on video. *News of the World* video. Which our rivals on News were only too happy to hand over. He was sacked. Everyone laughed at the madness of this story. But deep down it struck a nerve – that could have been any one of the sleazy bastards who worked here.

16

Samrai Warrior

I quickly phoned Paul from my New York hotel.

'What the fuck's going on?' I demanded. Becoming sharp with the lesser mortals in the food chain. Just like my bosses were with me. The Murdoch way. That keeps everyone in line.

'I've just had my boss on saying that the police are pouring shit all over our child sex story.' Paul ignored my slights. Like most Indians he ignored the status anxiety and focused on the payday.

'Fuck them off,' he said, always reassuringly decisive in a mini-crisis. 'I've had heat on me as well. The chief con sent round a couple of coppers to lean on me. They were spitting feathers, jumping up and down, saying that I was bringing shame upon the whole of Warwick, that I was making the police look like dick-heads by exposing all this crime every week.'

They had a point – Paul and I had been turning over villains and darkening doorsteps in Warwick for just over six months now. We turned over an immigration scamster called Ranjiv Malik who sold fake Portuguese passports to illegals. He also ran a marriage con in Warwick. A Warwick-based people-smuggler had also been plastered all over the paper as a result of Paul's tips. And we'd also exposed a local sex-pest.

Warwick wasn't a hotbed of crime – it's just that Paul was tied to helping out his dad at the shop and in the chippy. That meant all of his stories had to be local. Resourceful to the extreme, Paul had an uncanny way of turning a little early morning gossip over the counter into a *News of the World* story. His drinking problem also prevented him from doing stories in different parts of the country. Reading between the lines, his dad didn't want him straying too far from the family manor in case he went on a bender.

'Well, what exactly are the police saying?' I asked.

'They're saying that if I don't stop dealing with the papers, they're going to send me back.'

'Send you back where?' I asked.

'Prison – the police said they'll send me back to prison. I'm still on licence.'

Paul Samrai had once been one of the richest and most successful young barristers in Britain. After being called to the bar, the UCL law graduate specialised in immigration, setting up practices in London and Hong Kong. During the late 1980s, he lived the dream with a Docklands flat overlooking Tower Bridge and an ambitious wife who loved money.

But Paul wasn't happy. Like many second-generation Asian kids, he had been pushed by his father through school. He was living his dad's ambitions rather than his own. An outsider by nature, Paul had been picked on at school, despite winning a place at a very good one. Now in the rarefied, all-white circles of the bar, Paul felt out of place again. Secretly, Paul was nurturing a bohemian desire – he wanted to be a journalist instead of a high-flying legal eagle.

Lured by the prospect of easy cash and a misplaced sense of adventure to satiate his inner lack of fulfilment, Paul relocated to Hong Kong, to take advantage of worried Chinese who wanted to get out before the handover. Cleverly, he found loopholes in the law, through which he could obtain British passports and visas for rich businessmen. By pretending that they had been educated in the UK. Then he got into bed with the Kowloon Triads. Then he started forging documents and fraudulently obtaining British passports. In 1994 Paul Samrai was busted by Scotland Yard and flown back to the UK in handcuffs. He was convicted and jailed for immigration fraud. Inside he met Peter Trowell who taught him the ropes of freelance tipping. When he got out, Peter hooked him up with me.

Stood there in his dad's sweet shop, in which he was forced to work in penitence to restore the family's honour, I was getting one of my first lessons in how some police propaganda works. If some constabularies police don't get the press they want, they bully people with threats and smear tactics.

'Well, do you give a fuck?' I asked.

'Not really, but I've got to be more careful about doing stories for the *Screws*. I'd rather not go back to jail.' Prison had shaken up the middle-class Indian boy. Unlike us at the *News of the World*, Paul was genuinely scared of the authorities. Unlike us, he didn't think that he was untouchable.

'I'll carry on doing stories,' he vouched. 'But we'll have to cool off on Warwick for a bit, spread our wings a touch. I'll square it with my dad so that I'm not chained to the shop so much. If I can prove to him that I'm making good money from the papers, and that it's a proper job kind of thing, then it should be OK.'

'Good,' I thought. I couldn't afford to lose Paul. Too valuable a contact. Samrai was a gatekeeper into two hot-potato issues that Rupert Murdoch wanted demonised. The undeserving poor and illegal immigration.

A few weeks later a hollow capsule of air was turning over in my guts. Conference, and I had fuck all for my list. Desperately I rang Paul.

'Hi, mate, have you got anything for this week?'

'Nah, mate, not much. Fuck all going on . . .'

'Fuck's sake . . . I'm desperate, mate.'

'Well, there's one thing?' Paul said. 'What about a sex pest terrorising a local estate?'

'That sounds good. What's the story?' Like a salesman, Paul could sense that it was a seller's market. So whatever shit he had to flog, he polished it up pronto and put his best spin on it.

'One of the fellers who comes in the shop told me about a dirty old man. A nonce in fact, on one of the estates close by, who keeps preying on the kids and that.'

'That sounds good, mate. What does he get up to?'

'He fondles the local schoolgirls, plies them with drink etc.' Paul was vague on the details. Sounded like a load of bollocks to me but beggars can't be choosers. So I chose to go along with him and not probe him too hard in case the story fell apart under closer scrutiny.

'Can we expose him?' I asked. 'Can we turn him over?'

'Yes, I know all the people on the estate. I'll get you into him, and you can get him on tape, boasting about wanting sex with the young girls.'

'I like that,' I said.

I rushed into conference. Pitched it up, hard.

'OK, what about this?' I told Ray. 'An investigation into one of Britain's most depraved sexual predators.' I hyped up the tip and oversold the story. 'I've got a steer from one of my contacts about a twisted council estate resident who is grooming young girls after plying them booze. He then lures them to his lair and forces them to have sex with him.'

I knew this type of story would play out well in conference. The new buzz word doing the rounds was anti-social behaviour. The country was on stand-by to go into a General Election. And the New Labour leader Tony Blair was fighting on a ticket of bashing the unruly idle poor. The burgeoning underclass, that had been out-of work since the early '80s, were clogging up the sink estates. Being poor wasn't against the law yet, but their behaviour could be criminalised if a raft of new offences was trumped up. My job was to demonise anti-social behaviour to pave the way. The underclass, along with other on-trend vulnerable sub-groups, such as single mums and asylum-seekers, were now fair game. Unusually, the *News of the World* seemed to be supporting New Labour and Tony Blair. Slavish support of the Tories had been dropped. Little did a lowly functionary like me know that Tony Blair had courted Murdoch by flying half way across the world to see him. In 1997 Blair and his press aide Alastair Campbell flew to Sidney to address a Murdoch conference – I assume my Editor Phil Hall had been there to take note of what needed to be cooked up. To make it work for everyone. To manufacture the consent.

I kept overselling my pervert story to Ray, stating that the target was ritually violent and abusive to his salt-of-the-earth neighbours – council estate peasants. Our Readers. Our Punters. That needed our protection. In the end, Ray went for it.

'I quite like that,' he said. 'Sounds like a load of bollocks, but if we can get the whole estate up in arms about him, that could work.'

I was dispatched up to Warwickshire to turn him over.

If you had a story to feed to the bosses, then they'd get off your back for another week. That's all that mattered. That brief respite from the heat of battle. That feeling of isolation-tank contentment that you had survived another seven days at the cutting edge of the most competitive newspaper in the most cut-throat tabloid market on the whole of the planet. If I can cut it here, I can cut it anywhere.

So, it was around a month before the New York mini-break that I got to Warwick, and, as usual, the story was definitely not sold-as-seen. I checked the target out. His name was Derek Coop. In reality, he was no more than a poverty-stricken odd-bod who kept himself to himself. Got a bit grumpy when the local hood-rats wound him up. I spoke to the neighbours and they didn't really have anything bad to say about him. OK, he was a bit of a dirty old man. But didn't every estate have a person like him hanging around? Derek Coop was special needs. The type of person who needed help rather than to be exposed by the *News of the World*. He reminded me of a man who used to hang around my area where I grew up. We used to call him Dirty Dave. He was a bit slow and trampy. He used to stash porno mags on a disused railway line. Now and again, Dirty Dave robbed knickers off people's washing lines – but he wasn't a monster and he had to endure a life of bullying and hate crime, as so many disabled people do. Similarly, there were allegations that Derek Coop was a flasher.

I knocked on his door. Like most fellers like him, he lived in squalor. But he had a caring daughter who did her best to look after him. The poor girl was at the end of her tether. I lied and smiled that I was there to help her. To offer protection from the people who had it in for her dad. Tape on. Kindly, she offered me a cup of tea. Reporter's trick: always accept one as it builds trust and is an excuse to stay in the house longer.

'What's all this I hear about your dad being harassed by the local yobs?' I asked her.

'He's not a pervert, like they make out,' she said. 'He's just had a nervous breakdown since being made redundant. The neighbours accuse him of doing all sorts, but he doesn't know what he's doing half the time. We've asked the social for help, but there's nothing. We've fallen out with the lot of 'em. The kids shout at him and give him stick.'

Strife on the estates between residents was increasing – I'd noticed it. As society was becoming more selfish and hard-faced, people were turning on each other. Community spirit was dissolving in favour of dog-eat-dog.

The daughter carried on: 'Far from being a pervert, the kids use him. He drinks a lot, so the kids who play truant come and have a drink here. My dad doesn't know what he's doing?'

I felt really sorry for her. She broke down in tears. I couldn't face phoning Ray and telling him this was a non-runner. Have him scream down the phone. Instead, I did what every *News of the World* reporter did when faced with a listed story that didn't stand up – I made it work. Who was it going to be? Me or the defence-less Derek Coop and his lovely daughter? One of us would have to be sacrificed up to Ray and that was that.

Wedgnock Green was my kind of place. I surveyed the battle-field of ideas. A tattered rim of 1930s parlour houses, set around a weedy half-oval of contractor-maintained grass. These were my kind of people. Conclusion – I knew I could manipulate the residents into saying pretty much anything. Feeding off their greedy desires and petty hatreds. To slag off old Coop and serve him up like a roast chicken. Estates are riven with politics and grievances just like offices – I was certainly better at playing this kind of chicanery than boardroom poker with Rebekah Brooks and Ray Levine. I went to work.

As usual, the first witness was a 15-year-old paperboy who worked for Paul Samrai. He said: 'Coop offered me cigarettes and vodka and then urinated in a bowl before locking me in a bedroom.' Course he did.

I popped into Coop's next door neighbour at number 13. Their sour-faced teenage daughter let rip with irrational babblings – perfect for *NoW* quotes. The 16-year-old schoolgirl said: 'Coop has propositioned me dozens of times. He talks dirty and has shown me porn mags.' Took me half an hour of wading through unusable mundanery about Coop to get that. Hardly Ian Brady, but I could spin that up to make Coop look like the real thing.

I scamulated up some quotes from No. 10, No. 16 and No. 17. I exaggerated incidences of low-level anti-social behaviour into horrific acts of dangerous and criminal intent. In short, I demon-ised the vulnerable loner who lived in the decrepit parlour house with the overgrown garden so that he would become a hate-figure up and down the land. By the time the piece was written up, it read like he was the most dangerous man in Britain.

Ray called up: 'Can you draw a little map of the street with a big arrow pointing to the pervert's house? And then all the other houses where the people are in danger.' Sure – an official looking graphic will only heap more grief on Coop. On the way back to the office, I got a herogram from Ray: 'Well done, mate, fucking great story.'

Headline: 'Pervert on The Green.'

Picture Caption: 'Monster – Coop and his hell-hole home.'

Intro: 'We expose Britain's most depraved neighbour – Dirty-talking fiend's booze lure for kids.'

Strapline: 'One scared lad told the *News of the World* how Coop dropped his trousers, tried to kiss him and begged him to perform a sex act.'

I was pleased with myself. The tipster Paul Samrai got a couple of grand tip fee and I went back to my hovel in Holloway to crash out from fatigue.

Come Tuesday, the cycle was repeated. I started swaggering out of conference mantraing my new motto: 'Let's go and destroy someone's life.' Before hitting the road later that day to do exactly that. To another unsuspecting member of the public. Living in a nowhere town somewhere. Who hadn't done much wrong. People started getting turned over left, right and centre for doing nothing at all. These were the good times.

17

Angry Men

A few months later, I was desperate for a similar hit. Ray called me into his office. 'Have you got any good stories?' he asked, not looking up. He was examining several small diamonds and gold rings layed out on a soft black cloth on his desk. On the side, he sold jewellery – wedding bands, engagement rings, trinkets – that he bought off his mates in Hatton Garden, mostly, offloading them to members of staff at a discount. One time he sent me round to one of his mates with a stack of cash – Ray thought I was a good bag man because I looked pretty tough. Holding a monocle magnifying eye-piece to his eye, and without looking up, he said; 'That nasty neighbour story was good – have you got any more like that?' I phoned Paul: 'Have you got any more of those "nasty neighbour" stories? They want more of them.' New Labour were on the ascendant – the green light was given for a programme of mass criminalisation of the underserving poor, in a bid to pave the way for ASBOs.

'Yes,' Paul said. One of his mates had told him about a very angry man-type who lived in Coventry and was upsetting the estate. True, lorry driver David Jerome was a nasty bully – but did he really deserve to take the title off old Coop and become Britain's next nastiest neighbour?

A few hours later, after a good reception in conference, I was stood outside David Jerome's house, destroying his life. Jerome was irascible – so it wasn't hard for me to wind him up and get the money shot: him chasing me and the photographer down the road with his Alsatian, just like one of those timeshare fraudsters do on *Watchdog*. The picture was irrefutable proof that he was guilty of being nasty. In truth, this 'investigation' was no more than a local story. But again I hyped up the quotes from the neighbours and even got his wife to slag him off.

Headline: 'Say Hello to the Worst Neighbour in Britain.'

Picture caption: 'Bullying Jerome hurls abuse and threats at neighbours.'

Intro: 'This is Neighbour From Hell David Jerome – he's so nasty even his wife wants him out.'

Another new trend was also creeping into stories. Celebrity culture was dawning and every story, no matter how far removed from showbiz, had to have a celebrity reference. News executives had decided that their readers were so stupid that they could not understand anything unless it was refracted through the prism of a soap opera. Everything was getting more disconnected from real life. The *News of the World* were picking on David Jerome for being from the underclass. As part of a cooked-up story. Then selling the story back to the underclass who bought their newspapers. But saying that he was different from them by packaging it up as a soap opera so that they could relate to it. Tabloid culture was now entering the world of twist at warp speed. To boot, all showbiz references had to be high up in the story – a prominent place in the first few paragraphs. Hence in my third paragraph on this story was: 'Foul-mouthed Jerome, 55, is a real-life version of *Coronation Street* troublemaker Les Battersby.' Without this line the story would not have got in the paper and it was an excuse to use a big picture of a *Corrie* star. Within five years almost all off-diary tabloid stories had to have a celebrity mentioned in them.

This would be the language that the elite would use to simultaneously communicate with and distract the masses. Big Brother –
that is the other Big Brother from George Orwell and not the
reality show – could not have achieved a tighter manufacture of
consent.

No one ever batted an eye after my gratuitous attacks on the
defenceless. Unpeople, whose destroyed lives became my stock-
in-trade. A sign of the times. Britain's once proud working classes
had been reduced to cowering husks of suspicious and divided
groups. Community spirit, trade unions and mutual support
replaced now with poverty, smack heads robbing old bingoites,
and people living on the street. I was employed to make sure that
the truth that led to this state of affairs was never aired. How the
peasants had been battered down with economic shock therapy
and rampaging free markets. Instead, the vices of the poor were to
be blamed on themselves. My job was to fabricate the evidence,
painting a picture of a neo-Victorian Britain whose ills were self-
inflicted. To this end, Paul Samrai's stories were a perfect fit. A
logical step-up from stunt-ups. Tales of the unexpected that
weren't exactly false, but not exactly true either. Not quite full-on
falsehoods with walk-on parts for paid-up pretenders. But using
genuine people who were selectively tarnished and fitted up and
couldn't fight back. A kind of soap opera using real-life people.
An early pilot of *The Only Way Is Essex*.

'Let's do it to them, before they do it us,' I laughed, as I bailed
out of conference a few weeks later. A Big Swinging Dick now. A
Big Top Operator on The Street. I was high off a successful pitch.
Ray liked my tip about a vampire sex cult. All becoming routine
now. 'Can you book me a train to Weymouth in Dorset, please?'
I asked Tara, as I brushed passed the secretary's desk. Mixing it
with a bit of saucy banter, as though I'd been working here all my
life. 'And a little hire car, if you wouldn't mind.' I was getting used
to the corporate slack afforded to the successful functionary.

A few hours later I was playing Pac Man on a table-top video
game machine, in a deserted amusement arcade on the

whitewashed seafront of another town that beckoned nuclear war. Today, you'd get a grand-and-a-half for a sit-down console like that in a Notting Hill junk shop. But back then, the retro cocktail table was no more than a meeting point for bored teenagers in another coastal stretch with a high rate of petrol-sniffers. No wonder the kids were turning into blood-suckers around these parts. Teenagers need tower blocks, multi-storey car parks, decent clobber, big footy teams and good music. I was there to meet my contact, a disgruntled ex-member of The Family, an alleged Satanist sect based on psycho American Charles Manson's infamous cult, now made up of the best virgins Dorset had to offer.

Over a cup of Burger King tea and a Whopper with onion rings that I'd shit out within minutes, I asked the contact to introduce me to their self-styled leader, a bearded former car-robber called Wayne Phelps. A few minutes later, we were sat on the crumby floor of Phelps' housing benefit bedsit, soaking up the patchouli oil jozzies and the gothy posters. Seaside towns were rapidly becoming a great source of stories because the big cities were using their looming Victorian rooming houses as dumping grounds for council estate jetsam. Squeezed out by right-to-buy. Designated low credit scores. Community-care types, the disabled, drug addicts, special needs, single mums, anti-social families and petty criminals had turned the picture postcard into a bully's paradise.

'Hi Wayne,' I said, giving a slight bow, 'You don't know how much of a great honour this is. Your name is spreading far and wide. The reputation of The Family has reached London. Me and my friend Paul (Paul Ashton – *News of the World* snapper, later picture editor) are also followers of the Carpathian religion. We've heard about your great work. Respectfully, we've come down to ask your permission to set up a branch of our own.'

Crushed by a life of abuse and low self-esteem, Wayne was visibly blown away that someone had finally recognised his talents and come all the way down from London to seek his wisdom. His acolytes, a couple of pot-heads and girls wearing dirty tracksuit bottoms, were bewildered. But I knew Phelps' prison cunning wouldn't take long to roll with the flow. Within seconds he puffed himself up, and looked at his friends as though to say: 'I told you so – all this stuff I've been telling you about my powers is true.'

'I'll have to make sure that you're proper vampires,' he said to me, getting carried away with himself. 'We're a serious outfit and we've got no time for time-wasters. We drink each other's blood about once a month. It's a ritual that makes The Family stronger. And the girls like it as well.'

Every part of crap Britain has a Wayne Phelps. The Dungeons and Dragons kid who's taken it a bit too far. Escaping into the fantasy world a bit too deep, probably to blot out the care home he's in. Or the broken home that's fucked him up. Banned from Games Workshop for robbing. Glue-sniffer. Rat breeder. Ouija board cutter-outer. I've met a few of these Warhammer-types who live a double life as a wizard of Mordor. Wayne called himself Vandarl, after an ancient Transylvanian, but quickly realised that he could get sly wanks off the local slags, by drama'ing up their sea-grey life in a mean, ageing town where happiness is a warm bus shelter. I got on to what was going on within seconds – no more than bizarre game of spin the bottle run by an over-active imagination. Given 50 grand's worth of fee-paying education, Wayne would be working in the theatre today. But them's the breaks. I was actually nearly reduced to tears thinking about Phelps. The squalor he lived in. Filling me with pity. The little life he'd literally dreamt up, down here on his own. He was only doing his best – I had loser mates like him back home. Not vampires – but just fucked-up doleite lads. But what am I going to do? Ring Ray and tell him that my Dracula tip, that so spell-bound conference just a few hours before, is just kids who've watched *The Lost Boys* too many times? Or do I take Phelps' low-level role-play and manipulate it up into a big 'Hammer House of Horrors Devil-Worshipping' exclusive that would excite our demographic because there were lots of mentions of virgins, the word 'sucking' and flashes of firm young breasts?

Let's Do It To Them, Before They Do It To Us. Phelps had to go, no two ways about it. By patiently asking leading questions, I was able to get Wayne to come out with all kinds of bullshit on tape.

On the size of his cult: 'We've got about 80 members now.' (In his dreams. All bollocks by the way – Wayne had never met 80 people in his whole life.)

On girls: 'Around 10 are still at school, mainly girls. I've had sex with most of them. But we don't see that as wrong. My current girl is 15 and she has lovely firms breasts. She'll go for as long as you want her to go . . .' etc. (I suspected Warhammer Wayne was a virgin himself. But the pervy detail would go down well with the Sunday League footy players that draped the paper over their thighs in the car on the way to the game.)

Drug dealing: 'I used to make £200 a day selling speed. But with The Family I get to meet a lot of kids and I'm sure we can build a market there.'

Arming for a Waco-style siege: 'I've bought a sword and a gun. Weapons are expensive, but we need more to protect ourselves.'

More ego-massaging and more egging on and within minutes, Phelps has gashed his wrists a little, and was daubing black magic symbols over the face of a teenage girl. However, the pièce-de-résistance of my blag was to persuade Phelps to put on a blood-rites ritual at the local graveyard. Initially, Phelps had said no, explaining that it wasn't a full moon.

'But I must see how you do it with my own eyes,' I blagged. 'You've got to teach me how to make a sacrifice so that I can go back to my cult and show them how to do it correctly.' Phelps and his gang fell for it and later that night we entrapped them into our hire cars and off we went to a stone altar in nearby Sandsfoot Castle. To be fair, it wasn't hard to blag them. One of the more backward disciples lived in a village where he said the people at the bottom of the hill didn't speak to the residents at the top because of a feud that had gone on for hundreds of years. It was that kind of scene.

'By the way,' I said, helping Phelps to get on top of the grave-stone. 'Do you mind if we take some pictures so that I can show our followers exactly what you do?' Cue photographer Paul Ashton gets out his 15–20 grand's worth of professional cameras. Within minutes, with a bit of direction from me, Phelps had slashed his wrists with a rusty razor and a 15-year-old girl was sucking out the dripping gore.

Barely able to contain my laughter, I said: 'What's that like?'

She said: 'Wayne's a strong leader. It feels good to belong because we're so close.'

Phelps added: 'I am ready to kill for my followers and they are ready to die in sacrifice for The Family.'

One of his mates called Bobby chipped in: 'We do this every month. Wayne's blood tastes sweet. It's beautiful. I will die in honour and in battle for the Family.'

The story made a great splash.

Front Page Headline: 'Vampire Sex Cult Preys on Virgins.'

Inside page headline: 'Blood Lust. Investigation: Sick Black Magic Sect.'

Caption: 'Feeding Frenzy: Maniac High Priest Phelps grips his schoolgirl recruit after forcing her to drink blood from his slashed chest.'

Suckers: 'Bobby and Carr feed off Phelps.'

Strapline: 'Victim Loretta – Phelps must be stopped before he kills a child – he terrified me.'

'Sick menu – Phelps snacks on Bobby's arm.'

Strapline: 'Twisted Satanist turns teenagers into sex Zombies.'

Intro: 'An evil vampire-worship sect has launched a terrifying crusade to lure and defile schoolgirl virgins all over Britain. *News of the World* investigators witnessed sickening midnight scenes as Satanist high priest Wayne Phelps paraded his latest 15-year-old victim. In the ruins of a Dorset castle the pervert boasted how he robbed the girl's innocence and forced her to be a sex slave.

"I enjoy sex with young girls," he roared, "I've even had virgins in graveyards."

Already one disturbed victim has been admitted to a psychiatric unit after suicide attempts. But still Phelps' shameless disciples – dubbed The Family – vow to spread their sleazy web nationwide.'

It wasn't long before I was seeing this type of story on the box in the form of Trash TV. *Vanessa*, *Trisha*, then *The Jeremy Kyle Show* were characterised by obscenities, explosive guests and in-studio fighting. The underclass playing up like dancing bears for the underclass watching them at home on daytime telly. The next day I was inundated with herograms. Like a thunder-flash from the gods, the Editor bestowed on me my first picture byline. Proudly, I posed in my Dorset bed and breakfast in my old dog-tooth sports jacket while Paul the photographer took my portrait.

But the ultimate accolade was waiting in my in-tray back at the office. Carefully, I opened the envelope and unfolded the headed notepaper. The deep blue of *News of the World* letterhead solid like a bank. A herogram from Stuart Kuttner praising me for landing a world-beating exclusive without incurring extravagant costs. He used it to lecture his high-spending reporters. Rebekah flew past in a flurry of red hair: 'Great hit on the vampire,' she cooed. 'Really spooky – the readers love it. We should do more of that kind of thing.' She smiled knowingly. I wonder what she was cooking up.

18

No Excuse

'Sign here,' bleeped Kuttner, handing me the form for my first cash advance. 'Thanks, Stuart,' I said humbly. 'I'll spend it wisely.' The Cunt passed over the envelope containing £800 to his new golden boy. I was a good bet. The cost-cutter. The reporter who delivered like a B-movie producer – on time and on budget. Not like the Fake Sheiks and the Low Level Nevilles of this world, with their helicopters and entourages of bodyguards and tape-transcribers. Their toppy Max Clifford buy-ups wiping out budgets like footballers' wages. Draining the Cunt of his colour like embalming fluid. The Cunt smiled approvingly at his tame functionary. 'I won't let you down,' I replied, almost clipping my heels together, before backing out of his office gently.

Flash money for a hooker job. Shirley Ann Lye had been on. 'Got a facking good one for you,' she cackled. I could smell her house-white breath down the line. Straight down the Wine Press. In a whirlwind fluster of booze and hangers-on, she intro'd me to the former manager of pub rockers and Live Aid openers Status Quo. A relaxed deal-maker in need of a few quid since a fall-out with the band. The ex-Quo guy told me about the young daughter of a top Law Lord judge-type VIP who was working as a high-class hooker in a London clip joint. Good story. Nice upmarket sleaze – the advertisers'll get a stiffy on over that. Not to mention our porno mag-reading, woman-hating demographic. Icing on the cake will be a decent Sunday-for-Monday follow in the *Mail*, whose lower-middle-class readership also loved a good hate. By that time, poor girl will probably have topped herself anyway. All good stuff.

Before we got off to the sex club to check out the story, Shirley wanted me to meet a couple of shifty-looking, hang-dog ex-coppers in the corner of the Wine Press. One of them was called John Ross, notorious for breaking the story about the death of MP Stephen Milligan, who was found wearing stockings and suspenders with an orange in his mouth. Ross was a former detective sergeant in the Flying Squad who worked closely with the *Sun*. He was later cleared of bribing a serving officer for a story.

'C'mon,' Shirley implored, 'Ross is an important person to know in this game. I'll introduce you. We can get some good stories off f 'im and I'll split the tip fee with him, if they make.' But I was half-suspicious of delaying tactics. That she had her eye on the £800 flash money in my pocket: a free night out. So I blanked them, fucked them all off. I couldn't be arsed with coppers, never mind dark-horse ones and early retirement merchants. Too much of a mad, incestuous scene. Hurt, hard stares over the bar. Anyway I had no time. Drunk up. Too much of a bigshot these days. Got enough contacts. I was keen to crack on with the Quo man and the tale of the judge's daughter.

'Let's go and destroy her life,' I said as we hit Fleet Street and hailed a cab. We headed down to the hostess bar off Regent Street where the Status Quo guy had made small talk with the girl in question, on a jolly a few nights earlier. Inside, the livestock were parading themselves among the foreign businessmen and Russkie-mafia types. Crammed into a dark holding area above the old-fashioned cabaret floor. Wide-eyed, heavily made up Anne

Bancroft look-a-likes. Short leather skirts, hard bodies, fighting age. Gymed-up to death at expensive Chelsea health clubs and kids at private school. You wouldn't believe how much money these high-class brass make. And you wouldn't believe the respectable houses they leave behind when they come out to work. Secret lives and desperate housewives.

Their merry dance involved eyeing up the punters to see if they're for real or blagging it. Checking out their Rolexes for fakes. Looking for the Arab regulars who'll take back two or three of them at a time to their Bedouin tents, pitched up on the roofs of the better hotels. None of the girls want to pick up a dud John by accident. A time-waster who isn't going to drop at least a grand on them for a few hours' fun.

After about 20 minutes at the bar, the contact ID'd the target sitting alone under a dim gaslight-style lamp in the corner. Tape on, right over. Sweet nothings were forbidden by the moody-looking management. Unless the punters ordered a bottle of bubbly to go with the raspberry velvet coverlets and false flowers on the cocktail tables next to the disco. No wonder Ray said I would need £800 – one bottle was £150 and the girls were encouraged to get the clients drunk and ply them with more. A basket of thin, reheated school dinner chips was a cool nifty. Who was I to complain? That's how these places made their graft.

Shy and pale, I could tell at once that Claire wasn't really a pushy tart, hell-bent on bleeding me dry. Much younger than the cougar cattle at the bar. Nervously, she fiddled with her auburn hair and I could tell she was as embarrassed as I was. But it wasn't long before I had her laughing, flirting even by the second bottle. My cover story was that I was a self-made music mogul, who owned a recording studio and a string of coolio indie retail shops. Coyly, she giggled from under hair held in place by one of those posh-girl Alice bands, her head slightly tilted to one side. Something of the Princess Diana about her. Something vulnerable.

'Oh, I wish I had a boyfriend like you,' she suddenly lamented.

'My parents would be so proud. You're young and successful. You're exciting, and you've built up this big business all on your own. You're the kind of guy they want me to marry.'

This is going in the right direction.

'What do they do?' I asked. She tee'd me up like a dream. 'Your folks, that is . . .'

'Oh, well, my dad's, well . . .' she hesitated, so I smiled encouragingly.

'Well he's a big-wig in the legal profession,' she whispered, right off the bat.

'Wow, that's cool,' I said, lining up my next leading question. 'D'you mean like a barrister or something?'

'No. Well, yes. Kind of. Literally he's a big-wig,' she giggled again. You couldn't help liking her. 'He's a judge.'

'Wow. Mad one.' I said, trying to appear nonchalant, eyes dipping into my tray of pound-per-chip McCain's served up by the gangster bastards that ran the place. Claire wasn't stupid – she'd been to one of the top public schools in the country. I didn't want to spook her so early on, so I let her fill the pause. Holding your tongue and fighting the urge to work the tape, is one of the hardest things to do on an undercover job. We want her words, not mine. The spectre of the *News of the World* Legal Manager Tom Crone was lecturing me from his bed, in my head.

'My dad's kind of well known,' Claire went on. 'He's a judge. Or at least he was. Now he's been promoted, and he's actually the boss of all the other judges.' Insecure, she was relieved to tell me this, as if to put some distance between herself and mutton low-life, jealously looking over from the pen where they waited to be picked out.

'Kind of like the Lord Chancellor kind of thing,' she continued. 'But with a different title . . . I don't know exactly, but he's quite important anyway.' Bingo! The story was true – and I had the first key admission on tape. Now I just had to wheedle out his name.

No problem because then she started spilling her heart out. These tarts and their hearts. The way they carry on.

'But I don't really get on with my parents.' she went on. 'My dad's a very successful guy, very driven. So is my brother. He came down to London and got a big job, making loads of money. Me, I've done nothing. I'm the black sheep, I've achieved nothing and I've let everyone down. That's why I'm here, working in this place. Well, at least, until I can get it together anyway.'

Claire looked a bit red-ringed blubby around her eyes. I clocked the scratches on her bony arms. A self-harmer? Eating-disorder? A St Trinian's snorter? These left-on-the-shelf IT girls – being posh fucked them up Tamara-style. All that status anxiety, even at an early age. Too dim to cut it in the professions. Too flaky to catch a Cityboy and settle down. I felt sorry for her. She was clearly depressed.

'My dad'd freak out if he ever found out if I was working in this hell-hole, doing this – hostessing, getting paid to go with men.' The phrase 'go with' weighed down on the sentence. I gulped guiltily, draining the dregs of the £35-a-glass relabelled Asda champers. Well, he's going to fucking flip on Sunday, I thought. When he sees a picture of himself, grinning in his ermine fancy dress, next to a grainy Kodak disposable of his Little Princess, splayed all over my hotel bed in her suzzies. And splashed all over the World's Greatest Newspaper. M'lud is going to hit the fucking roof, no two ways. I wouldn't want to be at the next Christmas dinner with them all.

Hostess bar protocol prohibits Johns from propositioning brasses in the bar. But after 500 pounds' worth of acidy heartburn, and customary dropsies to the slippery maître d', Claire was finally given safe passage to leave the premises by an Albanian doorman. Next stop, the hotel. The crucial point in the night.

The plan was to get Claire to offer me a menu of sexual services, along with a price list on tape. (Legal deal-breaker.) Get her to pose up for some saucy pics. Before making my excuses and leaving. Mentally, I ticked off the 101 things on my legal and journalistic checklist. Before leaving the bar, I slipped off into the cold, smelly bogs – a forgotten-about cost-centre in a vice industry cash cow – and covertly checked the quality of the tape. Flushing the toilet as I went, to hide the noise of the playback. For fuck's sake – as I suspected. Very crackly and noisy background from the cattle market. Plus the '70s Saudi-friendly disco music was washing in and out of Claire's voice recording like a ghost at a séance. Frustratingly, I'd now have to go over all of the previous admissions I'd got out of her in the bar, within the controlled environment of the hotel room, just to make sure we were all shipshape again. The only problem was that I was getting tired now. And it never worked out as good second time as it did the first. Finally, while I was having a piss, I phoned the snapper outside to tell him to get ready to take a picture of Claire and me coming out of the jazz bar. 'I'll stand under the street lamp,' I told him, 'so there's enough light.' Then, a second one of us going into a hotel. This time the lights of the lobby, come Sunday, would illuminate Claire's sordid double life, for all to see.

Outside, the night air suddenly knocked me out. Making me a little unsteady on my feet – the bubbles had gone to my head fast. In the cab, I got a bit of the twirlies, battling to stop the enclosed leatherette spinning around. I was losing focus. Inversely, I started talking more jarg to Claire. The more Claire asked me about my pretend life, the more it got real. I started boasting about all the top bands I had signed to my record label – Oasis, the La's, the Happy Mondays, the Beatles. I told her about my imaginary dance label. Holiday homes on Ibiza and Santorini. Recording studios in Cotswolds country mansions. But it wasn't only the booze talking. By that time, I had told so many lies in my life, that falsehood now blurred into truth as routine. I actually began to believe my own blags, and felt more comfortable in them than in the harsher outside world. The irony was that deep down I was trying to escape reality – trying to get away from the job and all the terrible things that went with it.

Claire was falling for it big time as well. Falling for me, in fact. I began to feel protective of her. After checking into our room, I tried to get focused again. But couldn't shake the gloom that I'd broken the cardinal rule – never get drunk on a hooker job. My head was getting clouded.

I realised that she hadn't asked me for any money yet – you can't call her a brass if she doesn't charge money. So I brought up the subject. Astonishingly, she wasn't really interested. Was this girl really a hooker? Had she done this before? Eventually she agreed to take a few hundred quid off me – an essential element of the story if I was going to describe her as a prostitute.

As soon as we got inside, Claire jumped on to the bed. Without prompting, she started to peel off her clothes excitedly. Her dress, a dark blue twin set rimmed with white piping and a thin belt. The kind that you might see on a Tory MP's wife overlaid with pearls, slipped around her ankles.

Oh no!!! 'Wait there,' I said, panicking. 'Let's just chill out first and order some drinks off room service.' Anything to stall her. But by now she was pissed as well and bang up for the good times.

While I was on the phone to reception, she started tugging at my belt playfully. 'Take it easy,' I said. 'Plenty of time for that later.' I turned side-on to blank her. But when I looked back, she was laying on the bed totally naked. Her body was curiously smooth and plastery white. Not honed, but thin and mildly curvy. With small cup-shaped breasts. An aristocratic figure from a bygone age on a modern girl.

Leaping up on to her knees, Claire gripped the waist of my trousers and skilfully dragged them down. I was trying to get her away. But within seconds she was through my boxies, and pulling me towards her. A starburst of twirlies exploded in my head. Before I knew it, Claire was locked on. How could I resist? She was champing at the bit. I closed my eyes. For a brief moment, I drunkenly submitted to the pleasure.

'Fuck!' I opened my eyes. Snapping out of it immediately. Yanking myself away from her.

'What are you doing?' she said, clearly hurt.

'I can't do it!' I blustered. She looked surprised. But the damage had already been done. There was no doubt, that for however brief a moment, it had definitely happened. May not have been enough to draw DNA – no more than a few seconds in fact – but if it came down to it, I'd definitely had sexual relations with that woman. The one who looks like a naked courtier in a seventeenth-century oil painting hanging above a staircase in a stately home. The one now kneeling before me, looking confused. No denying it. I was bang to rights.

Fucking hell – what had I done? Black swirls tailed through my brain. What had she done? How on top was this? I'd blown nearly £800 flash money. Bagged a great fucking story. Then gone and fucked the whole thing up, over a momentary lapse of reason, right at the end. What a fucking beaut! I sobered up quickly. I was getting sloppy.

I fronted it out, as best I could. It's funny. At that time, it seemed so fleeting, that it wasn't much of an effort to automatically delete the incident out from the running order of the job. And carry on as though nothing had happened. A natural coping mechanism, I suppose. To clean the scene of the crime from the enormity of the fuck-up, in this poky half-cut hotel room.

Meanwhile, Claire carried on, urging me to come to bed. I blundered on, still needing to get more chat on tape. In order to stall her advances, I said that I couldn't have full sex with her because I didn't have any condoms.

'See if reception have got any?' she asked, calling my bluff. 'I can't take all this money off you, and nothing happen. I'd feel guilty. Plus I like you. I want to sleep with you.' Sounds corny, but she started giving it all the 'you're so different' and 'I'd like to see you again' and going on about how her father would love me, and how she wanted to see me again on a proper date. Maybe I could meet the parents.

With no other reason than to buy time, I called down to reception. 'No,' gruffed the night porter.

'See, they've got none,' I told her, 'so we'll have to leave it till another day – no way I'm shagging you without a bag on.' I got what I needed chat-wise and then started to wrap up operations.

'Maybe we could do this again,' I said, as she put her dress back on. 'Look, I really like you and that, but I've got an important meeting in the morning, maybe we could get together tomorrow night. Don't worry about the money – keep it.' With that, she got her kit on and I bundled her out.

19

Blown Out of Proportion

At 8.30 am the next day I checked in with Ray on the phone.

'Sorted,' I said, the half-a-blow job hangovered into obscurity and not looking such a big deal now.

'Got her on tape, offering me sex for dough,' I informed him gleefully. 'And she says her dad is definitely a Law Lord.' Within a couple of hours we'd got Claire's real name and identified her father in *Who's Who* and *Debrett's*. Pulled pictures of him. Not that we needed any, but the flimsy justification we cobbled together included a few court cases in which the big-shot judge had condemned prostitution. But all day the dread was pulsating in my stomach. Of what was about to come.

I filed copy and after conference Ray came on: 'I'm about to send this tart story over to the back bench but before I do – I've got to ask you – did you fuck her?'

Gulp! 'No, course not,' I said, which was true. 'The job's all bang on, everything on tape.' The thing is, as every vice reporter knows, silent japery of a naughty nature rarely comes out on tape anyway – a few groans and slurps here and there – so you can't prove anything anyway.

'OK, good. Well, if it's all shipshape, front her up on the phone,' said Ray, 'and see what she's got to say for herself.' TP3 in ear. Tape on. Slowly, dialing the number. Not wanting to do this.

Me: 'Hi Claire, how's it going?'

Her: 'Hi Graham, I'm so pleased that you called – I've been thinking about you.'

Me: 'OK, that's nice, because I've been thinking about you as well.'

Her: (Cue coy giggling) 'When can I see you again?'

Me: 'Whenever, but I've got something to tell you first.'

Her: 'You sound all funny all of a sudden – everything OK?' Her voice cracking a bit.

Me: 'Funny. What do you mean, funny?' Not quite Joe Pesci in *Goodfellas* but a bit stern just to warm her up.

Her: 'A bit distant, as though, er, you don't know me or something.'

Me: 'Well, yes, you're right. That's because I'm not really who you thought I was.' I could imagine her heart sinking – how many times had she been deceived by men. How many times had she been deceived.

Claire: 'What do you mean?'

Me: 'I'm not a really the music industry person who took you out the last night. My real name is Graham Johnson and I'm an investigative reporter.'

Her: 'Oh.'

Me: 'For the *News of the World*.'

Her: 'Oh. No. Fuck . . .'

Me: 'Yes, 'fraid so, Claire. And the reason I wanted to talk to you is because we're writing a story about you being a prostitute selling sex for money even though your dad is a top Law Lord.'

Pause – time to sink in.

Her: 'What do you mean? I don't understand.'

Me: 'We're going to expose you for being a prostitute in this Sunday's newspaper. What have you got to say?'

Claire broke down, sobbing and screaming.

Her: 'Graham, please don't do that. How can you? I trusted you. I thought you were my friend.'

Wow! She was not only slow but naive as well.

Her: 'I told you about my dad because I thought you were a nice guy. Please! Please don't do this! I'm begging you. Not now – I've got a lot going on in my life, and it'll push me over the edge, ruin my life. My dad doesn't even deserve this. We don't even speak any more – his life has nothing to do with mine. Please! Please! Ple . . .'

'Great!' I thought as she pleaded for mercy. In a way, I was relieved. Didn't mention the blow job at all. Consumed with the shock, Claire mustn't have thought it significant. May have even forgotten it, after all she was a drunk charlie-head.

Over the next few hours Claire called me several times, each time getting increasingly desperate.

'If you run this story, I'm going to commit suicide,'

Always a tricky one. But to tell you the truth, we normally didn't give a fuck. I remember one time when a man, who'd been fronted up by the *Screws* for child-molesting on a Saturday, topped himself that night, just before the paper hit the street. In the newsroom, a small cheer went up. Another scalp. Plus dead men made life easier – they can't sue. On another occasion a swinger, who'd been turned over for no more than dabbling in a bit of suburban wife-swapping, was exposed. Took his own life after pleading that he'd lose custody of his kids if his divorced wife found out. 'Fuck his family,' the reporter said, before the paper published the story. It was true – he did lose his kids, then his life. By now, deep down, I was even secretly reassured that Claire was drifting into whacko suicide territory – there was hope that she might take our sordid secret to her grave.

'Is that you Graham?' It was ten o'clock the next day. This time Claire's voice was crisp and steely on the end of my moby. Gone was the flaky self-harmer with a mouthful of paracetamol.

'How can you run a story about me selling sex for money,' she said with dismissive formality, 'when I gave you a blow job, after you paid me?'

Fuck!

Cringe-worthy conversation that followed isn't in it.

'What do you mean?' I protested weakly.

Her: 'Don't you remember? I pulled your trousers down, fiddled your zip and, well, went down on you?'

Me: 'No, that didn't happen, Claire.'

Her: 'Well, yes it did, Graham. You let me perform oral sex on you in the hotel and what's more you liked it.'

Me: 'You're talking nonsense and you know it.'

Her: 'You asked me to stop. I did.'

'You're making this up,' I said, speaking over her, as though, by drowning her out, it would make what she was saying less credible. 'You're just trying to get out of the story.'

Her: 'No, you are making this up, Graham – like you've cooked up this whole story about me and my dad. The fact is I gave you a blow job which is against the rules – the *News of the fucking World*'s rules of engagement and now you're denying it. Call yourself a reporter – you're a fucking disgrace and sleazy shitbag one at that.'

Wow! Both barrels. Gone was my cocky bully self. Put in my place. Speechless.

Her: 'At least I've got the decency to admit I was working as a hostess.'

'You're a prostitute,' I rebutted weakly, trying to take the moral high ground – a good place to launch a bullying counter-attack from.

'You sell your body for money. You take cocaine. You break the law. And now you're trying to drag me down into your sordid little world by smearing me. Well it just won't work. I will ask you once again: what have you got to say to our readers about your degenerate behaviour?'

I am the tabloid evangelist.

Her: 'What have you got to say about yours?'

Fuck – 'What a heartless cunt she is,' I thought. Trying to embarrass me like this.

'You're lying and you know you are,' was all that I could think of.

Claire's lines were delivered thoughtfully and I was beaten. I could tell she was being coached and more worryingly I could sense that she was taping me.

Minutes later, as I slouched at my desk, head in hands, an ominous green message flashed up on my terminal.

RL: 'Can you pop into my office a sec?'

Ray asked me to close the door – must be on top. 'This girl's just been on to me,' he said. 'This tart. She's alleging that you didn't make your excuses and she performed oral sex on you.' Alleged! Already all the jargon was coming out. All those terms they use in disciplinary hearings before they whack you. He was making it sound as though I'd fucking raped her or something.

'Fuck off, Ray, she's blagging,' I rebutted. 'She's just trying to get the story spiked. Yesterday she was threatening to do herself in. Today, she's making up all kinds of stories to force our hand. She's a fucking fruitcake.'

Ray went through the motions. Probing, man-to-man stares. A few questions. But in the end, like a public inquiry, I knew that Ray was always going to back his man.

'OK, I believe you.' said Ray.

'Phew!'

Funnily enough, slightly emboldened by Ray's support, my worst fear now stopped being a sex scandal and became losing the story. Like all crazed *NoW* reporters, I was desperate to get the story in the paper at all costs – even though the sensible thing would have been to lie low and gently bin it. That was just the brainwashing kicking in.

Ray must have mistaken this eagerness as a sign of my innocence and sent me round to bang her address. Front her up face-to-face and shut her down with my revenge. Now standing order: when under attack, go on the offensive. However, Claire wouldn't come out of her posh West London mansion flat, but she called me on the mobile instead.

'Not only did I give you a blow job,' she attacked, straightaway. 'But you would have shagged me except you didn't have any condoms.'

'No way,' I said to her.

When I got back to Wapping, another fear-loaded message flashed up on my computer. RL: 'Office now.'

Ray: 'When you were on that hooker job with the Law Lord tart the other night, did you or did you not phone down to the hotel reception for some condoms at three in the morning?' He was secretly taping me to cover his own back – must be getting serious.

'Yes, I did,' I admitted. Good job I did admit it as well, as the call would have been logged at the hotel the duty manager could have confirmed it. So by coughing to it, it made the rest of my story look good.

Ray: 'OK, it's just that this tart is now saying that not only did she blow you off, but that you were desperate to fuck her, but you couldn't because you didn't have a condom on you.'

Me: 'That's bollocks. In fact, the exact opposite is true. I was using the fact that I didn't have any condoms NOT to shag her and I phoned down to stall her.'

Ray shook his head, bored with the technical deets already. 'What the fuck is going on here?' he said, arms outstretched.

'I know what you're saying,' he went on. 'But it doesn't look good, does it? Phoning down for johnnies at that hour – looks like you wanted to shag her but that you were worried about catching a dose off f her, d'you know what I mean?'

Things got rapidly worse. Two things started working against me.

1. Claire was middle class and not the usual powerless peasant that I picked on. Once the middle classes get it together, they quickly become organised and effective and take no shit. They say complicated things.
2. Claire lived in London. The thing about London is that

anyone, no matter who, is never more than two steps away
from knowing the right people. No one gives a fuck if you live
in Liverpool, or Blackburn or Barrow or somewhere – who are
you going to know? No one. The local shit kicker lawyer who
gets smack-heads off robbing charges. No one. But in London,
if you want to get hold of world class libel lawyer, the cleaner
next door probably irons his shirts.

Not the case down in that-there London. It turned out that
Claire had broken down in front of her brother, who was some
big deal person in some corporation somewhere. Of course, this
being London, he knew some PR people, who in turn knew some
fixers who were specialists at dealing with the *News of the World*.
The PR gunslinger, that her and her brother had ended up getting
into bed with, was none other than John Ross, the surly-faced
ex-copper who I'd fucked off in Wine Press just a few days earlier.
Claire and her brother had paid John Ross to neutralise the story.
Now he was trying to destroy my life. John Ross had sat Claire
down, got the full story, locked on to my little *faux pas* and knew
exactly how to use it against me. He was going for the throat. To
boot, the hard-faced twat had tipped off a broadsheet reporter,
who was looking to do a dirty number on me in *Private Eye* or
something. If only I'd taken time to meet John Ross a few days
earlier, and bought him a drink at the Wine Press, told him how
great he was etc. Maybe this all could have been avoided and
laughed off as a lads' night out.

Then Shirley Ann Lye threw her oar in, kicking off that she
hadn't been weighed in for the story. John Ross had inadvertently
told Shirley that I'd fucked one of her stories up by not making
my excuses. Now she was calling me up from the Wine Press pay
phone, humiliating me in a loud voice.

'You dirty little cant,' she boomed. 'Caught with your pants
down, then finkin' you could put one over on me by not paying
me for the tip. I'm not paying the price of a sleazy facking blow
job.' Then she was going on to Ray blackmailing him to get paid,

even though the story hadn't gone in the paper. Fucking hell! Could any more people get to know about my vice? I was getting a taste of my own medicine.

The following week the story was quietly dropped. The £800 written off. Kuttner deducted it from my expenses on the drip over the next few months. Paul McMullan was furious.

'Any other reporter would have been sacked for that,' he exploded from nowhere one day before conference.

'You got caught bang to rights. But you're Ray's Golden Boy. Phil Hall likes you. You're being protected.' The gossip was that the PR gunslingers and freelancers, John Ross and Co., who had known about my minor scandal, had been paid off to drop their story on me. Bitterly, Paul listed a few other fuck-ups I'd notched up, which I thought had gone unnoticed. Next only to Bill Clinton's, it was turning out to be the most expensive and troublesome sex act for a good long while.

A few years later, one Saturday morning before Christmas, I was doing a bit of yuppified mincing around the Portobello Road market. New girlfriend on arm. Massive Starbucks in hand. Designer bags full of overpriced bric-a-brac hanging of us like baubles. Out of the corner, I saw a skinny girl sat on the curbside outside a pub. Nursing a handbag and a mobile phone, as though she'd been out all night. I recognised her instantly – it was Claire. Flustered and trampish, now though. Still a waif, still a worrier. Was she on the gear? Hard to tell – but her skin was sheeny white and greasy. For a brief moment, we caught each other's eyes. I was heartbroken. I wondered if her dad knew his Little Princess was hustling on the street. I wanted to sweep her up and rescue her. A faint smile broke from under her scraggy hair, as though reaching out to talk. But I walked on, grey and jowelly, a busy London life beckoning. The fear still raw. Not yet having come to terms with my past.

20

Summer of Discontent

A few weeks later I was sat in a cramped London flat with the secret gay lover of the right honourable member for Harlow, Essex. The *News of the World*'s single best contact Max Clifford had declared war on the Tories. He blamed them for destroying the NHS. To spearhead his crusade, Max had offered the *Screws* a big buy-up story about an affair between curly-haired Tory-boy Jerry Hayes and his 18-year-old ex-Commons' researcher Paul Stone. If the story panned out, then Max would be paid approximately £100,000 for the tip, a percentage of which would go to his client.

My job was to baby-sit Stone, until I got the order to put in the usual taped call. That meant getting Stone to slyly call Jerry up unawares. Then to script a conversation in which they would reminisce about their 18-month affair. An involuntary confession by Hayes which I would tape for evidential purposes. A simple task but a lot of pressure.

Being part of one of these big *Screws* set-pieces was like being involved in the build-up to the Gulf War. Rebekah was our Stormin' Norman Operational Commander. Ray was her Chief of Staff. For the first time, I was having to report directly to Rebekah, obviously a great honour. So I was on my best behaviour. For the first time also, she seemed to be handling the story day-to-day instead of the Editor. Obviously a step up the ladder for her as well. Surveillance vans were scattered all over London at various addresses. Reporters making covert inquiries at key locations. A team back in the office, secretly bringing together various bits of copy, backgrounders and pics. Inquiry agents pulling records, phone bills and other data.

Then the phone rang. It was Ray: 'OK, put the call in now.'

I picked up Stone's landline phone from the coffee table. Placed it on a rug in the centre of his living-room floor. I summoned the gay lover to kneel down next to it. Looking him in the eyes, I instructed him carefully: 'I want you to ring Jerry up and get him talking about how much you like each other and get him talking about all the dates you've been on and all the times you've had sex.' I pulled out a memo, that we'd got off Max Clifford, detailing all the info on their various liaisons, to prompt Stone if he began to fuck up. Slide the record button. TP3 on. Earpiece in.

The blag worked like a dream. Jerry didn't suspect a thing, coughing to loads on tape, proving that they were lovers. The next day it was front-up Friday. My job was to watch Jerry's constituency home in Essex all day so that I could warn the desk when he left for his surgery meetings with the locals. Getting out of bed had been a nightmare. A foggy cold morning. Plus, my head was blown with pain. An abscess had exploded under a rotting molar, decayed by too many years of Mars Bar breakfasts on the road. My mouth was drenched in brown tooth tincture. I battled to plug a hole in the stinking enamel, the edges blackened, with a sodden ball of cotton wool. Crunching Anadins three at a time. But taking the pain because Rebekah was the emir and if she asked me to run into Jerry's and blow myself up, I would have.

I was determined not to show-out in Jerry's leafy road so I hung well back from the house, a large detached where he stowed his wife and three kids. I was parked up over the road, next to a garage. The nosey-bastard owner, a Little Englander meddler-type, kept clocking me. So I edged further down the road. So far back, that I ended up watching the wrong house for eight hours. What a fucking bell-end? But the pain was driving me nuts.

I could have fucked the whole job up if Jerry had slipped out that afternoon without me knowing. Luckily, he turned up at his surgery nearby. And guess who was there with a problem for him to solve? None other than Rebekah Brooks. Rebekah fronted him with the allegations. He coughed. She slimed him up massively with her legendary charm. Expressing her sympathy. Talking him round into making a confession. Instead of fucking her off as he should have done, Jerry later rang the office to thank them for the way she had handled the story. Can you believe that? The *NoW* destroys his marriage and outs him in front of his kids – and he thanks them. He said: '. . . she came to see me at my surgery in Harlow to tell me of the story that the *News of the World* was breaking about me the next day. It was a terrible moment for both of us. And she was amazingly kind, offering to fly me and my family abroad and arranging blocking cars to stop unwanted pictures by the paps. I declined both.'

Let's be clear about this. This was not an offer to protect him. This was not an offer of kindness in his interests. These are stand-ard buy-up tactics to protect our story. No one, especially Rebekah, could give a fuck about him. She wanted to get him and his family into a hotel in Spain or wherever, so that a rival paper could not get to them. Simultaneously, teeing the whole thing up, for what's known as a 'week two'. An exclusive follow-up the week after, in which the *NoW* would get Jerry to do a sit-down, talking about the ordeal, giving his side of the story. All that Rebekah was doing was trying to persuade the target to give her a second story before the first had even be published – for nothing. You've got to hand it to her. She was cute – she probably reckoned that it was better to get into him for a second story before the first story came out because afterwards he was likely to be fuming. There was no amazing kindness about it. And Jerry didn't see this. Even him, a clever politician who plots and schemes for a living. All that bollocks about blocking cars, that's not for his benefit – once again that's for our benefit. In the run-up to the story the *NoW* has shelled out thousands of pounds on surveillance vans getting pics of Jerry, as well as buying any photo material that Stone had. The blocking cars would have been to stop rival papers getting pics that would spoil ours. Jerry and her became mates and he's still sucking up to her to this day for trying to destroy his life. But that's the thing with people like Jerry. Members of the political class who crave power and status, they are especially vulnerable to tabloid Stockholm Syndrome. Even when Rebekah was giving it to him. Even after the headline 'Tory MP Two-Timed Wife with Underage Gay Lover' appeared that Sunday. All he wanted to do was praise the powerful. Mad but true.

Spring turned into summer like a montage in *The Graduate*. Tinged with melancholy and foreboding. I went through the motions on autopilot. Telling lies and destroying lives. Like a Shakespearian portent, the clouds on the horizon wouldn't shift. The stress levels rising like the sap in my suburban back garden. My girlfriend Angela told me that she'd had an abortion because I wouldn't commit to getting a mortgage. I wanted to move out. At work, I was getting bigger and more complex jobs. My body was cracking under the strain because I never had time to go the doctors. An' abscess on my tooth one week. The shits the next. Can't breathe through my broken nose, the result of a playground accident and several fights afterwards. Sinuses on fire. Life in the big bad city. No time to go to the News Int. private hospital because I'm stuck on a watch in the middle of nowhere.

A few weeks later we did a big number on Jonathan Aitken who was about to fall on his sword for perjury. We got the domi-natrix that spanked him to a hotel in Watford. Headline: 'Four in a Bed, Whips and Orgy in a Gothic Mill.' It wasn't my job, but I got called out because the Hilton was just around the corner from Angela's place. I was stressed out and handled it badly. I got

annoyed with the buy-up for taking the piss with the room service. She took a disliking to me, so I got pulled off the job. Nothing
like that had ever happened before – it was a bad omen.

Tony Blair got swept to power but we still kept the pressure up
on the Tories. Murdoch must have had it in for them for some
reason. On the next job, the paper assigned its best big-shot
photographer. I was going up in the world. Steve Grayson was a
former plumber. Turned disco DJ. Turned senior investigative
photographer. Steve could turn his boxer's hands to anything –
and turn you over as soon as look at you. His blags were legendary. A fast-moving combination of bluff and bluster, like an Ali
shuffle on fast-forward. So incredible it made you laugh out loud.
But backed up with action so hard-edged and unpredictable, it
made your balls suck-up into themselves with pain, in sympathy
with the mark who'd been on the end of them. In the context of
the *NoTW*, He made me look like a child who'd lied about his
homework.

Steve was the Fake Sheik's personal photographer. Or, rather,
equal partner. A position of great status and freedom in a hierarchy of shit-eating and oppression. He and Investigations Editor
Mazher Mahmood flew around the world. Five-star hotels. The
best spook gadgets money could buy. Unlimited budgets. Like
Vegas magicians, they created illusions of such glittering gran-
deur, they suckered in the great and the good, one after the other.
And on Sunday left them dripping tears over their tea and toast
crying, 'What the fuck happened there?'

I'd first clocked Steve about a year before, when he walked into
the Features department.

Without daring to look up too much, I observed his manner-
isms through a gap in the monitors – and it was a fascinating
mixture of contradictions. It was as though Roy Keane had
wandered into the dressing room of a Sunday League side by accident. A team of shit-kickers and amateurs that he was being
forced to play in an FA Cup round. Steve looked down on us or
so it seemed to me. Like we were jokers. Playing-at-it,

£400-a-week shifters and six-month contract merchants who couldn't stand up a flower in a vase, never mind a world exclusive. Later, when I spoke to him about it, Steve was horrified to learn that I thought he was arrogant. 'I would would never think that,' he said. Genuinely hurt. But that was the contradiction – Steve could be overwhelmingly humble and kind at the same time. Steve worked mainly for the News department, which was considered a much more mature and professional outfit. To him, or so I thought, we were cheap-suited chancers who couldn't even afford a real Rolex, an essential prop on the kind of high-roller jobs that he and Mazher specialised in. That was my first impression anyway. I guess the tough exterior was just a way of coping with the unnatural atmosphere at the Screws.

Then we found ourselves working together. On another big *News of the World* set-piece where everybody gets turned over – and my role in it was proof that I was moving up. Married Tory MP Nigel Waterson was carrying on with a prissy-looking academic at the London School of Hygiene and Tropical Medicine. The Editor Phil Hall had been tipped off by a couple of unsigned poison pen letters. But we had to get the proof. And there was only one way to do that – snatched pictures of the couple together. Preferably backed up with surveillance logs and videos of Waterson's late-night trysts at his mistress's London pad.

Steve pulled up at Warren Street in his *Scooby Doo* hi-tech surveillance van. He got out and showed me a doubled-up bin bag, with a big knot flowering out of the top of it.

'Do you know what this is?' he asked me.

'Yes,' I said. 'It's a bin bag.'

'Very funny – but do you know what's inside?'

'Rubbish?' I guessed. 'That's what I use them for, mate.'

'OK, well, if you're going to be a smart arse, I'll tell you what's inside.'

'Go on then.'

'Shit,' he said. 'That's what's inside. It's a bag of shit. A big bag of my shit.'

Steve walked across the pavement and put the bag of shit in a bin on the street. I laughed.

Steve had been watching the woman's house all night. Instead of pulling off to use the bog somewhere, he'd shit in a bin bag, like the SAS do in Northern Ireland. In fact, it's pretty much standard operating procedure for Who Dares Wins-types, even if they're in the middle of the desert. They defecate in bin bags and store them up in their Bergens, until they get back. So as to leave as little trace as possible for the enemy to go on. When on watches, Steve didn't like to move the van so as not to arouse suspicion, never mind getting in and out for a piss break. Once he was on the plot, he was on the plot.

Steve gave me a little tour of his van. Showed me the mini makeshift bog by the sliding side door – no more than a waste paper bin, lined with a bin bag for the use of.

'Very good,' I said. He laughed.

Steve was a serious operator and I was determined to impress him. On surveillance jobs, it was common practice for reporters to skive. Reporters and photographers would make a cut-throat pact to go home rather than spend hours and hours staring at a brass knob on a door they were supposed to be watching. If the bosses phoned either of them to check in, both parties would say they were with the other at the address and back each other up. I wasn't big on skiving as the Force inside me was too strong. The fear of losing my job was still overwhelming. But on the odd occasion that I was late for a job, I opened the window of my bedroom, stuck my head out and checked in with Ray on the mobile, pretending that I was on the plot somewhere.

I could always tell that Ray was trying to catch me out – listening to the birds tweet in the background when it should have been six-lane motorways or a nightclub instead – the soundscape of that particular job. But on other occasions he went much further. Jumping on to his motorbike and racing down to the job, to catch reporters out. My colleague Dominic Mohan was turned over for this. After suspecting Dominic was blagging him from home, Ray zoomed around to Dom's flat. In his leathers, like a man on a mission. Parked up outside. Called Dominic on his mobile and smiled as he observed Dom stick his head out of the window to answer the call. Bang to rights. A sackable offence.

Increasingly, Ray and Dom weren't seeing eye-to-eye. Ray was trying to edge him out. Panning his stories in conference. Giving him shitty jobs. More and more, Dom was looking like a loser in a thick-weave suit and unpolished shoes. Tombstones in his eyes and no one wanted to talk to him. But Rebekah had a soft spot for the bowl-headed friend-to-the-stars. When he asked for a transfer, he was shipped off to the *Sun* to be a showbiz reporter. I thought it was a demotion and his career was fucked. But what do I know? Showbiz became the new currency of power. He went on to be Editor of the richest and most powerful newspaper in Europe. Now it was his time to hunt down the skivers.

Anyway I didn't skive once for three weeks on the MP Waterson watch. It wasn't boring, sitting off in the cafés in a nice part of London, sipping cappuccinos. Perving off the students on a summer's day. Steve regaling me with tabloid tales of derring-do. And we made sure that the mistress was followed at all times. It was on watches like this that the ability to spin car regs came in very handy. This was incredibly important in identifying who was coming and going from the MP's London pad, his home in Eastbourne and his mistress's flat. If I had to follow them in a car, or any visitor for that matter, I could find out who owned the car and where they lived. Both Steve Whittamore, and another inquiry agent called Skinner who was on the firm, could spin car regs. (£150 to £200). I used to ring Steve with the reg and the make and model. He would ring a couple of his mates in a regional office of the DVLA who then sold him the address and DOB of any registered car owner. They billed Steve £70 per reg. Despite being illegal, spinning regs was widespread. Most of the time there was no public interest, and they were bonking MPs like Waterson, celebs, or people who were shagging celebs, or selling them drugs.

Eventually we got enough pics of Waterson and his mistress

together that we were able to splash on the story. 'Top Tory Dumps His Wife for Lover – Poison Pen Letters That Shamed Hague's New Whip.' After I monstered him on his doorstep for being a degenerate, the MP was forced to announce that he was divorcing his wife. I was the tabloid evangelist.

'See you on the next one,' I said, as Steve packed up and got into his van.

'Yes, it's been good working with you,' he replied. I knew we would work together and the next one would be a big one.

But for now, it was back to the grindstone. Week after week, I kept banging out stories all summer. A Paul Samrai job about a paedophile who had been released from prison – and was now living on the same street as his victims. I turned over a church in Birmingham for being a den of sin – the congregation were hookers and drug-dealers. Easy-peasy – I disguised myself as a smackhead and got into them by going around selling faux-shoplifted universal bag-head fare – cheap batteries and razor blades. I exposed a straw man after fashion icon Gianni Versace was killed in Miami. Samrai found a man selling fake Versace jeans on the day that he was gunned down. Or, after the details had been fed into the scamulator, a ghoulish rag trade boss raking in blood money on the back of the great designer's death. Another paedophile story – a pre-emptive strike for Sarah's Law that would later make Rebekah's name in the tabloid world, about parents who declared a poster war on a local pervert. As summer was drawing to a close, I exposed Britain's biggest video pirate for churning out hundreds of thousands of counterfeit blockbusters and porno movies. When I got home I went straight to bed, exhausted.

The light had barely faded when the phone rang: 'Have you heard the news?'

'What?' I was crashed out on Angela's cast-iron bed. She was out clubbing with some doorman she'd met.

'Princess Di's dead.' Someone from work was giving me a heads-up.

'Fucking hell,' I was pissed off. Even though I was shattered, I'd at least have to show willing by calling Ray and offering to come in. Surprisingly, he was calm. 'Don't worry,' he said. 'We're going to change up obviously, but there's not much Features can do now.' The story was well covered by the night team on news.

'Great!' I said. Turned over and went back to sleep.

It was a good job that I snatched the rest, though. From that day on, for weeks afterwards everything went Di-ballistic. When I got in on Tuesday morning, three or four monitors on the Picture Desk were taped off with scene-of-the-crime ribbon. Apparently, the police were investigating whether the paper had been sent gory pap pictures on the night, showing Di's last moments in Dodi's totalled Merc SL under the Pont de l'Alma underpass. A hot potato because the paps that had been chasing her at the time were now getting the blame. I gave all that a wide berth and didn't ask too many questions – it was at times like that even little comments got people whacked off the floor. Of course, I was shown the unauthorised pics later in secret. The paper then phonily announced that it was no longer going to run any pap pictures as part of a new code of practice – yes, as if.

Then came Princess Di's funeral. Of course it was a massive deal. I was sent down there as an unaccredited roving reporter to see if I could dig up any cranks in the crowd. The problem was, there were hundreds of thousands of them. Ghouls from every part of the planet, who'd come to cry over a woman they didn't even know. I was genuinely confused. It was one of the few times that I lost all faith in the British public. Maybe I'd got it wrong – maybe they were actually peasants who deserved to be fed a diet of royal romps and skateboarding parrots. Maybe Rupert Murdoch and Rebekah Brooks were right about them and John Pilger was wrong. I used the funeral as a test of my blagging-into skills. To see how many restricted access areas I could infiltrate. For most of my career as a reporter, I never carried a press card or ID. I didn't need one. If you didn't believe me, so fucking what? You'll soon know about it come Sunday.

A week later, the big Di splash that the Editor was planning fell down on Friday night. Nightmare. We needed another to fill the void quickly. Phil Hall sent around a memo: 'We need a splash. Ring around your contacts.' I was determined to impress him. I stayed up all night phoning people, desperately trying to drum up a story, preferably one with a Di angle. Then I got a lead – Paul Samrai phoned back and told me about a con he'd been inside with. Multi-millionaire Benham Nodjoumi was a big time arms-dealer who had been jailed for rape and fraud. On the hoof and not expecting a reply, I sent him a letter-headed fax, in the name of a phony export company, asking whether he could supply banned landmines. Anti-personnel devices had been Princess Di's last big campaign before she died. Astonishingly, the Mr Fixit faxed back last thing at night. Saying that he could get hold of 46,500 landmines at £10 a pop. Bingo! Splash about evil land-mine-dealers that'd have Princess Di spinning in her grave – even though she hadn't been buried yet. Next day, Phil Hall stopped me in the corridor on the way to get a cup of tea. 'Great work,' he said. 'Well done.' I was elated.

The mad thing about all this is that it's all complete and utter bollocks. Not that it was a stunt. Just that it wasn't done to help Lady Di. Or the little kids in Cambodia or Rwanda with no arms or legs. But all done just to help us. To get a story in the paper. Total fresh air. Princess Di's 'ban' on landmines. Tony Blair's 'ban' on landmines. All 100 per cent propaganda. They've got more chance of banning Page 3. Or enforcing 'no ball games allowed' signs on the estates where the *NoTW*'s core readership dwell. For almost another decade the RAF was still using the BL755 'multi-purpose' cluster bomb. Not really a bomb at all but an air-dropped landmine. The BL755 explodes into dozens of little spider-shaped mines. Children are especially prone to stepping on them.

The leaves turned and I carried on turning over people at break-neck speed. All the usual stuff, but at the beginning of October one story stuck in my mind. It was just a bog standard investiga-tion into car-ringing. Posing as Scouse car-robber, I got into a 'crooked mastermind' called Francesco Pisanu. Pisanu had developed a fail-safe stolen car racket in which he could fake the identity of cars twice – and pass off twice as many write-off car wrecks as new. By spinning the reg of a red BMW M3, that Pisanu was trying to sell me, I was able to find out that the original chassis had been obliterated in a car fire years previously and then rebuilt with stolen parts. No big deal but it worked like a dream.

One Sunday shortly afterwards I got an abusive phone call from a heavy. It was connected to a story that I'd written. The anonymous caller said: 'Your mother sucks cocks. We're going to find you . . . etc.' All the usual stuff – this happened frequently – and I brushed it off nonchalantly whist watching the Sunday afternoon war film on the telly.

'Yes, mate, of course you are,' I intervened now and again. The last one came on about five o'clock just as the depressing *Songs of Praise* period kicked in.

'You fucking cunt etc.' He said that they'd get me outside work and break my arms. His parting shot was something like: 'You'll never write another fucking word in that rag again.' I don't know why, but it always stuck in my head.

21

Beast of Bodmin: The Build-Up

I was stood at a grey, deserted desk not far from the Editor's office, worriedly flipping through some dailies. Saturday evening, the paper put to bed. Newsroom eerily quiet. But I didn't fancy going home – the stress levels in Watford had now reached the same as at work. My relationship had broken down and I was desperately waiting to do one into the new Dockland's pad that I was buying.

A slight tension gripped my shoulders – I hadn't had a story for a week, the last one being the car-ringing gangster. A recurrent viral infection, triggered by stress over the last six months, had also been making me angry and depressed. When the delirium hit, I got confused – and manically horny, for some reason. 'What the fuck is going on?' I'd complain, but no one would listen.

'How's it going, Graham?' she cooed, like a Warrington-version of Jessica Rabbit. The fragrant Rebekah Wade was stood at my side. Panicky, I stood to attention.

'Much on?' she asked, flicking absently through a roughed-up copy of that day's *Daily Telegraph* on the bench.

On paper, Rebekah Wade should have been sexy. Tall and slim, an English rose with a killer streak, deadly as nightshade. But in the flesh she was strangely sexless, her femininity scraped barren by a corporate zealotry incongruous with her alabaster skin and floral prints. Rebekah Wade was, in my view anyway, the type of person who gave capitalism a bad name.

Not that I was perving off her. When being addressed by Rebekah, it was essential to mask whatever thoughts you had with the 'right attitude'. Free thinking, reflection and creativity were put to one side. A narrow set of *News of the World* views was acceptable – an unnatural process that led to mental turbulence. Brainwashing the polite and professional way is the subject of much research in Jeff Schmidt's book *Disciplined Minds*. It takes a critical look at salaried professionals and the soul-battering system that shapes their lives. In this unusual one-to-one with Rebekah, the right attitude was obedience. Servile gratitude that she had singled me out for her pet project.

'I'm trying to work up some good investigation ideas for next week,' I replied, trying to look busy. Rebekah pointed at a page lead in the *Telegraph*. 'What about this?' she said. 'A sighting of the Beast of Bodmin Moor by 15 Cornish councillors on a bus.'

'Wow!' I said, marvelling at her genius for spotting it. 'Great story!' Speed-reading it, but like an exam question that won't go in, getting nervous in proximity of power. Worried in case she thought me unworthy, I immediately began blagging her that I happened to be a bit of a Beast expert.

'Yes,' I announced, 'when I worked at the agency, one of the snappers got a picture of a big cat down there, silhouetted against the moonlight and all that. Big story – the *Sun* splashed on it.'

The flames in her eyes roared up like gas jets. Of all the desires that consumed Rebekah's extreme ambition – that's what she craved most. Editorship of the *Currant*. But first she had to impress Rupert. Prove that she could handle the warm-up Sunday hot seat. Before being let loose on the cash cow that had serviced his acquisition debt for 30 years. Bankrolling BSkyB. War-chesting his imperial campaign in the US. No one could be allowed to fuck that up.

'The Hound of the Baskervilles,' she said. Thin lips curling up at the end like the Joker. 'Fog rolling across the moors, mysterious howls in the night . . . I like it.'

'Yes, the smuggler's caves, Agatha Christie, pirates,' I babbled. 'I know Cornwall well. I did my training down there for a couple of years – spooky place.'

Bigging up my authority but digging a hole at the same time. All true by the way – I'd started off my journalistic career as a £90-a-week trainee at the tiny *Falmouth Packet* newspaper, whilst doing my NCTJ course at Camborne College near Truro. The question was – was it about to end down there as well?

'I want you to go down to Cornwall,' Rebekah suddenly ordered, 'and do a story on the Beast. You never know . . .' She smiled knowingly. 'There could be something in it – these are councillors after all, so they're hardly nutters. And look at this picture of a paw print,' handing me the *Telegraph*. And sure enough, there was a moody pic of a shape in a bit of mud.

'The councillors might have been pissed,' I said. Silence, like a Cheshire frost settling over the upmarket village she'd been brought up in. I'd clearly exceeded my banter.

Rebekah then mentioned a series of pieces that the paper had done on UFOs, a kind of real life *X-Files*.

'Our readers loved it,' she went on, as though she had unearthed some hidden truth about the workers that Karl Marx had overlooked.

'Remember your spooky vampire story, on the front – I think we were up that week.' Meaning that circulation figures had risen. 'People loved it.'

The first thing you learn about news executives is their complete ignorance of their readers. Readers, disparagingly referred to as punters, were imagined to be peasants with very basic levels of reason. No one really knew, because Wapping was cut off from the rest of the world, and reporters ate their sandwiches at their desks. The Chief Executive Les Hinton lived in a fairytale enclave of Wapping known as 'deep carpet land'. Where the wages were just as unbelievable. The waistcoats had colourful patterns on them. And the corporate slack flowed in abundance. Below him, the Editor moved between his subjects, on the other side of the high camera'ed-up walls, in a chauffeur-driven limo.

However, what was thought to be known was that punters were to be titillated with royal stories and celebrities. And distracted from important issues that affected their lives by unexplained phenomena such as UFOs, ghosts and phantom beasts. Confused by what Marcus Aurelius described as 'miracle-workers and jugglers' who talked about 'incantations and the driving away of daemons and such things'. Horoscopes and make-overs bulged out of the new lifestyle sections. Of course, the biggest distraction of all was the sport on the back pages. The Premier League was the modern equivalent of what the Roman's called 'bread and circuses'. The gladiators and chariot races that superficially appeased shallow citizens. But the irony was that readers were still the biggest single mystery to the management. Even to the New Labour-style focus groups that the Soho agencies were billing them for.

Rebekah piped up again with another stroke of genius: 'I want you to get dressed up as Sherlock Holmes and I want you to investigate these unexplained mysteries. I want you to go to the Himalayas and find out about the Yeti. Has the trail gone cold on Lord Lucan? Is he still alive? I don't know. I want to know. Is there a monster in Loch Ness? I want you to go there and see. And whereabouts is Shergar? Is he still alive somewhere?'

Shergar? The Derby-winner that was kidnapped by the IRA. Machine-gunned to death in a stable and turned into dog food. No, he was definitely not on this plane. But she was on one – there was no stopping her now.

'Firstly, however,' she said, 'I want you to go to the moors in Cornwall and do a number on the Beast.'

Who was going to tell her that these things aren't real? I looked around. A few weary reporters had come back from Henry's Wine Bar, after the customary pint between off-stone and first editions' dropping. They had had their heads down. No one wanted to break the bad news – Father Christmas didn't exist.

'What the fuck was that all about?' Hadn't noticed, but Ray had been nervously eagle-eyeing us *Goodfellas*-style from behind his venetians. But not having the bottle to interrupt us. When the coast was clear, he darted over.

'What was she saying to you?' he half-whispered. Shadily, looking from side to side, like a street dealer in one of my stories. For the first time I could sense vulnerability in him.

'She wants me to go down to Cornwall and take a look at the Beast of Bodmin.'

'Fuck's sake,' he seethed, backing up. It was obvious that Ray was deeply fearful that Rebekah was taking too much of a shine to my good self. But I didn't play him for it. I was still an office politics Bambi. And in the jungle, Ray was still a big beast.

'The Beast of fucking Bodmin. Are you taking the piss?' he wretched.

'No, and I've got to go dressed up as Sherlock Holmes, with a cape on and all that.'

'Oh for fuck's sake.' More emotional this time, shaking his head in denial. As though I'd told him that the economy was collapsing or something and that we'd all have to head for the mountains. 'What the fuck is that all about?'

'I don't know. She said it's part of a big series – she wants to send me to the Himalayas to investigate the Yeti. Go after the Loch Ness Monster, Shergar, Lord Lucan – the works, mate.'

The word 'mate', a little slight assertion of my new status.

'No way – you sure?'

'Yes way,' I said.

I allowed a measure of gloating to rise to the surface. Rebekah was putting me in the know instead of him. Was she teaching the Great Raymondo a lesson? Had he fucked up in some way that I wasn't aware of? Either way, in Fleet Street terms, this was my big break. Even though I found the whole idea of dressing up as Sherlock Holmes for Rebekah gimpish and humiliating. There

was a whole history of arsehole reporters dressing up as chickens
or Mr Blobby or whatever for daft stories. I was always of the
opinion that it demeaned the status of my illustrious profession.
Especially me – I was a serious, hard-hitting investigative reporter.
Booting in doors. Taking names. Crusading for Truth and Justice.
Not some fucking work experience kid in a panto costume

'Well, who the fuck's going to be Dr Watson then?' asked Ray.

'Elementary, mate – you are.' I knew I was pushing it. But it'd
been a gruelling Saturday and taking the piss was fair game.

At least he laughed. 'Fuck off. It'll have to be Ricky,' he said.

Ricky Sutton was a contract freelancer who'd just been poached
from the *Sunday Mirror*. He went on to get famous for being the
reporter who got into *Blue Peter* presenter Richard Bacon on a
night out. Then turning him over for cocaine.

'OK, I'll talk to Ricky. You hire the costumes. And talk to
Pictures to see who they're sending.'

22

Upholding the Claw

The train edged out of Paddington. The shuddering start to our journey. Into the heart of darkness. A real-life *Boy's Own* adventure. To find the Beast of Bodmin Moor. Bankrolled by the most powerful media conglomerate in the world.

First class. Feet on the seats. Snug in our carriage. Smug in the way that only those cocooned within the corporate belly can be. The phony life-support system of our age. Sat opposite, Steve Grayson was making the most of the free tea. An unusual decision to assign the Senior Investigative Photographer to a fluffy feature involving fancy dress.

'It came right from the top,' Steve explained, as the scratchy greenbelt of Outer London melted into the rolling racing green of Wiltshire. 'The Picture Editor told me that Rebekah had asked for me personally.' Shaking his head. The caper clearly well beneath him otherwise. Or thats what I thought anyway. Steve would never knowingly look down his nose. Dressed in high-waisted jeans, belted-up over a cheese cloth shirt, Steve's momentary pang of professional arrogance jarred with the pair of old women's glasses that hung from a lanyard around his neck. A crafty touch of the effeminate. To deflect away from his inner cunning. Only occasionally did the battle that raged beneath the surface, a titanic struggle between humility and pride, well up like bubbling oil. But that was just my first impression. Functional fixation, focusing on the parts of him that the *News of the World* brought out.

'I was supposed to be doing a big drugs investigation that was all set up with Scotland Yard this week. Catching Mr Big and all that. Guaranteed spread. But at the last minute I got pulled off it, to do this.' Steve wasn't happy. But he was professional enough to let it go. 'Rebekah's in charge this week,' he then reminded us ominously. 'So she is obviously desperate for this load of bollocks to work.'

Freelancer Ricky Sutton, the junior member of the team, was sat at a table on his own. Get-the-teas-in insecurity written all over his face. What the fuck is he doing here anyway? Oh yeah, I forgot. Dr Watson to my Sherlock. I made a little show of contemptuously turning down one of his beers.

'I'll have a drink later,' I snarled. 'Tonight, after we've taken care of business.' A little suck-up to Steve. To make sure he approved that I was the don. Serious as cancer, even on a panto story. Steve reciprocated in the unsaid. Letting me know that I was the top dog on the job. As least on the scribbler side anyway. Our bonds from the Waterson MP job recalibrating seamlessly, like switches on the railway beneath.

Then something unusual. Just as we were about to pull into Bodmin Parkway, after a ball-aching five-hour journey, Ricky got a call from Ray. The boss told him that he was getting pulled off the job – even before it had started. Another story was bubbling up in London, so said Ray. Extra bod needed back at base, PDQ, I'm afraid. Ricky, the disappointment visible. To be missing out on the hijinks. The career-lucrative Editor's Special slipping off him like loser's luck. Cosy glances between me and Steve. Our group-think solidifying just nicely thanks.

I couldn't resist a sly gloat on top – that I was no longer the arse-wipe junior. Run-ragged at will by the Desk. Jerked between pins on a map by posh, piss-taking executives. Like doomed Tommies in the trenches. Finally, someone had taken my place as the *Screw*'s non-person. Ricky, who'd not yet passed that magic, unseen line to respectability, was now the new knob-head.

'But what was really going on?' I asked myself, kicking back in the seat. The countryside flew past like scenery in a puppet show. Getting more raggedy. Gloomier. Deeper. What was the bigger picture, trickily flickering away in the background? That was the real question. Steve and I traded knowing daggers. We were being left down here. Swinging in the wind. On our own. The Editor's Special, ours alone to savour. Our Thing. For Made Men only. But why? What was the real reason behind Ray's sudden U-turn? To keep Ricky's prying eyes away? To exclude his uninitiated ways? So that the masters of the dark arts could work their magic? In private? Or was it really the case that Ray needed Ricky to work on another story? Who the fuck knows? All of it a total head wrecker. Agendas round here were deeper than 'Who shot the president?'

Bodmin Parkway was a ghost station. Autumn light fading fast. Too late to do proper pictures. Steve knocked off a few frames. But the plan was to get up handy the next day. Do the rest early doors. Then send Ricky on his way. Back to the office with the film. Darkness descended over the moors. My hotel bed was snuggly. Raindrops tapped on the window like a niggle.

Sun up. Morning Glory wank. Straight on to the clean sheets. Be dry in an hour – did chamber maids ever notice these things? Did I give a fuck? Not really. By now I was selfish to the point of mania. Downstairs on autopilot for The Full English. Then straight down the bog before we got off. Five or six papers, slid under my door on expenses, turning to mush on the sweating bathroom floor. An animal marking out his territory. Going through the motions.

Then we drove out on to the moors in the hire car to do the photo shoot. Dressed as Sherlock Holmes and Dr Watson. In the costumes we'd hired from London before we left. Steve couldn't remember Ricky being around – maybe he'd gone back. Neither of us gave a fuck anyway. It didn't matter. We knew we were the only ones that mattered. Steve took pictures of me creeping around a disused watermill, near an abandoned copper mine. Stooped over a magnifying glass, held half-way between my face and the ground. The classic Holmes pose. Hooked calabash pipe, favoured by actors because it stayed in your mouth without you holding it, freeing up your hands for the shot. Swished-up in tweed plus fours and matching cape. Run up in pretty crumby material, I thought, the way fakes are. Topped off with a checkered deerstalker, which looked incongruously tattier, as though it had been brought in by mistake from another get-up.

Ricky's Dr Watson tramped behind or was he? Already turning into a mirage – like a dream. But his tension was real enough. Stressing, because he was going to get bollocked by Ray if he didn't get off quick. The show was interrupted by a happy-clappy family of outdoor walker types. Off-handedly, we explained to the outsiders what we were doing. Dismissively, in fact, the way film people do to onlookers on location. The walkers fascinated by the glamorous media people who laughed a little too loudly. Curious about how they made their living from doing pointless things. But slightly scared off by their over-confidence.

After Ricky had left, both Steve and I kept up the pretence of taking the job seriously. Neither of us wanting to be the first to speaketh the taboo out loud. Plodding on, playing it straight. A charade for each other's benefit really. But deep down, both knowing that our fragile manufacture of consent was built on a fraud. Understanding that it wouldn't be long before the parts wore out.

That afternoon, we went to interview one of the councillors who'd claimed to have sighted the Beast. The planning committee chairwoman was a bit gruff and guarded, the way the Cornish can be. Cornwall brought back bad memories. I'd first come down here four years earlier, to do unpaid work experience on a small newspaper in Truro. Skint and desperate to escape the depression-ravaged City of Infinite Doom. By night, I rented out strangers' bedrooms for cash to crash in. By day, I shoplifted Chinese chicken wings and shampoo from Marks & Spencer. Security-wise, it was wide open down there because everyone was so babes-in-the-wood. But the hardships born by robbing and roughing it were worth it in the end. Like an Ayn Rand hero battling against the fury of Anglo-Saxon capitalism, I eventually gegged a staff job on the local *Falmouth Packet* weekly.

That afternoon, I interviewed a few other Beast of Bodmin witnesses. Then Ray asked for some quotes from a zoologist. A respectable academic who'd lend authority to the piece, which was rapidly becoming thinner than the unlined blag-tweed on my cape. But none of the universities that I called would play ball. Academics are scared of their own shadow because of all this peer review bollocks they stress each other out with. Unless it's one of their own scams of course, such as blagging some funding, in which case they'll come up with the right numbers, right off the bat. They really are the pits.

In the end, the only person who would speak to me on the record was a crank who claimed to be a Beast expert. Calling himself a crypto-zoologist, whatever the fuck that was. Dedicating his life to the search for animals whose existence had not yet been proven, such as unicorns and Bigfoot. For fuck's sake! What was going on? This was the *News of the Screws*. The World's Number One Guttersnipe. Not the fucking *Fortean Times*. What the fuck was Rebekah doing? Lining herself up with all these whacked-out *National Enquirer* types? I was a stormtrooper in the world's most vicious nuclear news holocaust. The bones of my victims crunching underfoot. Now I was chasing ghosts around like Dan Aykroyd. But crypto-person would have to do. Any turd can be polished up into an expert. Just watch the pundits on the news, if you don't believe me. I did a phoner with him from my hotel bed. Wasn't so bad after all – I could boost his phony credentials by throwing in some of the expert-sounding techno-talk that he came out with. Quite nicely, his pseudo-scientific term for phantom cats was ABCs. AKA Alien Big Cats. Which had a kind of nice, *X-Filesy*, kind of FBI ring to it.

'They're also called cryptids,' he added.

'Yes mate,' I said. 'I can imagine. I'll call you back when I get some more evidence . . . you can cast your expert eye over it and tell me what's what.' Knowing that he'd say anything about anything if I asked him – or paid him. Either way would do. I rang off and turned over for a little kip before tea.

When the pressure is on, a day feels like a long time in journalism. I checked in with Ray that night. A sliver of impatient menace in his voice. Disappointment that I didn't have anything dynamite to feed Rebekah. Ray said that the Sherlock Holmes photos that Ricky had couriered back to the office had been too 'light-hearted'. But most of the pressure was self-made. Coming from the remnants of my own soul. My desire not to let Ray down. Not to let Rebekah down.

That night I discussed the grave situation with Steve. Based on what Ray had said, we concluded that Ray was under pressure from Rebekah to make her pet project as sensational as possible. So that she could impress Rupert Murdoch in Phil Hall's absence. Subtly, the thrust of the story was changing. Instead of pretending to look for clues to the Beast's existence, now the imperative was to find the Beast itself. Oh dear!

'Ridiculous,' said Steve. 'It's never going to happen. Forget about it.' Instead he set about cheering me up over dinner in the hotel restaurant. North London Jewish of the old school – funny, over-the-top, sharp. One minute he was puffed up on his own self-importance. The next he was down in the shit helping you to save yourself.

The next day was Thursday. Always dreading the 10 am check-ins with Ray, on jobs like this. Having to endure his poisoned pauses. Made worse because I didn't have fuck-all to fill them with.

'They're turning up the heat, mate,' I reported to Steve afterwards to keep him in the loop, crunching the gravel over to the car. 'They're upping the ante – they want bigger and better.'

'What can we do?' said Steve, holding out his arms in an over-the-top expression of comic hopelessness. 'The fucking thing doesn't exist – we've got more chance of finding Lord Lucan.'

'Don't tempt fate – they want that story for next week,' I said. 'Let's concentrate on our ABCs for now.' Similarly, Steve said he was getting calls off his partner Mazher Mahmood asking when he would be back – the Fake Sheikh had some big stories line up and was getting frustrated with Steve's absence. Or so Steve claimed. In addition, the picture editor kept calling asking 'How you getting on?'

Bodmin's mind-blowing doomscape should have taken me out of myself. A jagged bed of granite covered by a worn blanket of peat and moss. Strewn with rock ruins. The black skies rolling in low and claustrophobic. Propped up from collapsing by mysterious tors. Dotted all around. But I was too highly strung to allow nature in. Steve and I headed off to the outskirts of a village where a recent sighting had been made. Into a little copse on the edge of a row of light-coloured cottages. Talk in the pubs and snugs of scratch marks on the trees there. 'Stick to the road, lads,' one of the piss-taking locals had shouted as we got off from the ale house.

'Why?' I said, looking out for the American Werewolf in Liskeard.

'Because if the farmer catches a couple of emits on his land, he'll feed you to the pigs.'

The Cornish, eh? Who says they aren't a good laugh? I was missing the city badly. Sunset over Lewisham. Lungfuls of clag off the A13. Getting stared-out by tooth-sucking gang members on the way to buy a pint of milk.

We made our way through the brambles, into the centre of the small wood. Suddenly, silent amid the yellow oak saplings on the forest floor. Shooting up through the carpet of dead brown. The soily smells, flashing me back to childhood. The virgin Cornish jungle wilder than I remembered. Moister and more mystical. Sure, there were marks on the trees, mainly thin birches. But grazes and scratches, just like you would see in any other wood.

'Who knows what the fuck they are?' I said.

'Look over here,' said Steve, pointing at clusters of loosely parallel lines on a tree in a diamond-shaped clearing of ash and maple.

'Do you think they're scratch marks?' he asked.

I looked at him, smiling. Both of us edging closer to the inevitable.

'How many claws is this fucking thing supposed to have?' he asked me.

'Well, if it's a puma, as everyone seems to think it is, then they've got five claws,' I replied,

'The scratch marks are usually about head height,' I added like Arthur C. Clarke on *Mysterious World*, 'because the puma gets up on its hind legs and reaches right up the tree to stretch itself. Like a normal cat does on a post.'

Steve looked at the most promising clusters more closely. One lot was a good fit – a bundle of five faint, parallelish lines. But there were also threes and fours as well. Randomly scattered about it. So it was no more than the wear and tear of Mother Nature, wasn't it?

'Well, they could be fucking anything, couldn't they?' Steve agreed. Both of us still moving around the unspoken. Like a pride of lions around a herd of elephants-in-the-room. Waiting for the other to pounce first.

'For fuck's sake,' Steve said. 'I may as well get some pictures of these anyway – what a load of bollocks.'

Steve boshed off some frames of the five 'scratches'. First using the bit of natural light, seeping through the disintegrating canopy of autumn leaves. Then on flash.

'Even with the flash, you won't fucking see them on the picture.' Gently opening the door for me to come in.

'They need to be thicker and deeper,' I agreed.

'Yes, they're way too thin,' he added.

Edging closer. Into the zone now.

'Well, can't we clean them up a bit?' I finally suggested.

Steve smiled.

'Get the dirt out of the grooves?' he said. 'Just so that they show up better. Against the bark?'

I began scraping the bits of old shit away.

'What about that?' I said. 'Is that better?' I wasn't exactly stunting-up the evidence yet. Just 'enhancing' it a touch. Sexing it up as they say at the Beeb. But definitely moving in the right direction now. To everyone's relief.

'Still, it's fucking shit, isn't it?' Steve said. Even after my handiwork. 'Could be fucking anything, couldn't it? The other branches scraping against the trunk? Scars from when it was growing up? Who the fuck is going to believe those have been done by a wild fucking beast? Not going to work, mate.'

'Well, we'll have to make it fucking work,' I said. 'Won't we?'

I began scraping away at the scratches with my finger again. Then a branch off the floor. Then a stone.

'Fuck it,' Steve said, pulling out a long jaggedy key.

'Give it here.' Steve nudged me out the way. The resigned superiority of the older tradesman. Carving out the grooves, where the spindly scratches had been. Wider and deeper. Steadying the oval bow of the key with his right hand. Pushing down on the blade with his left. Visibly straining, as the whittled curls of live wood fell away to the deck.

'Fucking hell,' he gritted. 'Who the fuck's gonna fucking know whether it was us? Or the Beast? Or the fucking local kids, anyway?' The scratches were now monstrous and terrifying. Looking like Freddie Krueger had crashed the Teddy Bear's picnic.

'That OK, d'you think?' Steve mused. Standing back to admire his woodcraft, like he'd put up a new shelf.

Finally, the taboo had been broken. The tension that had been holding us back evaporated instantly. The relief was palpable. Now, at last, we had exposed to each other our hidden inner spoofer. The dirty secret was out. Shared between us. No going back. Locked into a conspiracy of stunting from now on. That both of us would have to take to the grave. Our secret seeming more secure somehow. For having hatched it within the bowels of a dark wood. In the middle of a desolate moor. Far away from an office, which didn't seem as real now.

'Come here,' I said, grabbing the key competitively. 'Let me have a go.'

'They need to be big, fuck-off tiger marks,' I said, 'as though it's a fucking lion's den or something.'

Now that the secret was out, I wanted to show Steve that I was up for it – good at it. From then on, it'd become a mini-arms race to push each other to find out who was the most game.

Steve finished them off, until they looked ferocious and fresh. Then we did a few others. One lower down the same tree and a couple on different trunks altogether. Making sure to rub some soil back into the pinky-white scars. To age them a little.

The remoteness was making us lose touch with reality. Incrementally edging us on to more risk. Once the spoofing floodgates had been opened, there was no holding back.

I drew some paw prints in the mud.

'It doesn't fucking matter anyway.' said Steve, as he beavered away on the scratches. 'What kind of a fucking story is this anyway? It's a fucking fairy tale.' Panting. Going red with exertion. 'Catch the Beast of fucking Bodmin. Find the Abominable Snowman.' Sweating. Taking off his jacket.

'I can't believe she put me on it in the first place. No one will fucking believe it anyway. What the fuck does she expect us to do?' I got my Sherlock costume from the car and posed up. Examining the phony scratches and the prints with my magnifying glass.

23

Lost in the Field

Later that Thursday, after our first day of enhanced techniques, as the CIA call them, I checked in with Ray.

'OK, what you got?' he asked.

'Well, we think we might have found some, er, new evidence of the Beast,' I said.

'Really?' he perked up, genuinely keen.

'Yes, well, we, er, went to a place where there'd been some, er, sightings, in the past, you know, and one of the local councillors, from that, er, article, said that there'd been some unexplained scratches on the trees. So we went there.'

'D'you see anything?'

'Yeah, er, sure enough, mad one, we found some marks, some scratches, like.'

'Really?' raising his voice. Excited that he'd have something to feed Rebekah.

'What are they like? Where they made by the Beast.'

'Just lines on a tree, really.' Playing it down for effect. 'And some funny paw marks on the ground.' Deliberately underselling it, as though we were nonchalant.

'Nothing spectacular,' I went on. Double-bluffing it, as though it was something we wouldn't even dream about spoofing. But somehow my deep sense of shame, operating involuntarily in the background, was tugging it down even further. Long pause. Tapping of Ray on his keyboard, distractedly.

'But they look like claw marks,' I finally conceded.

By this time, I could sense Ray losing interest. After thinking about it, he probably realised that they were only tertiary evidence. Easily hoaxed, obvious and meaningless without a picture of the Beast itself. He flattened his voice deliberately. To signal displeasure. Before rallying a bit at the end and going through the motions.

'Can you get them checked out?' he asked. 'By your expert?'

Ray wasn't too keen on the crypto-guy. He was still pushing for a better commentator.

'Sounds like a nutter,' he said. 'You can take the pics of the claw marks to him for a first opinion, but in the meantime, see if you can get a better expert. A professor, or a zookeeper or something. If a proper expert says they're from a big cat, then it might be OK. File your copy as soon as and I'll have a look at the photographer's pictures in the morning.'

That night I filed around 1500 words of bollocks to the copy-takers over the phone. Steve pinged his pictures in, hoping that would satisfy Rebekah and we'd get pulled off as soon as.

Friday was a kind of day off, while we waited to see whether the mystery claws story would make. In the morning, I drove to my old journalism college in Camborne. Popping in to see my ex-tutor Gareth. Gareth was a very straight guy. An ex-hard-drinking hack from Wales, who'd seen the light and turned to lecturing to save his soul. I don't know why I went – the visit felt awkward. As though I was proving to him that I was a success. But it felt phony and premature. All the time half-ashamed inside that my career was mostly built on stunts and lies – the biggest one I was in the middle of pulling off, right now, under his nose, here in Cornwall. God forgive me. Gareth was such a straight-goer that I sensed he could see through my phoniness. He was pleasantly underwhelmed by my status at the *News of the World* – I thought he'd be more grateful. But that was just me craving approval again. Deep down, I think he was trying to say: 'Calm down, don't get carried away.' But I was too self-absorbed for it to hit home. As we shook hands, before I got off, he was gracious: 'You were easily the most ambitious in the class – you were always going to end up in Fleet Street.'

Then I drove over to Falmouth to lord it over my former colleagues at the *Falmouth Packet*. I was more bolshy here. My previous Editor John Marquis was genuinely pleased that I'd 'made it' in some fashion. The suave, sun-tanned former boxing correspondent, who was also too big for small-town papers, had tasted success himself in his own day. Flying all over the world to glamorous venues in Vegas and the like, to cover the big fights for Thompson Publishing. So he was on it and all smiles. The Sports Editor Leon Prynn took the piss, in a good-natured Cornish fashion, about being a big shot and a hard-hitter. Again, I should have decoded the secret message: pride comes before a fall. But by now I was desensitised to such an extent that I could only tune in to basic bodily functions.

That afternoon, both Steve and I travelled up to see the crypto-zoologist in person. To show him the pics of the claw marks. A bizarre, bespectacled nerd with stains on his shirt. Cramped-up inside an overheated, pebble-dashed council house. In one of those isolated urbanisations that you only ever see in the poverty-scorched Scottish hinterlands. Both floors filled with wall-to-wall glass cases containing reptiles, snakes and dinosaur-looking fish. Spooky posters on the walls of dragon sightings, werewolves in Hungary, and a black and white print of a dead sea monster in Canada. Back in the world of Wayne Phelps but nice and *X-Files*y, if it came down to it. With a bit of bamboozling, he soon put his name to the claw pics saying they were a straight-up puma.

Later that day, Ray called back with the verdict on the list line. 'No to claw marks. Rebekah wants you to stay down,' he said.

'She wants a picture of the Beast. Are you sure there aren't any new pictures floating about down there of fresh sightings?'

'We've spoken to everyone,' I said, 'and there's deffo no new collects.'

'Well, somehow we've got to get a picture,' Ray emphasised. 'Rebekah's still keen on the story and coming home is not an option.' My recollection is that he said: 'Somehow, we will have to engineer it in some way.'

I didn't know exactly what Ray meant by the word 'engineer'. But, instinctively, I took it to mean he was asking me to fabricate a picture. Ray had a different interpretation – he later denied he was suggesting Steve and I stunt-up a picture. he said that he meant for us to work harder and find a way of getting a good story. But I was so keen to impress, and on the back foot, that I didn't care to ask him to elaborate at the time. It was as though Ray was a superior being and I couldn't bear for him to be tainted with such problems.

When the call came in, I was sitting next to Steve in the car. Night-time was closing in. Steve kept badgering me to tape Ray to cover our arses. But taping superiors, though prevalent at the *Screws*, was never my style. I still looked up to my bosses. I still trusted them.

Whatever he meant, we took it that Ray was saying that a picture could be stunted and he was OK with that. Engineered = set-up = fabricated, to our minds. Ray wasn't exactly being explicit, but he was nodding us in a certain direction. That's what I concluded, anyway.

Either way, it didn't really matter to me, to be honest. By that time, I'd already made up my mind that a picture of the Beast would have to be stunted. Even before the conversation with Ray. It was inevitable. Surely, that's what everyone wants, I concluded. If you send Sherlock Holmes to Cornwall, you want a stupid picture of the Beast. It's that simple, isn't it?

The more I thought about it, the more I rationalised that Ray wanted me to stunt it. Maybe he and Rebekah knew that I was a demon stunt-up merchant all along. Maybe they had seen through the Nazi E-peddler, the fake-gun dealer and Princess Di's unofficial cannabis farm, from the outset. Realised that they were great pieces of fiction from the off, and come up with idea of Sherlock as a harmless outlet for my talents. That's what good managers do, isn't it? Bring out the best in their staff.

Afterwards, both Steve and I had a long discussion. Steve was under the impression that both Ray and Rebekah were in on it together. My position was slightly different. I thought that Ray was trying to inspire us to stunt, push us in that direction without actually saying it direct. Re Rebekah – I didn't believe that she had ordered Ray to ask us to stunt it. She did, however, create the right conditions for it to happen. By applying pressure. Forcing us into a corner. Where we'd feel we'd have no option. We both concluded that we'd sleep on it over the weekend. Then, if nothing changed, if the pressure kept up, we'd have no option but to stunt a picture the following week. We didn't know exactly how, yet. But again, we both agreed to plot and scheme on some options over the weekend. We both agreed to go back to London for a couple of days. Covering each other's backs if the desk called to check that we were still down in Cornwall. That night Steve headed off back to his plush property in Pinner. He was greatly relieved. He'd been extremely pissed off – the monstrous weather, the stress, the constant phone calls from the *NoTW*.

Triggered by my own stress, the virus crept back. Pressure on the back of the skull. Dark veil spreading over my frontal lobes. A raging heat infesting the front of my brain. I retreated into my mental cave to fight it. I couldn't face going back to Watford to see Angela. One time I'd gone back and found a young millionaire *Apprentice*-type getting dressed in the living room. I didn't go mad – I just went over to the fridge, popped open a couple of Pils and sat down with him. ' How's business?' I asked. Turned out he owned a merchandising franchise for a Formula One team.

'That's nice,' I said.

'I'll bring you a baseball cap, next time I come round.'

'Thanks,' I said.

Another time, I found her and Pulp's coke dealer, snorting off the five-grand glass table in the kitchen. The drug dealer started lecturing me for treating Angela badly. I just kept looking at my reflection in the smoked sheen of the table top, thinking: 'What the fuck is going on here?'

I stayed down in Cornwall. Lost and alone. The disease making me reactionary and angry – and for some mad reason sexually heightened as well. Like a predator roaming the moors, I tapped up a couple of girls I knew down there. One was the girlfriend of an old mate, a photographer called Shadow. Buxom blonde-type and an outrageous flirt. Played heavily on the devilish country girl thing. That was her hustle. She'd first come on to me in the Good Mixer pub in Camden one night. Blowing me kisses – and her digits – behind Shadow's back. Asking me to call her in sign language whilst flustering up her skirts. I'd always resisted because Shadow was such a nice feller. Now in my deranged werewolfian trance, it was a case of lock up your daughters. But when the time came, when the Beast came on to the phone breathing heavily, Little Bo Peep was too scared to come out to play. All talk. Another girl, who I knew from my agency days in Bristol, said she had settled down now and couldn't even slip out for a drink these days. The whole world seemed to be growing up and playing house. For me, anything outside my hotel room was too much reality. I like to stay inside, concocting fairy stories for a living. Like a lost soul, I headed to Newquay to get pissed. To cop for a slag, on my Todd.

Like a rabbit, I couldn't stay still. Darting from one impulse to another. Got to stay on the move. That was my medicine. On Sunday morning, I headed back to Watford. The transitory hope of the train giving me consolation. Being Oscar Mike stopped me from having to think about anything.

I spent the rest of Sunday and Monday crashed on the couch. Landline chinned up against my ear. Ringing round to find a stuffed puma which I could take back down to Cornwall on

Tuesday. By this time, I'd deffo lost it. In the field without any reasonable command or control.

I phoned my old stunt-up compadre Gav.

'I want you to get your hands on a prop for me,' I asked. 'No expense spared, and I'll pay you well. D'you get me?'

'OK, mate,' said Gav. 'No probs.'

'It's got to be a stuffed puma, OK? Failing that, a tiger or a panther or something in that mould, d'youknoworramean?'

'What about a lion?' Gav asked.

'Yes, if it's a girl one. But it can't be a King-of the-Jungle one. As that'll be too mad.'

'More low-key, like a leopard, I get you?'

'Yes, keep it a bit real, d'you know what I'm saying? It can't have a big main or hair around it, like in the cartoons. That'll look too on top.' I pictured myself getting back on the train to Bodmin. A big cat under my arm with its legs sticking out of the brown paper.

'OK. I've got it now. Who d'you think will have one, mate?'

Pangs of impatience welled up. Spikier than usual, sharpened hot by the virus. Dealing with *Untermenschen*, who weren't as resourceful as my good self, was a burden. Asking loads of questions. Holding their hands like on their first day of nursery. Get a job with the council, if you can't figure these things out for yourself.

'Firstly, try some prop-finders,' I sighed wearily. 'They are specialist set designers, companies that supply objects to film sets and the telly and that. From hats, to cars to blow-up dolls – whatever is needed to make something look right. Like an Aladdin's cave – they've got everything. If they haven't, for some reason, then try the museums – they'll rent out some of their dead animals, if you ask them nicely.' I remember paying Bristol City Museum a few quid. For lending me a stuffed bat in a glass case and a little robin nailed to a perch. At the agency, we set up a picture of them, together in a cage. Lied to the papers that they were alive and said they were mates. It was at the time of all those *Batman and Robin* films. So it tied in with all the hype around that.

'Then obviously try the taxidermists and the county homes and things.'

'OK, mate. I'll give it a whirl.'

'I'd do it myself, but this one is double-secret. You've got to put in the calls and front it, so there's no connection to me, because I'll be using it in a story next week.'

Then I rang Steve and told him what I was doing. But Gav's search proved fruitless. No one in Britain had a stuffed big cat for hire that week. Gav called me on Monday night with the bad news.

'For fuck's sake, mate. You're getting lazy,' I told him. Gav had recently moved to West Hampstead. It was all bottles of wine and spag bol. Hippy teachers and so on.

'I was relying on you.' Phone down. I rang Steve immediately.

'Sorry, mate, I can't get one,' I told him, deflated with failure. I bet he was used to Mazher, getting him anything he wanted.

'It's OK, mate,' Steve consoled. 'It was a long shot anyway.'

'What about using a cardboard cutout?' I suggested.

'What do you mean, mate?'

'Like a life-sized outline of a cat, kind-of-thing, cut out in plywood or something. We could paint it black, like a silhouette and put it far away behind a hedge. Snatch it from a distance. That'll do, won't it?'

'No, it's not going to work, mate – it will stand out a mile. Too suss.'

'Well, we're going to have come up with something. And fast, because we've got to be back in Cornwall tomorrow. And you-know-who will be on the phone early doors, wanting a big piece of meat to throw at Rebekah.' The spectre of Ray was hanging over us, hollowing our stomachs like Physics homework on a Sunday night.

'Well, it's going to have to be Plan B, isn't it?' Steve said.

'Do you mean the other Plan B we spoke about last week?'

'Yes, mate.'

'Well that's that, isn't it?' I said. 'No option, have we?'

''Fraid so, mate,' Steve said. 'I'll pick you up in the morning and we'll have a chat about it on the way back down.'

24

Dartmoor

Plan B was simple. Locate a puma in a safari park. Take a picture. Pretend it was the Beast of Bodmin.

The difficulty lay in maintaining the hoax. Believability depended 50 per cent on technical details. Twenty-five per cent on blagging skills (convincing the Desk that we'd actually seen a wild animal on the moors and snapped it). Then, most crucially, 25 per cent on Steve's authority. As Senior Investigative Photographer at the *News of the World*, if Steve Grayson put his name to the picture, then the grown-ups back in Wapping were more likely to swallow it. After all, Steve's cop-show-style partner back in the world was none other than the legendary Mazher Mahmood. The Investigations Editor no less. The Fake Sheik, for fuck's sake. Together, they had broken some of the biggest stories in the history of the paper. Steve's Big Top Operator status sucked up privileges like a life peer. Reporting less to the minions on the Picture Desk. Often going over their heads. Direct to the Editor. Even the Cunt was an open door to him – I'd seen Steve wander in. Slide contemptuously into one of his chairs. Tap him up for a fireside chat. Steve's professional pull was the keystone. The wedge of trust holding the whole caper up. For the common good, he had to remain strong.

For the five-hour journey back to Cornwall, we tilled over all the angles like Farmer Giles.

'Obviously, the most important thing,' I said, 'is that the safari park isn't recognised in the background.' Bombing down the M4, Steve turned to me wide-eyed and nodded madly, as though I was stating the obvious.

'That it's bland enough,' I continued, 'so that we can match it up with a similar landscape in Cornwall.'

'Yeah, course,' agreed Steve. 'It's got to be just grass or trees or something.' Under no circumstances could there be identifiable topography, such as fences, cages, buildings, telephone poles and pylons clueing-up the scenery for nay-sayers to latch on to later. Easily recognisable hills and roads and stand-out foliage, such as lone trees and rare plants, would also have to be avoided at all costs.

'And it goes without saying,' I carried on, 'that we don't want to ID the puma as one that belongs to a particular zoo. That'd be fucking suicide, wouldn't it? So it can't have any distinguishing marks on it. We can't have some ball-bag zookeeper seeing his puma in the paper and saying, "That's my Elsa" or something. Then we'd be fucked, d'you know where I'm going?'

'Like I've said,' Steve added, 'we're best snatching it at a distance.'

'Yes,' I said. 'So that it just looks like a generic pic of a puma, roaming around.'

An amorphous image of a Big Cat. Could be anywhere or anything. But because the *News of the World* are saying it's the Beast, it's the Beast. And that's that. Who's gonna say it's not? We're the *News of the World*. If you say otherwise, we'll destroy your life.

By the time we got to Exeter, our spirits were high. Excessively inflated by the warm glow of conspiracy. At the service station, I jumped out of the car readily. To get Steve a cup of tea. Eager to please. Feeling important that I was part of the plan. Comfortable that I was in safe hands. Of a VIP. The old biddies, in the queue for the till, made me impatient. The salesmen, with their tedious lives, shuffling about. Mugs who didn't know the score. As we got off, Steve seriously hoped that, in the end, it wouldn't have to come to down to Plan B.

'Maybe,' he mused, 'Ray has calmed down over the weekend ... and it's all been forgotten about now, d'youknowwhatImean? Hopefully, when you speak to him, we'll get pulled off.' But checking in with Ray was a brisk formality. During the call, he still sounded pissed off. Rebekah was still keen on the Beast, he said. Obvious that she still wanted a picture of a mystery cat. Plan B hadn't been a forgone conclusion up until that point. But in a way, now it was a relief. To know for sure that, finally, we'd have to put it into action. At least we had a firm objective. It seemed that Steve and I had talked about Plan B for so long that morning, on top of the several days of exploring the stuffed animal option, that in truth it felt as though we were already committed. That's the way you think when you're a young reporter. Once you've spent time on an angle, it's hard to give it up. Even though the results might be bad. A kind of self-destructive tendency.

Arriving back at the hotel in Bodmin, I did a ring-round of all the zoos I knew. Dartmoor Wildlife Park, on Exmoor, was the nearest facility containing pumas. Over the phone, the woman told me that the big cats were in pens, like giant cages. I preferred to go to a proper safari park, I told Steve. Where the big cats roamed more or less free over acres of territory. But they were miles away up north and no one could be arsed. That's the problem with Cornwall – it's fucking miles away from everywhere.

During the day I checked in with Ray. He was still pushing but was also telling us to rejig last week's piece to make it better. I had a solution but I couldn't tell him just yet.

'Don't worry,' I told Ray, bursting to tell him that everything was going to work out just great.

'I think we'll get some good stuff. It's all in hand, we're following some fresh leads. We've got some info on new sightings.' I remember Ray being slightly sceptical.

The next day we drove up to the zoo, around five miles away from Plymouth. On the way, Steve made an unusual decision.

'I'm going to shoot it on digital,' he announced.

'Why?' I asked, slightly alarmed at this last-minute aberration. Digital cameras were in their infancy. Very few Fleet Street snappers used them routinely. The picture quality was low and the cost high. Steve had been given one free by the *News of the World* only because he was so important.

'It'll be easier to Photoshop the image afterwards,' Steve explained. 'If the puma is in a cage, there's going to be metal bars all over the place. So I'll have to clean it up on the computer later.'

This worried me.

'Won't the Picture Desk be suss? If you suddenly change your usual camera, from film to digi?'

'No, it'll be OK. Trust me. If they ask, I'll just tell them the battery went on my film camera, after we were walking around all night, looking for the Beast.'

We'd already cooked up a basic back story to explain, when the time came, how we'd managed to get a picture of the Beast. For over a week now, we'd been telling the desk that we had been tracking the Beast at night. We'd even told them we'd bought a tent for £50, to make it more on the up-and-up. The bonus was that we were going to claim £25 quid each on expenses for the phantom nylon shelter. Going out on to the moors in the early hours. Looking for trails and listening for howls. Of course, it was all bollocks. After chicken and chips and a pint in the hotel bar, straight to bed. We'd had to lie to get Ray off our back. Anyway, the plan was simple – we were going to say that we'd snapped the Beast at dawn. On the way home to the hotel, from one of these bogus late-night missions.

'The battery went?' Sounded iffy to me. But I had to defer to superior knowledge. 'OK, if you're safe with that, then that's fine.'

But it got me niggling. Maybe Steve wasn't as streetwise as I thought he was. Me, I was a stunt-up imperator – I never went off-plan, no matter what. That's how you got caught. That's how easy it was for a guy to get whacked. Maybe Steve's standards weren't as high as mine. Maybe he'd never done a stunt-up. Maybe, God forbid, he was naive.

Sensing my uncertainty, Steve bolstered his position: 'The other thing is that I've got to think about the roll of film and the sequence of the negs. If I use a film camera, then the Desk are going to want to see all the negs. They are going to look at the order of pictures on the contact sheet, before, during and after the useable ones. And it's fucking hard to make that look kosher.'

He had a point.

'You've got to understand that when we get to the zoo, I'm going to have to get loads of frames of the puma to find the one that is usable. But with film, you can't delete the unusable ones. So it'd be obvious to anyone who saw the negs that they'd been stunted in captivity. Whereas with my digital camera, I can just delete the ones I don't use. So it just looks like I managed to get off two or three shots of the Beast, as it's come into view, all of a sudden.'

'OK, I understand.' You had to trust him. After all, he'd once worked as a freelance spy for the security services. Keeping an eye on foreign revolutionaries as they partied on in Soho nightclubs. In the '70s, Steve had been a top disco DJ. Perfect cover for being on the payroll of those fat grammar schoolkids they call military intelligence.

In the zoo's car park, Steve rotated a shortish lens on to the digital camera body. Stashed covertly into a green plastic bag. Waltzing in with his classic canvas Billingham would have attracted too much attention.

Drizzly Wednesday morning. A sprinkling of visitors shielded from the wind behind bare concrete walls. An old man, shod in a throw-away plastic mac that looked like a giant condom, was stooped at the entrance. A coach-load of kids crowded around the low fences of the deer sanctuary. All potential meddlers who would have to be neutralised during the business stages of the coup. Steve and I stood out like undercover coppers at a riot. Unshaven, dead-eyed city-types. Looking from side-to-side, whilst feeding the monkeys.

Snaked up a gravelly mud path, that led to a large enclosure. Boxed in with strengthened steel mesh. A dark-coloured puma loping around inside. Geronimo! Like the SEALs, who came to smoke Osama in front of his missus, we went in for the kill. Slow is smooth. Smooth is good. The good news – there was just enough free space around the puma. If Steve got in close, with a tight shot, he could get one off without revealing too much of the background. The bad news – the resulting photo might be too much of a close-up.

Bonus – each square of mesh, that formed the lid of the cage, measured around 10 cm by 10 cm. Just enough to partially slot the lens through. Saving Steve from having to shoot right on to it. Around the back, the access was even better. No mesh, just a dirty concrete wall. Topped off with a row of thicker steel bars. Widely spaced so that Steve could get the lens right inside. A bit further inside the bars. Not completely, so there'd still be some metal in the frame. But it was the best of a bad situation.

We waited until the other visitors had moved on. I kept watch at the entrance to the puma enclosure, blocking the path. While Steve papped away at the rear. Darting around the outside of the cage. Scoping it from different angles.

'OK, keep a close eye,' he said. 'I'm going to get a bit of a leg-up.' Steve hoisted himself up the concrete wall, so he could shoot through the wide-spaced metal bars. Dangerous game – if the puma pounced, Steve's hand was breakfast. More worryingly, he was putting himself on offer by exposing himself from the rear. As the park was on a slope he could be seen from the base at the bottom and from those higher up.

'Is it going to work?' I whispered, my adrenalin pumping.

'Fucking hell,' I heard. 'It's hard, but if I can get a bit higher, I can get a shot that will.'

'Go on then. Get up there,' I said.

Sure enough, Steve edged himself higher. Balancing with one foot on the concrete wall. Another precariously on the wire mesh. Cool as a cucumber. You had to admire him. Game he was. Streetwise enough not to show out. Under any circumstances.

In the old days, they called them *Luftmenschen,* or 'men of air'. The scallywags of Eastern Europe, who floated in and out of the shtetls, the poor Jewish villages. The underground fixers who lived by their wits and could get their hands on anything. Steve was a Fleet Street version of the man of air. No wonder the *Screws* had got their hands on him. He made things work.

'Someone's coming,' I said. Steve jumped down. Brushed himself off. Camera stowed in the bag seamlessly. Casually we walked on as though nothing had happened.

'Any good?' I asked.

'Think so, mate,' he replied. 'I think there's one or two frames which might work.'

Back to the car. Raced to the nearest pub, a large neo-Victorian Wetherspoon-style place with a yellow painted restaurant that sold cheap food. While I got the teas and scran in, Steve uploaded the images on to his Mac. The waiting was torture. I had to sit at a separate table. This could be the story that finally makes me. Or breaks me.

'Here you are,' Steve said, after about a quarter of an hour. 'Have a look at that.' I peeked over his shoulder.

My heart sank. A close-up shot of the puma's face stared back. Stretching its mouth, baring its teeth. Not quite yawning but not quite roaring either. Its pupils, like yellow jewels, beamed out from the dead centre of its eyes. A pair of perfectly erect ears stood up like pyramids on top of its head. Too close. Too ferocious. Too perfect.

But it was the background that really fucked things up. The fluorescent quality of the digi pixels tinged the colours with an unreal, jump-out feel. A fire of streaky reds, yellows and oranges, that matched the walls of the restaurant, striped the rear. As though the puma was pouncing out of an inferno. All in all, the picture looked like a car advert or something.

But I had to be careful not to offend Steve. After all, he'd done his level best. Under unusual and difficult circumstances.

'What do you think?' I said diplomatically. 'Is it too close up? Too dramatic, maybe?'

'See what you mean,' mmmed Steve. 'I'll try 'n' tone it down a bit, on the Photoshop.'

'OK, mate.' I said flatly. But I was still not convinced. If we sent this picture in, then we'd get wholly buzzed off. No back answers. Laughed out of court. Even air-brushed, the portrait nature of the shot was evidence of a close encounter with a puma. No other way of explaining it. That meant the story would no longer be just about the picture. But a whole new ballgame altogether. No longer just a third-person report. An ambiguous feature that tied in with the playful Sherlock Holmesy feel of the piece. Is this the Beast of Bodmin or not? Is this bullshit or not? A close-up spun the story into a different kind of journalistic animal altogether. Now it became a first-person account. A piece of reportage. An 'I-came-face to-face-with-a-ferocious-mystery-beast' kind of tale. That meant we'd have to invent not only a back-story but a first-hand account of the whole shebang.

All the time, I'd been thinking of more of a long shot. Of a puma sneaking through some grass or in between the bushes or trees. Like the Abominable Snowman or the Loch Ness Monster. Where you didn't really know what the fuck you were looking at. It was just a load of shite that you glanced at for a second. Bollocks for kids and bottom-shelf penny dreadfuls. A bit of crappy footage for *Arthur C. Clarke's Mysterious World*, before *Coronation Street* came on. Steve's picture, on the other hand, showed every detail. Right down to the spots on the puma's face and the perfectly formed triangle of its nose. David Attenborough would have given it an award.

Steve ate his burger and chips as he got busy with the Photoshop. I forked over my scampi, thinking about whether this was going to work.

'Do you think we should try somewhere else?' I suggested.

'Where like?'

'Well, there's the big cats at Longleat in Wiltshire. I don't even mind driving up to Knowsley Safari Park, just outside of Liverpool. I know it well. Went there loads of times as a kid. You can drive through these massive fields and the cats are hundreds of yards away. It's ideal for us. Do you get me? That's the kind of thing I had in mind.'

'OK, fair enough,' said Steve. 'I'll have a play around with it tonight on the computer. See if I can tone it down a bit. Make it a bit more real. We'll see how it looks tomorrow morning. If it looks too moody, then fair enough, we'll have another go somewhere else.'

On the way back, we drove past Dartmoor Prison. We both laughed.

'I wonder where all this is going,' I said.

25

Black Thursday

Sun up. Woke up. Sexed up. Steve's Photoshopped puma looked a bit better in the dark dawn of a new day. But it seemed like an old decision by then, anyway. Steamrollering on regardless now. Eight hundred miles an hour. Like those marines up the Baghdad highway. The momentum of the job was in charge by this stage. Carrying us along like a pair of pricks.

The next mission was to recce up a location. For the Close Encounter of the Furred Kind. Without too much hassle we discovered a perfect place – a dirt track, buffeted by hedges on either side. A conveniently short distance from the hotel. Credibly close to the lion's den in the spooky copse, where we'd chiselled out the claw marks exactly one week earlier. Like the government, it was all joined-up thinking.

We cooked up the deets. Choreographing around the scene, like a couple of homicide cops off *The Wire*.

'Keep It Simple.' Yawn. 'Stupid,' I lectured. Blowing Steve an early morning bad-breath kiss.

'OK,' he nodded, crouching down next to some tall weeds. 'We'll say it all kicked off at around 6.15 am – that's about first light – when the puma loped out of the bush around here.'

'Yes,' I said, picking up the baton and a handful of soil on one knee. 'Then suddenly the thing turns to us there, face-on, in the middle of the open track, because it sees us coming. Bosh! Bosh! Bosh! You get off three shots from, around 15 foot away, back there. Bingo! Job done. File by three. Home for tea.'

'Then the Beast leaps back into the undergrowth here,' finished off Steve, pointing to a hole in the bushes on the other side of the track. Whoosh! Gone! Splash! The rest is natural history.

We rushed to fabricate the evidence. Eager to get back to the hotel before breakfast finished. Our bellies hollow with worry. If this was going to work, we'd have to ring it in soon – before conference Wapping-time in fact. Otherwise, we might miss the boat and it might get held over till next week, which was out of the question.

I squashed down the brambles at the pretend entry and exit points on both sides of the track. Then I sculpted out a few paw prints in the mud, around the pools of rainwater on the ground.

'Maybe it had stopped for a drink?' I said.

'Who the fuck knows?' said Steve. I carried on, carefully mimicking the exact indentations that we had seen a day earlier inside the puma's pen at the zoo. Accurate spacing was important, too, Steve reminded me, as I did so. A kind of cabin fever had set in by now – we'd been in-country too long. Operating out there, without any decent restraint. Totally beyond the pale of any acceptable human conduct.

By half-eightish, I'd been up for nearly four hours. Mid-morning listlessness dragged under my eyes. A dry, tinny taste clagged up my mouth. My mind was saggy with sleep fog. Dozed off in the car on the way back to the hotel. But no sooner was I asleep than I was jolted awake, by Steve pulling into a sloping road, that led into a sleepy tree-lined hamlet.

'OK. If we're going to do this, we better check in now,' he said. 'Liz usually gets into the office around this time.' Steve looked at me ominously. 'OK, are you sure you want to go ahead with this?'

My head was heavy with fatigue. But three reassuring thoughts clouded my vision. One – I'd always got away with spoofing before. Two, at the end of the day, it was only a bit of laugh, wasn't it? And three, there were no safer hands to be in than Steve's. While I was trying to focus, a sign appeared from God. In front of the News Int. company car that we'd brought back down from London. A jet-black cat crept out into the road. From under a tree-tangled street sign, and walked right across the lane into a yellow cottage. Of course – it was the omen for me to say 'No' to Steve and fuck all this madness off right now. Were we insane? What the fuck did we think we were up to? I turned to Steve.

'Yes,' I said, not wanting to let anybody down. Weighed down by all the energy already spent on it so far. 'OK, let's do it,' I said. But this time, I didn't follow it with a gung-ho catchphrase like usual. There was no, 'Let's do it to them, before they do it to us,' now. For some reason, my heart wasn't in it.

I sat in the car pathetically. While Steve wandered up and down the lane, on the moby. Gesticulating in gross motor movements, whilst telling the story to the desk. As though animation proved it was true. Journalists never like to talk to their bosses in front of anyone else. I overheard him recounting the story, first to Pictures Assistant Claire Wood, then to Act Pic Ed Liz Cocks. The gist of it was how we'd seen the Beast of Bodmin an hour or so earlier. I wound the window down to earwig.

'I don't know whether I got the picture yet,' I heard him say. Lacing it up with false real-event uncertainty. 'Because we've only just pulled off. It was fucking mad. Fucking scared shitless, d'youknowhatImean?

'But anyway, fuck's sake, we're on the way back to the hotel now. We're not hanging around here any longer. The fucking thing might come back and bite us on the arse. No, I'm fucking serious – it was dangerous. So I'll see what I've got when I get back to the room and whack 'em over in a bit.'

Hero or what? He came back to the car buzzing.

'She was fucking ecstatic,' he said. 'Nearly wet her-fucking-self.

They love it. Not a fucking word. If it was anyone else, she would have been, "Fuck off, you're taking the piss. Either that, or you've dropped a fucking trip. It's a fucking spoof." But because it's me, she knows it's all on the up 'n' up.'

'That's good,' I said.

But already I was getting jealous. That he'd got in there first. To steal the glory of the Beast for himself. Cheeky twat. Making me look like a tool. Just down here to carry his cameras and a fresh pair of undies for him. Sleep-deprived furies were raging me up. These four-by-twos – they're always taking your graft off you. 'Who put this thing together, me that's who?' Tony Montana's indignant mantra, madly looping around my head.

Frustrated, I kept speed-dialling Ray to check in. But he kept going straight to answer machine. Impatience and fatigue were shredding my nerves. Worried, in case I got a bollocking off him. For not getting him the big news first. I didn't want to make him look like a cunt. Walking into the office and getting ambushed unawares by Beast-mania

Joyrided back to the hotel at car-chase speed. Steve pinged his pics in to wild applause. Then fuck. Rebekah came straight back on to him. That's when I thought, for the first time, 'What the fuck have we done here?'

From then on, the conversations got very messy. Mainly because everyone had different opinions about who knew what. Steve was convinced that both Ray and Rebekah knew the pictures were stunted. I disagreed. My position was slightly more convoluted – I believed Ray was a kind of catalyst. Who'd lit the fuse. But was not responsible for the resulting explosion. That side of the Chinese Wall was down to me and Steve. I assumed Ray would twig for himself and let us crack on. However, the crucial point was this. To maintain protocol, I could only communicate with him as though he had no idea whatsoever.

As far as Rebekah was concerned, deep down, I didn't really think she was in on it. But I assumed she would suspect foul play because it was all so expedient and just too damned good to be true. However, I also thought that she'd wave it through with a nod and a wink. As it was a calculated risk in her own interests to do so – to get a good story. Of course, again, I would have to speak to her as though she was totally innocent as well. The script would have to play out like I was conning her. Her position was too important, too pristine to be contaminated. Like a private military contractor who was killing babies on the side, I'd have to remain reliable and deniable at all times. On her side, she'd have to reciprocate with a straight bat. Pretending to check out the story. To protect herself. But not pushing it too hard. One of the great skills of being a tabloid editor. Both Steve and I agreed that no one on the Picture Desk knew or would ever know. As was the case with Kuttner.

The already complex cross-wires were further mangled by the method of communication. Most of the conversations took place on speakerphone. With all of these people talking at once over each other. So, Steve and I would have to follow different rules of engagement simultaneously. Hiding one thing from one person, while communicating something else to someone else at the same time. It was going to be a hair-trigger combination of double-meanings, mind-reading and timing. On top of that, there was a fourth dimension – a layer of independent observers and secret fifth columnists lurking about. Listening in to find out if there was any conspiracy. Reporting back to different factions, who they were loyal to.

Let's just say, it wasn't exactly a culture of openness and transparency. Years later, I understood completely how phone hacking was allowed to get so out of hand. With everyone ratting on each other. It was simple – exactly the same type of conversations had been going on. I could imagine a Spaghetti Junction of cover-ups, calculated risks, half-truths and lies. All glossed over with a veneer of corporate respectability. No big deal – isn't that's how Big Fat Westerners get through the day? Isn't that why we rule the world? I'd complain, but no one would listen. No fucking wonder they ended up shutting the whole thing down. Like a ruptured reactor.

The toxic mess threatened to spill out, sliming up the whole world for all time. No single building in history had ever been the home to so much dissembling. Once a chain reaction like that starts, there's no containing it so it's a good job they did – by closing it down forever.

During the first chat with Rebekah, Steve was more than happy to play ball with her – after all he was convinced that ultimately she was the Mr Big pulling the strings. To his mind, she was having to go through the motions of quizzing us simply to convince all the people at her end and cover her own back. That said, Steve's blag was word perfect – Peter Cook-esque in its droll understatement. Like he was telling her that he had just shagged Christie Brinkley and Cindy Crawford in the bogs. But with the delivery of a gasman reading the meter. I loved him now. It's true – these good North London boys, they really are the chosen ones. I assumed he had to prove to her that his blag was good. So that she was confident that the scam was airtight.

Then gulp. At 9.45 am Ray called me. Turning on the breathlessness, I told him something like. 'Yeah. Yeah. Yeah. Blah. Blah. Blah. And then it just walked out, in front of us. Cool as fuck.

'Just as me and Steve were walking across the field. Then, the next moment like, it was gone just like that. Blah. Blah. Blah. Bollocks. Bollocks. Bollocks.'

'Well done, Graham.' But his voice was light with blag-bonhomie. Brittle with caution around the edges. Not knowing whether to shit or comb his hair. Of course, there could never be any explicit reference to 'engineering'. Not in a million years – are you fucking stupid? Even though I believed he knew what was going on, or at least could work it out, the Chinese Walls were well and truly up by now. Suddenly slammed shut, like a secret chamber in *Indiana Jones*. Too late for polite conversation now. From then on, it was strictly gangster-speak on the blower. Fresh air for the Feds. Never talk over the phone, d'you get me? Where everyone knew the score. But everyone tap-danced around the graft like it never happened and it wasn't there. In a merry dance of multi-level, shape-shifting conspiracy. Looming but silent like a car bomb that was about to go off. So that if it ever came on top, everyone can plausibly deny everything. And the shit can only ever flow one way. Gravity-wise, and straight on to heads of the minions below. Leaving the powerful to seal the airlock. To head straight for the bunkers in Deep Carpet Land. At News Int. force protection was a well-honed drill. Once a caper was underway, it went without saying that everyone would have to behave. Both in public and in private, that the Beast was all on the up-and-up.

In a strange way, I was glad not to have to speak to Ray about stunting-up. I didn't have the bottle. It felt squirmy and embarrassing. He was too sacred. Like having that talk about the birds and the bees with your mum and dad. Once a peasant, always a peasant – I actually felt it was my duty to shield him.

But Steve had other ideas – he wanted to be able to talk freely about the stunt. It was frustrating for him. But no chance – by then it was already out of control. A labyrinthian riddle of smoke and mirrors where nothing was what it seemed.

26

The Calls

After conference, Ray called again and spoke to both Steve and me. He said something like, 'Listen, they're great pics and Rebekah appreciates your efforts, being down there. But if they're stunted, you can tell us now. We'll all have a laugh and move on.'

But deep down, I sensed that his heart wasn't in it. Both Ray and I knew that if I'd have confessed now it would have been extremely serious because it was taking the piss out of Rebekah on her big week.

'Mate,' I said, 'I've told you what happened. I saw a big cat. And we're not just saying this because it's raining down here and we're desperate to come home.' Steve said that he thought Ray was having to put on an act because other people were listening in. On that occasion, Assistant Editor Garry Thompson and a female Pic Exec were next to Ray. Ray was making himself look good.

A few minutes later Steve was getting the same shit direct off his line manager Liz Cocks. Rebekah must have put them up to it. I later found out that Rebekah was saying that she needed reassurance before midday, because if it was kosher, she was going to ask Exec Chairman Les Hinton for more budget to fund an extra-long print run on that Sunday. Hooray! Big sales for her.

Steve and I knew that Kuttner would be cautious. Sure enough, when informed, he thought that there was something about the pictures that made them almost too good to be true. Not only that, but if he or any of the execs would have looked just that bit closer, they would have seen a clue to their falsehood. At the bottom of the photograph, there were three symmetrical and parallel dark lines – the remnants of three photoshopped-out railings from the puma's cage. Later Steve said that he had deliberately left them in their as an insurance policy against taking them seriously. But for now Kuttner failed to spot them. But he tempered his suspicion for the greater good. Adding that he would never have expected someone like Steve to stunt them. Or a relatively junior reporter like myself to take such a large risk with my career. So for him, on balance, it was a 'yes'.

Some time later Ray called again on speaker phone with Senior Associate Editor Harry Scott.

'I want you to get hold of a professional hunter,' he explained. Great, I thought, the heat's off for a bit and Ray is playing along nicely. Makes us both look good in front of Harry. 'I want you to lay a trap for the Beast at the spot where you saw it. When we catch it, we can put it in a cage and get proper pics. Then hand it over to a zoo or something.' If he wasn't so serious, I would have laughed. What a fucking palaver! That's the thing with tabloid newspapers. They don't know where to stop. At heart, they're extremists. You give them a picture of the Beast. No it's not good enough now. We want more. We actually want to own it now. We want it to be ours. That's why, in the end, tabloid newspapers are doomed. They will always destroy themselves.

'OK, Ray. That's a good idea. I'll get on it straightaway.' I felt like saying don't bother. Our Beast already lives in a zoo. But I didn't. I liaised with Ricky Sutton who started ringing around to find a real-life Jungle Jim. 'Look in Yellow Pages,' I told him. 'Under H for hunters.'

Next up was the big set-piece with Rebekah that we were all dreading. On speakerphone. With Rebekah and Kuttner up front. And Ray and Liz lurking about in the background.

Steve stiffened. He wasn't happy at all that Kuttner was getting involved. So far he'd only had to lie to senior execs who he thought were involved in the scam – that was Rebekah and Ray. He was more than happy to merry dance with them all day long. But Kuttner was a different matter. Steve felt he was now 'being put in an impossible position'. Where he was having to lie to Kuttner, who wasn't at all fair game, because he wasn't in on it. Nor did Kuttner have a direct interest in it. Steve had to make a split-second decision on the spot – confess to Kuttner there and then. Drop Ray and Rebekah in it, with them listening in. Or blag on and hope for the best.

'On the spur of the moment,' he told me afterwards, 'I decided that the best course of action would be to maintain the pictures were genuine.'

First off, Rebekah came on quite strong. Trying to put us on the back foot. Or the back paw, as we laughed later. All for show in front of Kuttner, Steve concluded, and played along.

'You simply can't have a picture of the Beast,' she crowed. 'And if the story's not true, you should say now.' To rebut her, I did my pièce-de résistance, blagging Rebekah in the most important phone conversation of my life.

But Steve went on the offensive. Volleying the shot right back over the net like Björn Borg. 'D'you know,' he said to her, backing her up in this charade, 'I am so pissed off. You do a good job and you come up with a story and picture scoop like this and all you can do is kick us in the bollocks.' In his own mind, Steve was lining himself up with Rebekah to convince Kuttner.

Rebekah was taken aback. This was the turning point, she said later, when she was convinced the pics were genuine. No one could say that she wasn't taking all reasonable steps. Like we had assumed, it was Steve's stature that was going to carry the day. But the icing on the cake was a little sideswipe he took at Ray with everyone listening in.

'We're not going to do what Ray Levine wanted us to do,' Steve told Rebekah and Kuttner. Pause. As everyone held their breath.

What the fuck is he going to say, I thought? Blow the gaff now? Verbal Ray up, for asking us to engineer a pic? Bring it all crashing down at the first big hurdle?

'What do you mean?' someone asked. 'What has Ray asked you to do?'

'Set a trap for the Beast,' Steve sighed. 'Ray has just asked us to catch the Beast. And we're not going to do it because it's bloody dangerous.' Steve's little verbal gemstone had the simultaneous effect of making the Beast blag more credible and attacking Ray covertly at the same time. Steve was trying to say something to Ray, under the radar. 'You've dragged me into this, you cunt, and now I'm going to make you look like a cunt. Even if I can't tell you straight, in front of Kuttner.'

Ray piped up in the background, somewhat chided. 'That's not the case,' he intervened, 'that I wanted Steve and Graham to trap the Beast. I simply told them to get an expert to do it for them.' Rattled a bit by the shot across his bows. Steve had well and truly put him in his place. Letting him know, that if it came down to it, he wasn't afraid of criticising his instructions in front of Rebekah and Kuttner. 'Don't fuck up in here,' Steve was saying to him on the QT. But a nice little touch to create fear of the Beast, as though it was real. Rebekah liked it. Kuttner swallowed it.

'It certainly sounds as if they're telling the truth,' Rebekah told her consiglieri.

'I've got little option other than to believe them.'

Kuttner agreed that it was a spectacular scoop on which we were both to be congratulated but that he had to be sure they were genuine.

To close the deal Steve said solemnly: 'I would never lie to my Editor and Managing Editor.' Amen. Everyone congratulated us on our 'memorable achievement'.

Battle Stations. Rebekah cleared the first five pages of the paper for our world exclusive. The PR people started to fix up TV interviews for Steve and me. Plans were made to accommodate the hundreds of press people who'd flock to Cornwall to revel in it. This had to be done because there was no infrastructure in the countryside to cope with an expected press invasion. A big international news conference was pencilled in. All the while, Kuttner and Levine were ringing us to check the details. Steve and I held the line fast.

But later that day, Steve was suddenly ordered back to London.

'What the fuck's that about?' I asked, the colour draining.

'No big deal,' he said. 'Obviously, they're going to use the pictures big, and they want me in the office.'

'Oh. OK,' I said.

'And I suppose they also want to hear the story again face to face this time,' he conceded.

'Mmmmm,' I thought. But there wasn't any time for a steward's inquiry now. I had to put on a brave face in front of Steve, even though deep down I knew this was an ominous twist.

'OK, mate. Stay cool,' I said. 'Don't fold under questioning, whatever you do.

'And, it goes without saying, watch out for all those rats. There's more snakes up there than at that crank's we went to the other day.'

'Fuck off,' he said. 'I'm staunch.' The man of air flexing his props.

'Well, good luck,' I said, as we shook hands like escaped POWs going our own way. 'I'll see you on the next one.' Lord Lucan. Loch Ness. Life on Mars. Whatever it might be.

27

Bad Friday

Imagine the worst day of your life. When something that you have invested in, falsely or not, fucks up so apocalyptically, that all you can do is lie down.

1. You get the Os, Us and Fs in your A-Levels, when you should have got Bs and Cs.
2. You're made redundant after twenty years of getting up in the dark, and working through dinnertime, because you didn't mind taking one up the arse for the company.
3. Your kids get really ill.
4. Your village is overrun by soldiers and massacred. Even though it's been there for 10,000 years.

As always of recent, mine began with a wank. Just like on the news, disaster days began same as it ever was. Room was top-off hot, because the dial on the cast-iron rad was rust-stuck on one louder. Over a luke-warm Full English/continental room service combo, on a too-busy tray off which lots of things fell off on to the floor, I watched the *Big Breakfast*. Then buzzed off a few peasants talking bollocks on *Kilroy*. Before turning the sound down, best way, when Richard and Judy came on. Switching back and forth between them, and keeping an eye on the racing on Channel Four.

All the while I was writing up the story on a 1980s laptop – my notebook. Before singing it down the telegraph to the copy-takers. Who didn't give a fuck that I was making history, just hating on my unprofessional stopping and starting. They had complained about me before now, the slags. Moaning that the new generation of reporters couldn't speak fluent *Sun*ese like the old guard, and were therefore wasters. This story'll show 'em, I thought.

So prawn sandwiches and tea on trays were coming through the door like tellies through windows on tour with The Who. Too busy even to get dressed and showered. Sat there in my boxies, hair stuck up on end, unshaven. Just the same as when I'd decided to become a reporter, watching Sky News on the couch, on the dole.

Then Ricky turned up with Jungle Jim. A youngish but slightly balding big cat tracker, who got excited when I told him about my brush with the Beast.

'I think there might be some footprints,' I added, 'so I'll take you to the exact spot, as soon as Ray stops hassling me for adds.' Deep down, though, I was worried in case overnight drizzle had washed away our corroborating evidence.

But Jungle Jim didn't seem that arsed, saying he'd look for droppings as well. Droppings! Fuck! Why hadn't we thought of that? Maybe we should have robbed some from the zoo, when we did the pic, and scattered it about a bit at the scene of the crime. Irrefutable proof. Instead, all Jungle Jim'll find is some of my old chewy packets and shoe prints from my Rockport boots.

A big steel cage was being sent down. With a dead sheep as bait inside it. Another *News of the World* photographer called Steve Burton, whose nickname coincidentally was Beasty, said that he was trying to get a chopper up, to do an aerial. A broadcast-quality film camera with a crew was on order, he said, to get footage of the Beast for a TV advert. I was pleased – I'd scrutinised both Beasty and Ricky. To see whether they'd swallowed it all, or were spying for the Desk. But Ricky seemed genuinely glad to be back on board for the big win.

Then Steve Grayson called from the office in London. I took it in private, without trying to make it look like a big deal.

'Everything's cool,' he whispered. 'Don't worry.'

'Thank fuck for that,' I breathed out, glad to hear from him.

'I got a fucking big grilling off Kuttner, mind you. But it's all calmed down now.'

'What d'you mean?' I asked, trying to size up the risk.

'You know what he's fucking like. He kept asking me over and over again, in his office, if it's real. Of course I said it was real, because it is, isn't it? It's a real puma. After I'd said that, he seemed happy, and he then went off to see the Chairman, because they'd want the higher-ups to sign off on a big telly spend.' Meaning they were going to buy costly advertising space on ITV and Sky. Bigging up the story, in the run-up to Sunday.

'It's going to be over the first six pages,' Steve added. 'And that's not fucking happened since Princess Di died.'

'For fuck's sake,' I said. Not knowing whether to defecate in terror or have another wank.

'But that wasn't the only thing. That fucking dick-head Ray Levine collared me by the photocopying machine. Started talking all kinds of bollocks, about me going on the telly on Saturday night.'

'Fronting the advert and that?' I asked bitterly. I pictured what Ray wanted, in my mind's eye. You know the model. Steve bouncing on to the telly, in between *Midsomer* and *Stars in their Eyes*, with mad bangy, bangy, newsy, newsy take-this-seriously music in the background, saying: "I'm the man who came face-to-face with the Beast of Bodmin Moor and lived to tell the tale. See my astonishing pictures of Britain's only man-eating monster. Read my spine-chilling story. Only in the *News of the World* tomorrow."'

'Yeah, course . . .' said Steve nonchalantly. A twist of jealousy tightened in me. Already, down here, in the back of beyond, I was being kept in the dark and edged out. Me and Jungle Jim chasing shadows. While Steve was lapping it up under the bright lights, telling Trevor McDonald how great he was.

However, he was far from gloating, to be fair. I could tell Steve thought it was all getting well out of hand. But what could he do? We were in for a penny, in for so many pounds by now that it'd pay the deficit off. Too deep. Too soon. So back-pedalling was out of the question.

'I don't know what the fuck Ray's playing at, talking bollocks like that, when I thought he knew the fucking score. I suppose he's just covering his arse like everyone else. But I told him to fuck off anyway,' said Steve forcefully. 'I blagged out of it, in front of everyone – there was a couple of Features' reporters sitting by there – saying that it'd blow my cover if I did a TV ad and I'd never be able to work undercover again. So he got the message – he's a cunt, isn't he?'

I didn't like Steve slagging Ray but what the fuck? He was letting me know that he was taking the weight above and beyond. While I was sitting on my arse. Out of the firing line. Scratching my bollocks in a hotel room.

Phone down. I was a bit freaked by all that officy, politicky stuff, to be fair. But I was too busy to get my head round it all – I had to crack on with honing the story, which intro'd something like this:

'Today the *News of the World* publishes astonishing photographs of the Beast of Bodmin Moor. Our exclusive pictures prove the existence of the mysterious big cat once and for all. The explosive images show a dark-coloured, puma-like animal prowling around a foggy field in a remote area of Cornwall. The Beast was caught close-up on camera for the first time after a blood-curdling encounter with a crack *News of the World* surveillance team. Photographer Steve Grayson and reporter Graham Johnson had been tracking the animal's movements for two weeks. But they suddenly came face-to-face with the monster shortly after dawn on Thursday morning. The Beast appeared close to the scene of several recent sightings.

Steve said: "It was the scariest moment of my life."

His photographs show . . . etc. Bollocks. Bollocks. Bollocks.'

The copy wasn't very well written because it was always harder to write falsehoods than true stories. But Ray was on the phone every two minutes with fresh queries.

A couple of hours later Steve called back.

'Fuckin' hell, that was a nightmare.'

'What?' I said, heart in mouth, wondering what had happened. He told how Kuttner had called him in again. Then suddenly taken him out for lunch, to the brightly lit News International canteen. To rattle him up a bit.

This time Kuttner launched into a solemn speech, to underline just how grave it all was. Saying how he and Steve had been in the business for a long time. How that made them understand how important it all was – the Beast, that is. To make sure that the paper got it right. That it was all kosher. Half this was genuine inquiry. But half of it was the old newspaper propaganda of pretending that even the stupidest of stories were very, very important.

Reciprocating gravity, Steve replied solemnly: 'On my life, I wouldn't mislead you, Stuart.' Kuttner put his hands together and looked him in the eyes: 'So be it – well done.' Then they shook hands to mark the momentous occasion.

'Do you think he suspects?' I asked Steve.

'Course he does. You know what he's like. But he chose his words carefully . . . In the end, we had to have close words, very, very close words, d'you know what I mean? I had to do this thing, to make sure he knew that I was being serious – that I wouldn't bullshit him.'

'What thing?' I asked.

'Oh, don't worry, forget about it, it's nothing.'

'Well, what thing? Tell me,' I pushed, lightening up a bit because we seemed to be home and dry. 'D'you mean like sexual favours? D'you mean you had to bend over for Kuttner to prove that it was all true?'

'Fuck off,' Steve laughed. 'It's just a kind of Jewish thing. Between us, our thing, d'you know what I mean?'

'No, I don't but . . .' I could tell Steve was kind of uneasy about revealing the secrets of the Protocols of the Elders of Zion. Especially to a gentile over the phone on the shabbat, so I laid off.

'Just to say that it's on the level . . . you know the score,' Steve added.

'Oh, I see. Wow, that's mad. D'you mean like a secret sign?' I said, taking the piss a bit. 'Like a funny handshake type-of-thing. On the square and all that.'

'No, fuck off. Just like something we say, it's no big deal.'

'I see. Wow! That's fucking sound. So that swung it?'

'Yes, he warmed up after that. He was OK a bit then.'

But the cracks were beginning to appear. Steve was clutching at straws. Religious deal-breakers or otherwise, I could tell he was rattled. The thing about the £300,000 TV-spend shook him. As it did me. That was six times Steve's annual salary and ten times mine. Steve desperately needed time-out to think everything through before his next move. As of now, the story had gone from being a knock-about Fleet Street caper in fancy dress, to knocking Princess Di off the record tables, to potential corporate fraud. World-wide corporate fraud – if they were shelling out 300 grand on ads then they'd be whacking out the pics on syndication to every paper on the planet – that was all big money. All alone, Steve needed to get out of the office hothouse, get home and get his head together.

But on the way out, he bumped into his main story hombre Mazher Mahmood. Steve couldn't face any more blagging – especially to his best mate on the paper. A bit of small talk then straight off. Not even mentioning the Beast. Mazher didn't realise the dilemma raging on behind Steve's unusually subdued manner. Steve needed to tell someone – but who?

28

A Night to Remember

But no bother. If Mazher had failed to decipher the emotional semiotics, then Wapping's very own Lois Lane certainly wasn't going to let it lie. According to Rebekah, she was already on to Steve. Like Darth Vader, she believed she had a sixth sense. A supernatural gift for sensing when Rupert Murdoch's interests were in danger. Later, as her stature went stratospheric, her followers spoke of a metaphysical energy field that some believed was God in action. Or at least Murdoch's representative on earth. The Force was strong with Rebekah.

Even so, Rebekah's special abilities weren't as powerful – or as consistent – as Darth Vader's. Over the next 15 years, Rebecca's sixth sense did not detect other forms of bad behaviour at the *News of the World*. According to her, she failed to pick up on crimes such as bribing coppers, mining illegal data on an industrial scale, and hacking phones – literally to death. All going on, as she looked on imperiously from the bridge. But despite her x-ray vision, on these occasions, Rebecca claimed she could see no evil. Nor hear it, in the form of tapped voicemails. Not even speak it, as part of her evidence, at those Parliamentary hearings which she got dragged along to. Saying fuck-all and tap-dancing through the raindrops. Except for the odd admission of paying policemen. After all that, despite all of her clever talk, it was apparent that her sixth sense had failed to alert her to the deadliest danger of her life – the one that would eventually bring her down and destroy her paper.

But no such luck for Steve Grayson. On the day of reckoning, when he'd come into the office, to front one of the biggest stories in the paper's history, unfortunately for him Rebekah's sixth sense was beaming over Wapping like a death ray. Things started to warm up when Rebekah clocked Mazher and Steve chatting together in the newsroom late afternoon. Phones up. Curious, she rang Mazher to ask him what he thought of his best mate's great success in snapping the Beast.

'What d'you mean?' Mazher replied. 'Do you mean the paedophile ring that Steve was investigating?' Referring to an ongoing story that they had been working on.

'No, not that kind of beast,' said Rebekah. 'I'm talking about the Beast of Bodmin Moor – the big cat that Steve got a picture of in Cornwall this week.'

'I don't know what you're talking about,' said Maz.

Fuck! Alarm bells. Rebekah said her heart sank. The scent of rats. Immediately, she put Maz up to ringing Steve, with a view to catching him out. However, by that time, Steve had also had time to think, taking his wife out to their favourite Indian restaurant, to mull things over. According to him, a kind of Last Supper before the balloon went up. The calm before the storm. Steve had already decided to confess. He'd concluded that there's no way on earth he could let it go ahead – especially after learning of the £300,000 spend.

But when Maz rang, Steve was taken by surprise. Mate or not, there was no way he was going to confess to Maz. The big heart-to-heart was for Rebekah's ears only. Plus he needed more time to explain to his wife – and then ring me, to put me in the picture also. On the hop, Steve conceded to Maz that there were some problems with the story. But according to Maz, he also stuck to the original version of events.

'Listen, I'm in the middle of a meal,' Steve told Maz irritably, 'I'll call you back.' Maz now claimed that he smelled a rat too. He also thought it was extremely odd that Steve hadn't volunteered his scoop during the day.

Maz rang Rebekah back. 'Don't run the story,' he told her. Rebekah told Maz to ring Steve back. To put the pressure on for the full script.

'Make sure that you tell him this,' Rebekah instructed Mazher. 'If we went ahead and printed a false story, not only would I lose my job, but everyone else involved would lose theirs as well for approving it for publication. 'Therefore he has to say now.'

Meanwhile, back in the Indian, Steve was telling his wife, for the first time, the whole truth about the Beast. Steve's wife was shocked. She told him: 'You're in an awful position. You're damned if you do reveal the truth and damned if you don't.'

Then Maz rang Steve a second time and told him the SP. 'I think Rebekah's on to you, mate. I think she knows that you lied.' Phone down. Maz rang Rebekah and told her to ring Steve for the big showdown. It was 10 pm on Friday night – a tense time on a Sunday tabloid when the final stories are being knocked into shape and the pages are being laid out. At about the same time Steve was ringing her.

'Isn't it about time you told me the truth?' Rebekah said.

'I'm not saying anything,' Steve replied. 'All I'm saying is that you shouldn't run the story.'

'What do you mean by that?'

'The pictures aren't genuine.'

'What do you mean?'

'They're not genuine, in the sense that they aren't pictures of the Beast of Bodmin Moor.'

'What does that mean?'

'Well, what I'm saying is that, they are genuine pictures of a beast – but it's a puma at Dartmoor Wildlife Park.'

BOOM! They think it's all over. It is now. The President is down. I repeat – the President is down. Tora! Tora! Tora! You name it – the sky had just fallen in.

'I'm sorry,' said Steve. 'But I'm glad it's come out. It's been playing on my mind heavily – the most important thing is that I didn't want to cause you or the paper embarrassment. And I couldn't go through with it all, knowing that you were going to spend a great deal of money on promoting the story.'

'This is not a good situation,' said Rebekah calmly.

Then, according to her, Steve broke down in tears. According to Steve, he never cried.

'It was the pressure,' he sobbed. 'The bullying from Ray Levine to produce a picture of the Beast.'

'What do you mean?'

'Ray insinuated that me and Graham stunt the photograph and the story.'

But the walls had already come up. The emergency glass had been smashed. The klaxon was sounding the alarm. Dive! Dive! Dive! Rebekah was bolting for the panic room in Deep Carpet Land, letting off some light suppressing fire as she went.

'That's rubbish,' she hit back. 'I heard you personally speaking to Ray about the Beast. I heard you talking genuinely and seriously to him. What would be the point of pretending to Ray that the picture was genuine if he had asked you to stunt it in the first place?'

'Well,' said Steve, 'me and Graham had agreed to stick to the story from the outset. Even if we were talking to Ray.'

Conspiracies are hard to describe at the best of times. The dark, inscrutable shadows of human nature. So subtle that it takes years to get to the bottom of it. You can't put your finger on it. It's why fraud cases go on for five years – then fall apart because no one knows what the fuck is going on. Despite 5000 boxes of evidence and sixty lawyers sitting there scratching their heads.

For Steve, it was his grassy knoll moment. Or, at least that's how I imagined it later, when he recounted the ordeal to me, his face a contortion of white worry and sweat. Steve was pacing around the room animatedly. It reminded me of that scene in the movie *JFK*, in which Joe Pesci played conspirator David Ferrie. When the dark forces finally get too much for him. Steve was ranting under huge stress. 'Oh man, why don't you fuckin' stop it? Shit, this is too fucking big for you . . . you know that?' Trying to unravel the claustrophobia of unknown forces that were manipulating him. That had holocausted his material world off the planet. Steve was pacing around the room animatedly. 'Who did the Beast? Who stunted the photographs? Fuck, man! It's a mystery! It's a mystery wrapped in a riddle inside an enigma! The fucking people who did it don't even know! Don't you get it?'

But this wasn't the movies. This was the reality of life inside a corporation so powerful that it didn't have to whack the president. It simply told him what to do. Perfunctorily, Steve was ordered into the office. Before he left his wife, he tried to call me twice. To tip me off that the game was up. But I was engaged on the phone – Ray Levine had beaten him to it. Taking advantage of the fact that I was still totally in the dark about all of the day's events. Sitting in my hotel room, 212 miles away, with my dick in my hand – literally. Not knowing any of this had happened. To tape me up while I'd still front it out like a fool.

My position was simple – never fold under questioning. No matter what. Secret rendition. Abu Ghraib. Torture at the *News of the World's* secret training camp in Libya. Didn't matter what you threatened me with. I was strictly a name, rank and number merchant. Loyal to the last. Or at least I was in my own mind. Or on this occasion until at least I got the nod off Steve first. There's no way I'd drop him in it. After extracting the verbals off Steve, Rebekah had glided over to Ray's office.

'The Beast story is a hoax,' she'd told him.

Ray's first reaction was incredulity.

'I simply can't believe that's the case,' he told her.

Rebekah: 'Well, call Graham then and see what he's got to say.'

The conversation went something like this.

Ray: 'Hi Graham. It's Ray.'

Me: 'Hi Ray. How's it going?

Ray: 'Fine, thanks. Have you got anything to tell me about this Beast of Bodmin story?'

Massive panic attack. Gulp! A kind of out-of-body experience.

Me: 'No. Why? What's up?'

Ray: 'Was the picture stunted?'

Me: 'No.'

Ray: 'Well, in that case, why is Steve Grayson telling Rebekah that the picture has been faked?'

Big gulping. World falling away.

Me: 'I don't know, Ray.'

Ray: 'To your knowledge, are the pictures and story absolutely genuine?'

Me: 'Yes.'

Phone down. Wow! Mad One. What the fuck happened there? Desperately, I tried to get hold of Steve. Speed-dialling like my life depended on it. Which it did. Engaged. Engaged. Calling him everything under the sun. Until eventually he picked up.

'Fucking hell, Steve, what's happened?'

'It's all over, mate,' he replied, his voice blank and heavy, as though he was on tranquillisers.

'What do you mean?'

'I've told her everything.'

'Why?' I asked, trying to suppress my bunker-style rage.

'They fucking knew, mate. They fucking knew. There's no point. It's all got out of hand. I had no option.'

'For fuck's sake, mate, what happened to bring all this on, all of a sudden?'

Armageddon.

'I don't know. Fucking hell. Maz threw his oar in somehow and told her not to run the story.'

'Fucking hell. Mazher?'

The Angel of Doom. Death from Above. The Fifth Horseman.

'What the fuck is he getting involved for?'

'I don't fucking know, mate. You know what it's like. But then she came on. I told her about Ray.'

'For fuck's sake, mate – I wish you would have told me. I've just had Ray on and I was holding out. Telling him flatly that it wasn't a hoax.'

'Well, I tried to call you – twice. I did. I did.'

'Fucking hell, mate – why didn't you try the hotel phone, in the room? You knew the number. We've been staying here for about two fucking years.'

'I know. I should've. Fucking hell. I'm sorry. But it was too mad. My head was all over the place.'

Memo to self: never let Steve become an international jewel thief or get involved with him in a raid on the Louvre or a heist on the Federal Reserve. You'd all end up in jail for a very long time. I was fucking livid – that was plain flaky. In the initial fury, I self-hated on myself to Woody Allen-style levels of soul-loathing for lining myself up with such a weak link. He was all over the place. What the fuck was going on with him? What the fuck was he doing? Letting the side down like that. Giving a bad account of himself. Crying and shilly-shallying all over the place like a big girl. What was he? A real man? Who could take the pain? Or a mouse that was going to squeal on his mates and start crying about it and saying this, that and the other? But that was just my anger. Trying to deflect the crisis away from myself. Steve had been put in a hideous position. What's more he'd done the right thing. And what's more he never fucking cried.

But what the fuck? The cat was out of the bag now. Again, in an act of intuitive stoicism that would later come in handy when I eventually went mad, I bit the bullet. There was no point blaming each other. Time for shoulder-to-shoulder and cool heads. Not for cut-throat defences.

'OK, mate. No sweat,' I said. 'So where are we now?'

'I told her all about Ray and him putting us up to it.'

To me, it seemed silly to do that. Why bother blaming Ray?

Yes, he did ask me to engineer a pic. But at the end of the day, I was thinking about doing that anyway. And it was me who decided to go along with it once he'd given us a steer. It was me. My fault. No one else.

But Steve was older than me. I still didn't trust my own judgement as much as I did his. He was a veteran of News Int. corporate politics. He also had a lot more to lose than me.

If it was purely down to me, I would have said fuck all. Blamed no one. The peasant's defence. That our Lords and Masters were above the sea-level shenanigans of their lowly charges. Why tarnish them? It felt like a betrayal. Go quietly. I knew deep down what was expected. Do your duty. Leave the tent, Oates of the Antarctic-style: 'I am just going outside and may be some time.' The act of a brave functionary and an English gentleman. That'd all go down well. Self-destructive humility always played out well in a corporation. A six-month lie-down in the regions until everything blew over. Then it just might be possible, with some goodwill that came from not rocking the boat, to slip back down to London and into the game again.

But I also had to think of Steve. He was putting me under pressure to go to town on Ray. I couldn't cut him loose. I decided to plot a middle course. Back Steve up. Tell the truth about Ray asking us to engineer a pic. But I'd also take full responsibility and hara-kiri myself at the earliest opportunity. If Steve wanted to take them on then that was his decision. I'd support him but I wasn't going head-to-head with the Death Star on a sticky wicket.

My head was wrecked. Then Rebekah came on.

'Listen, Graham, Steve has confessed everything.'

'I know. Yes. It's true what he's saying.'

'I want you to come back to London immediately.'

'OK,' I said. That's how it sounds when you get terminated with extreme prejudice.

Then Rebekah told Ray. Ray seemed to think that Rebekah was testing him. He phoned me once again to hear it for himself.

'Are you now saying that the pics were stunted?' he asked me.
'Yes.'

Ray asked me more questions, slowly and stilted, taping me. So what?

I lay down like a dead foetus on the bed. The only way you'd know I was alive was the panic. Waiting for the terror to subside. I wanted to speak to someone. But, with all this shame sloshing about, the last thing I felt like doing was facing anyone.

29

The Dark Side

That's that. Game over. That's how easy it was for a guy to get whacked. Step out of line, you get whacked. And, by Jove, had I stepped out of line. Steve got sacked for gross misconduct. I resigned. Under a cloud of shame so black it unnerved humans just to hear of it. These were the bad times.

I went quietly. Exit plan: find a hole, make like a mole. Why kick up a fuss? After all, it'd been me who'd fucked up. No one else. Me. That's who. Who put this thing together? Me, that's who. Who do I trust? Me, that's who. No one else's fault. I'd taken a big gamble. Like millions of young extremists before me – and lost. I was the man who'd put it all on red. Walking away. Taking it on the chin. On the steps of the casino, as the sun comes up, rubbing his stubble. That's life. Tomorrow's another day. Don't worry – I'll eat breakfast in the morning.

Of course, I had to say fair's fair. I might have cooked all this up. But I also stuck to the line that Ray was the big egger-on-er. That Rebekah was the original tool who'd come up with the brainwave. If it wasn't for her, we wouldn't have even been led into temptation, would we?

But my pronouncements were mainly for Steve's sake. Personally, I'd lost my bottle, shell-shocked into indifference and fear. But, crucially, I was still young. Could walk away from the crash site with my Adidas Gazelles intact. Start anew. Life was cheap.

But Steve was fifty-odd. Wife. Daughter. Big 1930s kennel with hand-built wardrobes in. Even a celeb-style dressing table with a ring of bulbs around it. A parade of well-stocked shops, just a nip-out-in-the-second-car-away. Bills, duties, expectations to meet. I'd seen it before. What happened to mates' dads. When the *Truman Show* illusion had been snatched back from them during alcohol-soft middle-age. Didn't matter what the reason. Redundancy. Nightmare divorces. Taxman coming through their door for the under-the-mattress nest egg. The outcomes were always the same. Heart attacks. Mental outpatients' unit. Even suicide. I owed it to Steve because I'd fucked his life as well.

But no one was listening anyway. A matter of indifference to me. In an early version of the stoicism that would later bring me back from the brink of madness, I rationalised the big picture. Rebekah wasn't really to blame. I'd been a shit-bag right from the off. I'd been stunting on and off for virtually all my time at the *Screws*. If it wasn't the Beast, then I would have probably fallen on my arse over something else. It wasn't her. It wasn't Ray. It was me. In fact, if you really thought about it, it wasn't even me. The Beast just happened. Accept your fate and move on.

I kept my head down. More sickened with worry. By how I was going to pay the big fuck-off mortgage. On my new Dockland's drum. I'd exchanged. But couldn't move in until it was done up. I'd already paid the fellers.

Angela booted me out of her house. Bin-bagged and cash-point ransomed. She got one of her shady mates – a wheeler-dealer coke-head fashion contractor – to rob my car. Hostaged it. Until I paid her back for all the salmon bagel breakfasts she'd bankrolled me for during the course of our life together. Then, when I'd finally moved into my pad near the river, she kept turning up pissed in the early hours. With a Beamer full of Grrl Power mates. Shouting around the flats like a fishwife, that I was bastard and a liar. (True.) Was such a fucking big liar, she screamed, that I'd even lost my job over it. (True.) I just lay there on the bed upstairs. Not answering the door. Even the police turned up. All the other yuppies in the neighbouring flats thought I was a wife-beater. Avoiding eye contact when I put the bins out. Fuck – when Mother Nature pays you back, she really fucking gives it to you.

Even the papers waded in. *Media Guardian* ran a story headlined, 'Trial by Tabloid', claiming that I'd bullied actor Paul McGann in the aftermath of his affair with Catherine Zeta-Jones. How dare they? A gross intrusion! Invasion of privacy.

It all dated back to a story a few years before when I was a freelancer before joining the *Screws*. Paul McGann had accused me of trying to ruin his life. But until now no one had dared run the story. The *Guardian* roared: 'A local agency man called persistently, trying to ingratiate himself with Paul by mentioning their joint Scouse background.'

McGann and his harassed wife Annie had kept tape recordings of my '80s-style, Rottweiler doorstep drill. When the Scousers-Against-the-World line fell flat, I turned Turk on the no-sell-out Monocled Mutineer with the old swarming.

'He tried various tricks,' the story went on. 'If the couple agreed to have their picture taken in the park, he would head off the *News of the World* "who are on their way". When that failed he sneered: "We'll get you one day when you're out Christmas shopping."'

All true, by the way. As I said, the persecution had taken place when I'd been a ruffian-and-scuffian freelancer before joining the *Screws*.

The *Guardian* added: 'The Liverpudlian agency reporter, who joined the *News of the World* two years ago, has called at regular intervals ever since and always been rebuffed.'

For me, this was natural justice. I'd dished it out for years as a nuclear news bully. Now I was getting a taste of my own medicine. Take the pain.

No one had noticed the article when it was first published a fortnight or so before the Beast. But now the two-page spread was being trumpeted as genuine proof of evil. In addition, the posh, privately educated navel-gazers at the *Guardian* diary section, some of whom have lived in houses the size of small castles, ran shorts saying that I'd never work again with such a despicable record of employment. Take the pain. I suspected that Rebekah was black-opping me in the background. Her PR was excellent. The ginger ninja's sixth sense was being lauded all over the place. A kind of Fleet Street miracle for which we should give thanks. A glowing puff in the *Evening Standard* cast her as the heroine of the Beast drama. Saving the paper at the eleventh hour. The coup even bringing her to the attention of Rupert Murdoch. Not surprising that she'd come up smelling of roses though – Rebekah's best mate was PR earth-ruler Matthew Freud. Whose ancestor Edward Bernays was the man who had single-handedly founded the PR industry. Full stop. Being part of the matrix is really useful when it comes on top.

Both Steve and I hired a tin-pot lawyer. Me, to tie up the loose ends. Steve to take the Evil Empire to an industrial tribunal. But the first solicitor was a piss-head and it was going nowhere. I went for a one-to-one telling off from Rebekah. The *Screws* psyops people set it up nicely. So that I had to do a humiliating walk of shame through the whole office. Snaking past rows of silent reporters. Heads bowed at their desks for the condemned man. Glimpsed the inside of Ray's office on the way past – still striped by shadows like Jimmy Cagney's death row cell. No eye contact. So by the time that I got to Rebekah I was a nervous wreck.

One reporter defied convention. Grinning vengefully from underneath his arm. His name was Ian Edmondson, who went on to great heights at the *Screws*. His colleagues used to say of him: 'Yes he is a cunt. But at least he knows that and that you know he's a Cunt Too. So at least you know where you stand.' As though that transparency was a grace in itself. I used to call him Cunt Too. Edmondson was later nicked for suspected phone hacking and is alleged to be one of the links that intro'd demon phone hacker Glenn Mulcaire to the paper. Which in turn led to the paper's collapse. RIP Cunt Too.

At first, the *News of the World* had tried to hush it all up. The execs made an offer to Steve: if he would say that he'd gone temporarily insane, then they'd sign him off for six months. Wheel him off to the Priory or whatever, for corporate realignment. Then, if he didn't make any waves, if the dust settled, they just might be able to sneak him back into the company on the QT. Vintage NI. Steve turned down the offer.

'Fuck you,' he said. 'She's the one that's insane and I'm going to fight it.' What followed was a mini-Enron corporate cluster-fuck of underhand chicanery that half made you think that 9/11 might have been an inside job. Even though it hadn't happened yet.

Steve accused Kuttner of knowing about the stunt. But of turning a blind eye using selective questioning to cover his arse. Steve said that during his grilling with Kuttner in the NI canteen, Kuttner had been awfully, awfully careful never to ask whether the photos were of the actual Beast. Suspiciously awful.

In a statement, Steve said: 'Mr Kuttner repeated the question that he had asked me earlier. "Were the pictures of a real animal?" I responded that they were pictures of a real animal. At that moment, I had formed the opinion that Mr Kuttner was deliberately phrasing the question in a specific way in order to continue to say truthfully that they were pictures of a real animal. In effect, it was as if Mr Kuttner had himself concluded that the pictures could not really have been those of the Beast of Bodmin Moor. But for as long as he did not specifically ask me that question, he could always say at a later date that he had no knowledge of them being pictures of anything other than that which they purported to be. Indeed of a real animal.' Kuttner denied Steve's account as being 'disingenuous'.

Steve also accused the Executive chairman Les Hinton of being in the background of some of the phone calls. Trying to make out that he had some knowledge of the Beast story. But there was no

evidence and Mr Hinton denied it. In addition, Steve accused
Rebekah of going red with embarrassment on the Saturday night
after Steve confessed. 'I accused her of being involved and she
blew up crimson.' Steve said. Rebekah denied this. But Steve also
raised some controversial issues: he said: ' Why didn't the executives ever ask for the contact sheets of the photographs of the
puma – then they would have seen that they were stunted inter-
mediately? To ask for the contacts was standard procedure and
they didn't follow that. Even when I went to file the contacts in
the photographer's room on the Friday morning, the other
photographers were taking the piss shouting "Meouw. Meouw."
Even they knew it was a stunt. You could even see the railings
from the cage in the picture. And why did Kuttner appoint
Rebekah to investigate the story after I confessed? She was
involved, so she should have been an indepedent observer.' But
no matter what Steve said, the *NoW* denied having any knowledge of the stunt and Rebekah said she hadn't gone red. Steve was
finished. F-U-C-K-E-D. Finished.

As night follows day, then came the dirty tricks. Basically, if
you take on the *News of the World* in a legal fight, they try and
fuck you in the same way that reporters turn punters over. They
spread it around the industry that Steve had stunted the Beast
because he was getting old. Desperate to prove himself again with
a big hit. They said that Steve had become bitterly jealous of his
own son-in-law, who Steve had got a job as a *Screws* snapper a few
years before. Because the son-in-law was now the favoured choice
on Mazher jobs. That's how ruthless they are – they even turned
his family against him.

Then, in an orchestrated campaign, *NoW* cointelpro got all
Steve's ex-mates at work to ring him up. Taping him saying
compromising things. Mazher rang him up. The US Editor. The
Birth Certificates Puller who taped everyone as a matter of course.
They even got Steve's own son-in-law to entrap him. Low wasn't
in it.

But Steve was a Jedi Knight as well. He knew the power of the

Force. The ways of the Dark Side. So he turned the tables on them. Like when the hero reflects the laser beam back on to the baddies with a mirror. Taping them up. Coaxing his entrappers to say terrible things about Ray, Rebekah and Kuttner. Like the showdown between Darth Vader and Obi-Wan.

But then the go-around got dirtier. The *Screws* accused Steve of trying to find out Mazher's secret address. Saying that the deranged fantasist was plotting to iron the Fake Sheik out in a revenge attack. But Steve laughed it off. Claiming that it was a set-up. Meanwhile Steve's legal bills were rocketing through the roof.

Then the *NoW* trained their sights on me. Though I wasn't attacking them directly, I'd agreed to be a witness for Steve at his tribunal. Making me fair game for undermining operations or to-get-onside. One day Paul Samrai turned up with my old boss Dan Collins, who'd since left the paper to become a barrister, then a book publisher. Got an odd feeling over the meet. Over a cup of tea, they kept asking if I was sure that Ray had asked me to engineer the pics etc. Amid the pervasive paranoia, I was suss that they'd been sent to tape me up. But I fought the impulse to go dark and stayed nice. Humility was my watchword.

Under gigapascals of molten pressure, Steve suffered with the effects of stress. Lost his big house when the legal bills reached fifty-odd grand. Lost the plot. Ending up in the gutter – literally. He got a job as a £200-a-week drain-cleaner in Soho. Where the chip fat is a foot thick on the sewer walls and the lice are as big as fifty pence pieces. So that when you look at them, he told me later, it seems as though the whole wall is moving. 'But you know what,' he told me. 'At least down there, you know who the fucking rats are.'

30

Look on the Bright Side

But there I was. Stuck in my new pad. A shit-load of easy-come, easy-go, pre-credit crunch Consolidated Debt Obligation-fuelled Brown Boom mortgage that had somehow been Credit Default Swapped on to my watch. That I now had to step up to. Not to mention the £700 wall-to-wall navy blue carpet which I'd just got laid. But that I'd soon enough have to rip up. To make way for the wooden floors that were becoming all the rage. But just when I was about to go under, and back onto my mum's couch, Mother Nature threw me a bone.

My saviour came in the form of Nick Pisa. A squeaky clean *Sunday Mirror* reporter of Italian extraction who used to work with me at the agency. Nick was a real-life, church-going Good Samaritan. Feeing pity, Nick asked me to go for a drink with the *Sunday Mirror* News Editor Andy Burn. Nick later went on to be a big-shot reporter who dominated international coverage of the Amanda Knox case. Making himself a huge amount of dough in the process.

Andy Burn was a fellow Scouser who'd made his name pulling life-saving *Coronation Street* exclusives out of the hat on a Saturday afternoon for his editor Bridget Rowe. I told him my tale of Beast woe. He laughed. Everyone in the industry knew I'd been turned

over. Over an overpriced beer at Chillies bar in Canary Wharf –
then no more than an eerie marblised office block that couldn't
give space away – Andy offered me a six-month contract on the
super soaraway *Sunday Mirror*.

For Fuck's Sake! Wow! Thank you, God! I'd just been handed a
first-class, round-trip ticket to The Resurrection. Unbelievable!
Bend over, Christie! Come on down, Cindy! The kind of miracle
you only ever read about in the *Bible*. In keeping with the spirit-
ual theme, I was determined to change. This time, I'd take the job
seriously, I vowed holily. No longer just a job – a career. No more
making up stories. No more fucking about. This was the *Mirror*.
The home of John Pilger. The left-leaning, social conscience of
Britain. With a mission to educate and enlighten its readers. Of
course, I knew it'd be difficult. Knocking the antics on the head.
Bit like being an alcy. Twelve steps and all that. I knew there'd be
times when I'd fall off the wagon. I knew it'd be hard to go from
Mickey Mouse reporter to emulating the World's Greatest Living
journo. Living in the long shadow of Hugh Cudlipp, Paul Foot
and the like. But listen. I was being given a second chance. I
wanted to give back. What was the alternative? Heading back up
the M1 to the City of Infinite Doom. Central heating up. Kecks
off. Skin up. Sky on. No, fuck you! I was back in the game.

On my first day, I was welcomed with warm smiles, cups of tea,
friendly faces. Lunch hours. Down-time. A leaving do for someone I didn't even know. But where I was fussed over like an old
hand anyway. Life at the *Sunday Mirror* was a dream. Genuinely
nice people. Not cut-throat. Ethos was: 'We can do the business,
but we can have a laugh too – and there's no need to go around
fucking everything up. Especially your work mates.' Like a refugee given sanctuary, I became fanatically loyal to my new home-
land. Of course, I couldn't help thinking that it was a second-rate
country. In my arrogance, a few weeks earlier, I would have been
like Ray. Wouldn't have wiped my arse on the *Sunday Mirror*.
Didn't even read it. That silly. I would have looked down on
Sunday Mirror reporters. Doughnuts and door-step cannon

fodder, to wipe the floor with on jobs. But that was just the *NoW* brainwashing. Or corporate culture as it's called. But now, magnanimously, these people were giving up their desks and helping me get used to the Apple computer system. It was as though I'd been released from the Hanoi Hilton. Where I'd been hanging upside from a meat hook for two years. In a dungeon with water dripping on my head. Then suddenly finding myself free. Recuperating in a friendly hotel. Staffed by a load of caring nurses.

But there was no time to fuck about. I needed some big hits fast. Having lost his *Screws* link-up (me), Samrai was drifting off into TV land. But I headed him off at the pass. Persuading him to come on board for the big win, back at the *Sunday Mirror*. Soon we were back in business. Turning over his fresh-out-of-jail buddies, one after the other. The first was a Nigerian 419 conman who was busy getting his Christmas money together. By scamming Harrods with dodgy credit cards. Headline: 'Santa Frauds.'

Then I did 'Steak and Kidney Pie Saved My Life.' About a woman who fell over badly. But her head was cushioned by her chippy dinner. Hardly a special report from Cambodia about the Killing Fields. But I was still on the bench – and had to take my chances when they came up.

Then my big break came. Around Christmas time. In the tabloid spirit of a bumper Xmas exclusive, it'd turn out to be the best present I ever had. What made it was its beautiful synchronicity. In one fell swoop, I would be able to show the *Sunday Mirror* what I was made of with a belter world exclusive. Simultaneously putting two fingers up to the *Screws*. By robbing one of their own stories from under their noses. Whilst fucking off Rupert Murdoch and his cronies at the same time. Not forgetting Her Majesty The Queen. Disgraced red-top hack Graham Johnson – come on down!

The saga began when my old mate Roger 'the Dodger' Insall was unexpectedly jettisoned from the *Screws* for unknown reasons. I don't know what had gone on, but it had something to do with a paedophile story he'd been working on in Sri Lanka. Roger had been secretly investigating Arthur C. Clarke for being a nonce.

Arthur C. Clarke was one of the world's best-selling writers – *2001: A Space Odyssey* etc. He was also host of ITV's *Mysterious World* show. Synchronistically, the popular paranormal programme had also been the inspiration behind Rebekah's brainwave to find the Beast and Lord Lucan et al. Somehow, it all made sense.

In addition, Arthur was also one of Rupert Murdoch's mates. A 'guru' in fact. After having come up with the theory behind the self-regulating geostationary communications satellite. Which of course inspired the Dirty Digger to invent Sky.

Consequently, the *Screws* wouldn't run Roger's paedophile story about one of Murdoch's mates. For obvious reasons, in case the proprietor got pissed off. Underlying this dilemma, there were even spookier simultaneous phenomena.

Coincidentally, Roger was also feeling some heat off the Beast fallout. Even though they were old mates, Steve had taped Roger up saying bad things about the *News of the World*. In addition, to boost his tribunal case, Steve Grayson was claiming that one of Roger's old stories was a spoof, denied by him. Oh dear! Part of a legal tactic to prove a culture of fabrication at the *Screws*. The upshot was bad blood between Roger and *NoW* Editor Phil Hall. One day on the bridge of the Death Star, Roger's NI career was asphyxiated by remote. To get revenge, he handed over the Arthur C. Clarke tip to the rebel alliance.

Immediately, I was dispatched to Sri Lanka to stand it up. My first foreign – very exciting stuff. But super-gravity-folding-in-on-itself levels of inner star pressure to boot. The problem was, by the time I arrived in Colombo, I had less than 24 hours to stand it up. But like the SAS, I was expected to be dropped anywhere, anytime in the world and sort it out.

First, with Roger's help, I tracked down some rent boys who claimed that Arthur C. Clarke had fondled them up at a seedy table tennis club where Big Fat Westerners played with the beach boys. Penniless, powerless destitute caste. Who'd been bummed senseless by Arthur and his harem.

But their testimonies weren't enough. Plus no time for a big investigation. Saturday morning. The desk were screaming down the phone for copy. Whole paper riding on it. Everything fucked if it didn't work. Only one thing for it – to blag a confession out of Arthur himself.

Bombed it round to his pad. But he was playing the old soldier. Laid up in bed with a muscular disease. His servants wouldn't let me in. I told them to give the great white chief man a message – that I'd come all the way from London to congratulate him on his knighthood. Stroking his ego was the only way forward.

This was the icing on the cake, by the way. We'd been tipped off that the wank-on-the-biscuit, shape-shifting secret rulers of the world were gonging Arthur up the following week. In the New Year's List. Prince Charles was coming to Sri Lanka himself. To do the honours. Once again the synchronicity was sublime. In the finest of Fleet Street traditions, the big plan was to fuck the whole thing up. For all of the nonces and their Establishment cronies. All at once. Put a bomb under the fucking lot of them. In one great, big, massive piss all over their weirdo parade. But was our dynamite good enought to do the job?

Needed to think fast. The timer was ticking. Got it. Jumped in the cab to the nearest flower shop. A street vendor with racks and racks of exotic Triffid-like bouquets. Bought the biggest, pinkest, most expensive bunch flowers on the stand. Virtually cleaning him out and filling the backseat of the cab. No camped-up predatory nonce in the world is going to refuse a bunch of bloomers. Or at least that was my *Carry On*-style tabloid view of these affairs then.

It worked. The serfs granted me an audience. On his bed, Arthur looked like death warmed up. Reminding me of when I was at the agency and I had to front a serial paedophile on his death bed. Like an old Nazi, the man then had stubbornly refused to confess. But old Arthur C. Clarke was too cocky for his own good.

I opened up with the pleasantries, tape whirring in my suit pocket, now drenched in the jungle heat.

'How you doing? . . . Aren't you great? . . . Isn't it nice that Prince Charles is coming to see you next week? . . .' etc.

But the pressure was on – the Desk screaming down the phone. I knew I only had a few minutes. So I hit him straightaway. Between the eyes like Carlos the Jackal.

'By the way, Mr Clarke,' I asked, using the old Columbo trick again. 'Just one more question – what's all this I've been hearing about you touching up underage boys down at the taboo club?'

At first, Arthur said it was just scuttlebutt from unreliable rent boys. Fair enough. But as I reeled off the names and claims of one witness after another, the old fox was forced to concede.

Like of all these satellite-inventors, he thought he'd use his some-what powerful intellect to chicane his way out of it. But this wasn't the Royal Society. This was a newspaper with a reading age of 14. Arthur's argument was that it was acceptable for him to have sexual relations with young teenage boys because in Sri Lanka the lads mature faster. The sun. The jungle. Hairy chests, whatever. I pinned him down to the age that he considered fair game – 14. Bingo! That was that. Bye-Bye, Dick-Head. I didn't even stick around to hear the end of the hypothesis. Within minutes I'd left the room. Throwing the flowers on the bed. Desperately in search of a phone to ring my copy in. Mission Accomplished.

The following week, Arthur C. Clarke refused his knighthood out of shame. Causing Prince Charles considerable embarrass-ment and face-saving relief at the same time. For years afterwards, he denied underage sex. Every six months he'd pop up on the World Service saying that he'd been turned over. His cronies in the corrupt Sri Lankan police backed him up. But he never sued. Even getting some apologists in the broadsheets to publish a denial. Boasting that he'd called in a favour from Rupert Murdoch. Allegedly promising him that the reporter responsible would never work again in Fleet Street. But by then I think Rupert was just humouring him. I returned home to a hero's welcome – and got offered a staff job with a big fat contract on the spot.

31

98/99

Over the next year, the plan was to restore my reputation. To widen my horizons. Started doing stories all over the world. In Croatia, I exposed a blackmailer. Trying to screw a cool mil out of F1 ringmaster Bernie Ecclestone. Threatening to smear his then wife Slavica in a sex scandal. I posed as Bernie's bagman. With powers of attorney to negotiate a deal and pay the villain off. Meeting the conman in a smoky, dockside bar in the rundown port of Rijeka. The blackmailer filled the venue with Eastern European mafia-types to intimidate me. But I fronted it out with my secret tape whirring away in my pocket. Coaxing him to admit that he was a chancer. Boasting that the scandal was a fabrication. Little more than a blag to criminally extort money from Bernie Ecclestone and Slavica the diminutive billionaire. When I got back to London, Bernie invited me round to his Knightsbridge office to thank me. He said I was scruffy, went to his safe and pulled out a grand in cash. I think he wanted me to buy a new suit, rather than influence me. But now, under my new self-imposed code of conduct, any kind of madness was strictly off limits. Financial moodiness was never my bag anyway. Born poor, die poor – that was my expectation. Though it wasn't a bribe, I'd only ever been offered cash once before. When I tried my hand at court reporting at the agency. By a dodgy solicitor on rape charges. He offered me £200 to drop the story. Mouthing the offer out and holding the cash up silently in the lift in case I was taping him. Of course I fucked him off. Just like then, I immediately reported the grand to the new *Sunday Mirror* Editor Brendan Parsons. We agreed to give it back straightway. Bernie was a bit pissed off that I'd told anyone. But we remained half-mates, going out for lunch now and again.

In LA, I got a good line on the George Michael cottaging story. When the former Wham! heartthrob got caught engaged in a lewd act by an undercover 'pretty' policeman in a Beverly Hills bog. The Beverly Hills cops, whose plush police station was better decorated than my flat (cream carpets/chrome desks), gave me the name of an airline steward who was arrested at the same time as George. Tracked him down and babysat him. To protect my exclusive, I had to pretend that I was the airline press officer when the *National Enquirer* turned up. Blagging them in my best *Starsky and Hutch* blowse Yankee accent that the steward wasn't commenting. It was flippin' hard because it turned out that they were all ex-*Sun* hacks from Manchester and Essex.

During the job, I fell out with the arsey American snapper that had been assigned to me. I had to tell him off for 'showing out' while he was trying to covertly snatch the target. I handled it badly, taking the old jingoistic Fleet Street line that: 'You wouldn't get a Brit snapper behaving like that. Driving down the road letting all and sundry see him. Yous' Americans – you're fucking amateurs.' He got very angry. But soon got his revenge. Later inviting me out for a pastrami. Being suspiciously nice. The sandwich tasted moody. The next day I went down with a violent stomach bug. Spewing and shitting all over my $300-a-night Beverly Hills hotel room. I called a doctor out at $500-a-pop to inject me up the arse with antibiotics. Convinced that the photographer had spitefully spiked my pastrami. But everything ended up OK. Taking the pain on the bed, I got a phone call in the middle of the night – it was a new editor called Colin Myler who just been appointed to take over. Colin Myler was a straight-forward person. I knew we'd get on well.

Then I spent six weeks flash-packing all around the States. Doing stories about Ernie Wise, Ruby Wax and the death of Linda McCartney. Every time I turned up at a BA terminal to fly back to London, the check-in lady would say: 'We've got a message for you: "Under no circumstances whatsoever get on plane. Call the desk. URGENT! URGENT! URGENT."' The BA people let me use the back office phone to get my new set of instructions.

Next stop France. Paris in summertime was hot but beautiful. Spent a month doing Princess Di death anniversary stories. £15,000 bill for freelancers. Another few on top for translators. A grand's plus worth of mini-bar. And a dry cleaning tab so big that the moody hotelier marched me round to a cashpoint in person because he knew I was going to do a runner.

Straight from there and half-pissed, I flew down to Cadiz in Spain to cover the shock arrest of Sexy Beast racketeer Kenny Noye. The whole pack was there. Staffers from ten different news-papers. Mostly bloated, bitter, middle-aged moaners. I never moved with the pack. Sharing war stories and swapping blankies. Of course, I fiddled exies like everyone else. But I didn't turn it into a homoerotic bonding ritual like some these old-timers did. The pack even had a mad hierarchy. With the senior reporter booking the tables for dinner and arranging the flotilla of cabs to hither and thither. Even as a reformed sociopath, I couldn't handle it. Lone Wolf. Always Move Alone. Welcome to the Terrordome.

The key to getting a good line on Noye was the local newspaper reporter. A tasty Spanish señorita called Carmen Torres. The grass didn't grow around town without her knowing about it. Ace translator. Good fresh lead digger-upper. Skin the colour of olives.

But her services quickly sparked a war. Between me and Team *News of the World*. Stoked up by the bad blood still bubbling up from the Beast. The *Screws* had sent their main cut-throat henchman Cunt Too Ian Edmondson. To hoover up the story. Cunt Too's henchman-in-turn was a slippery fish snapper called Nick Bowman. A thin-shouldered, hate-filled fag-smoker who was also mildly amusing.

Carmen suddenly became a prized trophy within this bilious circus. A status symbol more important than the story itself. Like white slave traders, we bid to win her loyalty. Of course, I won. Firstly charming her into the hotel pool for a midnight swim. Then back to the room. Then into her contacts book.

Cunt Too took defeat very badly.

'Factor X, mate,' I told him the next day. Carmen lounging around the hotel pool in a gold bikini. 'Look into your soul, mate. Look into your soul.'

In revenge, he turned me over in *Private Eye*. The diametric Orwellian untruth that he peddled to the magazine's infamous *Street of Shame* column was that he'd won Carmen. Then employing her as a double agent. To seduce me. Download my notebook of stories during pillow talk. Then slipping out of my chambers in the dead of night. To betray my best lines on Noye to her real amante – him. All bollocks by the way. But good rough-and-tumble all the same. Had to laugh.

One night the pack got pissed. Frustrated and desperate to get new leads, Fleet Street's finest broke into Kenny Noye's safe house. Smashing a window. Burgling his bedroom. Screwing his hideout to find some new collects. I never went. But Carmen and I continued to see each other for another year.

When I got back to London, a mad thing happened. The *News of the World* offered me my old job back. Oh my word! Blown away. What a fucking turn-up. It was like a vindication. But flattering at the same time. I went out for secret drink with the *Screws'* Editor Phil Hall. He told me how devastated he'd been over the Beast. Getting back from his hols to find blood all over the newsroom carpet. Then hearing that one of his favourite reporters had been ironed.

Phil said he'd been tracking me ever since at the *Sunday Mirror*.

One story in particular had convinced him to offer me my job back. I'd infiltrated a bent church and been ordained as a priest. In return for a back-hander. The mad thing was that it was all bona fide under church law. I got a dog collar. A certificate. Best of all – a legal right to perform christenings, burials and marriage blessings. Phil said the Exec Chairman Les Hinton thought it was such a piss-take that I should be rehired on the spot. Indulgence granted. Sins annulled.

Though I trusted Phil Hall, I couldn't help thinking that it was a nasty plot by Stuart Kuttner. To get me back on the firm for ulterior motives. So that I'd drop my evidence at Steve's tribunal, which coincidently was due to start the following month. Steve was suffering badly. One day he was unblocking the bogs at the swishy Oxo Towers restaurant when two journalists came in. As they were weeing and talking big-time newspaper stuff, Steve hid in the cubicle to hide his shame. I couldn't cut him loose and knocked the *Screws* back. Of course, I let the approach slip to the Editor of the *Sunday Mirror*, who bumped up my money.

In South Africa, I did a story about Princess Diana's brother having an affair. In between the jobs abroad, I was knocking out bread-and-butter guns 'n' drugs stories. As fast as Samrai could set them up. But I spent two years as a special correspondent. On the road. All over the world. Being sent from one job to another. Living out of airport shops. Cash on tap. Twenty different currencies stuffed all over my falling-apart suit.

When I got home, there were pints of milk outside my door. My car had been towed away for expired tax. Squatters in my flat. A broken-down motorbike on my new laminate floor. A Volly van full of wood on bricks in my parking space. Being a reporter had a devastating impact on your personal life.

I was getting all the plum jobs – but something was stirring in my soul. I wanted to do more serious stories. If I was going to go flying off round the world, with virtually unlimited budget and state-of-the-art surveillance gear, I may as well put it to good use. Instead, I was still getting sent to Florida. To interview Ernie

Wise. Or to LA to do a story about Lynn Redgrave. Frustrated and sleepless in Hollywood, one night I went to a 24-hour bookshop. Cleaning the shelves out of all their Noam Chomsky books. Chomsky is an American linguist who analyses the media. Exposing the interests that are really being served. Thirsty to understand how my profession works, I locked myself in my hotel room.

Chomsky explained that all the papers, whether *Sun* or *Guardian*, are run in the interests of the powerful and the rich. End of story. No back answers. Few exceptions. To bend the heads of the peasants. To stop any real dissent. To limit freedom and prosperity. Bang on! Having worked on the line in a propaganda factory, instinctively I knew this to be true.

But in many ways, he said, liberal broadsheets are worse blaggers than even the red-tops. As they try to disguise their hypocrisy by pretending to be kinder and more honest. Which, he says, is a load of bollocks. The *Guardian* is not the real opposition to power. Merely an 'acceptable face of dissent'. Brainwashing middle-class intellectuals into thinking that it sets the boundaries on what is 'appropriate' criticism. Anything beyond their norms is considered to be conspiracy theory. To be mocked. The limits of the arguments are set by a 'manufacture of consent'. Between those on the left and those on the right. Kept in place by a constant process of 'self-editing'. Preventing journalists from saying what they really think to their editors and colleagues in case they are laughed at. Or marked down as trouble-makers. All true by the way. I'd watched reporters self-edit for years. That's why most stories are basically similar. The same themes are repeated over and over again. Have you ever wondered why the papers are full of bollocks? I'd lost count of the number of times readers would say: 'I don't buy the paper any more because there's nothing in it?' Here was the reason why.

I was blown away by these ideas. But the next day it was back to Planet Nonsense. I had to go into the Hollywood Hills. To investigate why Lynn Redgrave was divorcing her husband. Over a secret love child that he'd fathered with her secretary. I'd come 6000-odd miles for this? I was confused. I couldn't be arsed. I made up the quotes. Or, rather, I attributed quotes that Redgrave's friend had told me she said. To Redgrave direct. I'd fallen off the wagon. I was gutted. I spent the whole day stressed out, worried and reflective. But on the other hand, so fucking what? What do the papers expect?

32

Slave

In a bid to satisfy the yearnings in my soul, I decided to do more worthy stories. The first was a campaign about child slavery. To expose the secret sweatshop shame behind globalisation. The big economic movement sweeping the corporate world in the late 1990s. Today, retrospectives claim that cheap credit was the main driver behind the glory days of the big boom. But slave labour was the other vice propping up the P&L accounts.

Paul Samrai gave me some good link-ups in South Asia. In Sialkot, Pakistan, I exposed the 10p-a-day children who made surgical equipment in filthy fume-filled factories – astonishingly for NHS hospitals. In the middle of the Rugby World Cup, I turned over the company that made the prestigious balls. The Gilbert company claimed that its world famous sports equipment was made in England. But behind the scenes, production was shadily subcontracted out to child slavery workshops in the Punjab. Then deep into the jungles of Assam. To find out the real price of your cuppa – little girls picking leaves in plush tea gardens for peanuts. No more than indentured slaves. Little had changed since the days of Empire. Except the new secret rulers of the world were multinationals instead of Rule Britannia. I loved doing these stories. But in tabloids they are generally derided for being 'worthy'. Why go to all the hassle when we can do a spread on Anthea Turner and Grant Bovey?

At the British Press Awards, I was a finalist for the ruthlessly competitive Reporter of the Year title. The nomination based on the Arthur C. Clarke exposé and a few other investigations. I was coming back in from the cold. Like the cloud from the Beast was finally dissipating.

But the *News of the World* weren't having any of it. Livid that I'd even been shortlisted. Like a personal insult for them. Even during the ceremony they couldn't help themselves from having a go. Getting up to a few dirty tricks. Sending people over to the *Sunday Mirror* table. Where I was chatting with our paper's dinner guest Max Clifford. To tape me up. *News of the World* Assistant Editor Harry Scott interrupted, trying to trap me. Saying, 'There's no way Ray asked you to stunt that Beast pic. Admit it now.' Thinking that I'd fold, half-pissed. With my ego running rampant because I was up for a gong. Trademark News International. Always pushing it too far. Always fighting when it's better just to fuck it off. Little did they know that the extremist win-at-all-costs attitude would one day bring it all on top for them.

Next day, hangovered to death, I headed off to Albania to cover the breaking Kosovo crisis. In the Albanian capital Tirana, I hired the country's only helicopter for $2000. To taxi me up to the mountain borderlands. Couldn't wait to do another proper story. But deep down I knew the script – war reporting is basically a blag. Except for a handful of dissenting, anti-war journalists such as John Pilger and Robert Fisk, the rest are fucking blaggers and chancers. I knew this from my days as a freelancer in Bosnia seven years before. A lot of highly-paid staffers sitting around getting pissed in hotels. Holding court with other gobshites. Whilst paying a small army of local fixers and ex-services privateers to do the dirty work on the front line. You wouldn't believe it how big a knob-head the average war correspondent is. It defies reason.

Then, at the end of all this, regurgitating the propaganda of the 'international community'. Ruthlessly self-editing in order not to offend any special interests. All that's left is to cook up some harmless refugee stories. The war pack even hold rave parties next door to the tented camps. I couldn't believe it. I've seen the most famous TV war correspondents do this.

But that's not the worst of it. Most of the war reporting done by these apparatchiks, even in the broadsheets and on the telly, is propaganda. Subtly controlled by NATO and the MoD. To make 'our' side look good and to demonise the bad guys. I took part in this fascinating charade. But only realised it later. Once you're inside the matrix you don't know what the fuck's going on.

Basically, the Kosovo war had nothing to do with a 'humanitarian intervention'. Which was the line used by Tony Blair to justify bombing Belgrade. NATO attacked Serbia to increase US influence in the Balkans. As part of a military strategy to control Russian power in Eastern Europe. But you wouldn't have read this in any papers at the time.

Before I went to Albania the demonisation of the enemy had began. One day I was in the office working on a daft story about Vanessa Feltz's new boyfriend. Mysteriously, I was asked to come off that very important piece. Told to write a backgrounder on Slobodan Milosevic's wife instead, who no one had ever heard of. But slagging her off for being an evil 'red witch'. Unusual, because we rarely did 'foreign affairs' stories like this.

In the build-up to the war, I also wrote a story about how the SAS were being deployed in the region. To execute warlords. Another story out-of-the-blue bigged up the RAF's latest smart bombs. Claiming that this campaign would be even cleaner than the Gulf War. With hardly any collateral damage at all.

As the conflict warmed up, I went along with ramping up all the stories about mass graves and Serbian atrocities. Almost all of these stories were false. Propaganda deliberately planted by MoD shadow-men. With the editors and political reporters. Then passed down to me to write up. But the best phony mass grave story I read was a howler in my sister paper the *Mirror*. About the metal ore mines in a place called Trepca. Where 'they' said 1000 bodies of Kosovans had been smelted and dissolved with acid by Serbs. The name Trepca, the *Mirror* said, would 'live alongside those of Belsen, Auschwitz and Treblinka . . . etched in the memories of those whose loved ones met a bestial end in true Nazi Final Solution fashion'.

But no bodies were ever found at Trepca. No human remains at all, according to the International Criminal Tribunal on the Former Yugoslavia. After the war the FBI and war crimes commission found no evidence of mass graves in the whole of Kosovo. During the bombing, NATO officials reported as many as 225,000 Albanian men missing. After the bombing, officials said the Serbs had murdered 10,000 Albanians. So far investigators have found the bodies of only 2,108 presumed victims, including some Serbs.

From Iraq, to Afghanistan, to Libya – the model is always the same. The ingredients of modern propaganda never vary. Starts with demonisation of leader. Then mass grave-spoofing. SAS saving the day. Finally smart bomb stories that disguise the true numbers of civilian dead. If the pudding needs over-egging then the issue of WMDs is thrown in, just like it is today. In the build-up to the war with Iran. I had to laugh when I was watching the Gaddafi caper unfold. I sat there in front of the telly watching Sky, ticking them off my list.

Saying that, I did get some good stories in Kosovo. Got an interview with the first Serbian prisoner of war. His pockets full of gold rings. Robbed at gunpoint from old refugee women. I paid the Kosovo Liberation Army fixer £3000 in cash for the pictures and interview. Promising him an extra £2000 in London. But of course we bumped him for the balance. Later he threatened to kill me, spending years trying to get to me. It's true – those Albanians never forget. Also I bagged a good story about how loads of the humanitarian aid was corrupt – with UN emergency supplies being sold off the back of a lorry.

But when I got back to London it was straight back on to skate-boarding parrots. Flew to Tenerife. After veteran TV comic Lenny Henry was accused of harassing strippers on a BBC bender. Behind the showbiz frippery, a menacing air of violence and shadiness hung around the story. The sunshine isle was controlled by one of Britain's richest gangsters, John 'Goldfinger' Palmer. Goldfinger was knee-deep in a gang war with his former enforcer. The main drag Playas de las Americas was a seething cauldron of smouldering underworld tension. Everyone, from the lowliest bar touts to the millionaire nightclub owners, encased in their bullet-proof cavalcades, was on trigger-finger red alert. Into the valley of death – I fear no evil.

I arranged to meet a small-time Brit villain in a wild west-themed bar. After he rang the News Desk, claiming to have pictures of Lenny Henry with the strippers. We got on well. Before he nipped off to the bogs, he agreed to sell me the pics for a few grand. But after ten minutes, mysteriously he'd still not come back. I nursed my pint for a further 20 minutes. Worried that he'd got cold feet and run off. Suddenly, I heard a commotion near the entrance of the pub. I decided to take a look. There he was, my contact. Lying on the floor in a pool of blood. Under the slatted wooden swing-doors. Surrounded by a horrified stag party. Paramedics trying to save his life. Throat cut. Eye gouged out with a knife. Slash marks all over his face and arms.

Later in intensive care, one of his mates tried to blag me off. Claiming that the attack had nothing to do with meeting me. That it was down to a long-running underworld feud over pub crawls. Tourists pay through the nose to go on 18–30-style organised drinking sessions. A trade so lucrative that gangsters had started killing each other for the concessions. Especially now that war had broken out between the island's godfathers and rival gangs were looking for protection.

But I suspected he wasn't telling me the whole truth. Later my suspicions were proved correct – the contact had been stabbed for talking to me. I was warned that he'd been deliberately targeted because another rival gang had also got hold of the Lenny Henry pics. But had agreed to sell them to the *People* for bigger money. My guy was stabbed to keep the pictures exclusive. Of course, the *People* didn't know any of this. Just business between local hoods playing at being paparazzi. Chequebook journalism was becoming a dangerous business. This was the first time that I'd noticed organised crime blatantly cashing in on a story. But it was a sinister influence that would go on to grow and grow. Especially as villains realised the amount of money to be made from the papers. Along with the potential to blackmail the growing number of young celebrities.

Later that night, I realised I was being followed. I was warned by some very heavy doorman to drop the story. My spider senses were exploding. Then I got a moody phone call. Telling me to get off the island. In the early hours I woke Carmen up – she'd come over to see me from mainland Spain on a flying visit – and we slipped out the back door of the hotel. Stealthily checking into another four star on the other side of the island. Under a false name.

I'd been involved in a similar situation a few years before at the *News of the World*. In which I'd been held hostage in a hotel. By some extremely serious villains. So I knew the drill and didn't want a repeat.

That story had started out benignly enough. Turning over a TV soap star for selling cocaine. Straightforward up-and-down. No big deal. Got the target on tape up to no good. Was just about to check out of the hotel when I got a phone call from a mate.

'You know that feller off the telly you're looking into,' my mate said. 'He's not just a silly actor, you know.'

'What d'you mean?' I asked. 'How do you know what I'm doing?' I'd been undercover for two days and no one was supposed to know what I was up to.

'Never mind how I know. I'm just calling you for your own sake. The guy you're on is the front man for one the biggest drug cartels in Europe.'

'Fuck off,' I said, the confusion setting in even more. 'He's just a two-bit actor off the telly selling a bit of gear on the side to look hard.'

'No, he's not. He's got himself wrapped up with some serious cocaine importers. Not only that, he's on their firm. He's agreed to be the licensee on a nightclub they've just opened. If you turn this soap star over in the papers, then he'll lose the licence. The club will be shut down.

'And the gangsters will lose all the squillions of quid they've invested in the front business.'

'Fucking hell,' I said, understanding the significance of the info immediately. Phone down. Down the stairs. Heading for the doors. But it was already too late. The lobby was full of roid head gangsters in baseball caps waiting for me. No escape.

I ran back up the fire escape. To my room with the freelancer I was with. We locked ourselves in. I pulled the mattresses off the beds. Jamming them up against the door. Shored up by a heavy-based table, a chair and a lampstand. Waiting for it to go in.

But instead the phone rang. The man on the other end was matter-of-fact. I could hear the sounds of a toddler in his arms.

'I'm downstairs. We want a meeting,' he said. The man turned out to be Colin 'King Cocaine' Smith. One of biggest drug barons in the UK. Worth an estimated £200 million. His senior partner was Curtis Warren, the richest criminal ever caught in British history with an estimated £300 million fortune. What followed was yet another bizarre merry dance. The *News of the World* opened up negotiations with the drug barons. The cartel boss employed a professional PR firm to talk terms on their behalf. The *News of the World* flew in a freelancer called John Merry, who'd been in prison with Curtis Warren. Merry negotiated my freedom in exchange for the coke story on the soap star being dropped.

Fast forward back to Tenerife. I'd managed to sidestep a similar situation by moving hotels in the dead of night. But it freaked Carmen out and I didn't see much of her after that. But before I got on the plane home I got a call from one of my contacts: 'It's a good job you got out of your hotel.'

'How did you know that I did?'

'Because they were watching you. If you hadn't have left, you would have woken up with them in your room with balaclavas on.'

33

Millennium Bug

Back in London. Back on to the treadmill of humdrum nonsense – spies at the Palace, rugby star drug shame, monkey meat for sale. Then I did one of the saddest and meanest stories of my career. The News Desk asked me to turn over a former *Grange Hill* star for drugs. Erkan Mustafa used to play Roland Browning in the BBC's much loved kids' serial. The chubby loner who'd helped front the show's 'Just Say No' anti-drugs campaign. Now the child actor had grown up and was on his arse. Trying to reinvent himself as a club DJ. Someone came up with the idea of exposing him as a heroin dealer – even though he wasn't one. Don't let the facts get in the way of good story. I set him up in an elaborate sting operation. Luring him to a plush hotel suite. Complete with a Jacuzzi and a couple of tasty girls hanging around. As is standard in this entrapment model, the inducement was a big record deal. I blagged Erkan that I was big promoter. I wanted him to play at raves in Spain and Dubai at £20,000-a-set. Roland wasn't too clever. After a string of leading questions he offered to sell me heroin. I knew he was just trying to please me as a thank-you for the blag DJ contract. Bigging himself up as a

gangster in front of the girls. The upshot was total annihilation on
the front page. I always felt guilty about doing those Mazher
Mahmood-style stings.

I finished off the year with another big drugs sting – turning
over the builders at the under-construction Millennium Dome.
For serving up coke, weed and pills on the job. No big deal. Most
big building sites these days are awash with gear. But everyone
was kicking the Dome to death. So it would have been rude not
to. Happy New Year.

The turn of the new millennium should have marked a para-
digm shift. Inspired by my child slavery series in South Asia, I
wanted to do more serious stories. About big, bad corporations
fucking everyone up the arse. Fucking up the planet etc. No more
silly drugs turnovers. No more stitching up straw men for cheap
thrills. Raising my game was the name of the game. Fixing my
sights on some proper targets.

But there's always one. Who wants to hold you back. Force you
to follow the same old self-serving agenda. A new hotshot News
Editor called Paul Field had been hired in from the *Daily Mail* the
year before. His sidekick Euan Stretch, who'd used to be all right,
had turned into an abrasive office arse-kisser.

Paul Field was one of the new breed of showbiz fanatics. An
elite corps of reporters and execs, rapidly coming up through the
ranks. Who championed near-saturation celebrity news. Building
empires within newspapers based on the magic they could conjure
up. Basically out of thin air – literally nothing. Energising impressionable followers with their showbiz expertise. A coup against
the old school was underway. To overthrow the greying editors
who still valued a version of hard news. Warped, tabloidy and
fake though it may have been at the core of their papers.

But one day fame evangelist Paul Field told me that from now
on it was all about Posh and Becks. They would lead the charge
on this regime change. I was genuinely astounded. Even a hack
like me. Au fait with total bollocks all of my 'career'. Even me, I
couldn't believe that this bollocks was the new currency. Hard to

believe, but true. Even harder to believe considering that his prophesy came true. Today that idea of people like the Beckhams dominating popular culture wouldn't raise an eyebrow. The idea has since been normalised. But at the time I was genuinely oblivious.

In order to guard myself against this impending doom, I went in to to see the Editor. Field wanted to mould me into a kind of poor man's Mazher Mahmood. Turning over quilts off *Big Brother* for shagging and cocaine. I told Myler it wasn't really my thing. Myler promoted me to Investigations Editor. So that I didn't have to deal with any showbiz knob-heads.

But the writing was on the wall. The knives were out. Externally, I had a veneer of fake toughness. Based on my streety image as an undercover crime investigator. But inside I felt bullied. The silent, mocking intimidation of office politics. Niggling away. Fostering self-doubt. Knocking self-confidence. I got flashbacks of the Beast. A watered-down version of career post-traumatic stress disorder took over. Sparking further spirals into low self-esteem.

In addition, I couldn't quite break out into the hard hitter I dreamed of becoming. To find proper targets I tried a different model of news gathering. Relying less on paid tipsters like Paul Samrai. Digging up my own leads. Especially on the burgeoning internet. I did a long-running investigation called the A-to-Z of Nazi Britain. Exposing the hundreds of odd-bod far right cranks. Hanging around under the surface in market towns and around suburbia up and down the land. Extreme right-wing Catholics such as The International Third Position. Front groups such as the Crusaders for the Unborn Child. Fascists who send Christmas cards with pictures of Himmler on. When the paper lost interest, I even went to a secret training camp in Poland off my own bat. Narrowly escaping a good thrashing. After being rumbled round the camp fire for not knowing the words to the Horst Wessel song.

Depression set in. Started skiving at home. Watching the History Channel. Blagging the Desk that I was on jobs. By sticking my head out of the window. Turning into £50 bloke. Going into Waterstone's, spending £50 on a CD, a Second World War book and an MOR music mag.

I got sent to Japan to track down the former wife of Barry George. The man wrongly convicted of killing Jill Dando. On such a sinker that all I could do was lock myself in the hotel room. Reading Albert Speer and *Into That Darkness* by Gitta Sereny. One day ordinary Germans were helping old ladies across the road. The next they were booting in doors and sending their kids off to the gas chambers. Though much less extreme, I understood the similar effect corporate propaganda had on confused functionaries.

I gave evidence for Steve at his industrial tribunal. Despite being warned that my salvaged career might go tits-up again. But I may as well not have – Steve never stood a chance. Even the reporters' gallery was rigged by the *News of the World*. To suppress reporting of the scandal. Flooded with News International placemen and agency reporters controlled by Kuttner.

Parts of my evidence were deemed 'not credible'. Which was true – I blamed everything on Ray. Instead of balancing it out by blaming myself as well. I never coughed to earlier spoofs. I tried to make myself look good. Giving them the babes-in-the-wood routine. To help Steve as well myself. But despite some very embarrassing moments for Rebekah, Steve lost. Losing nearly everything. Including his nerve. They had destroyed a middle-aged man over a daft picture.

Meanwhile, celebrity culture was mushrooming. Fuelled by a perfect storm of reality TV and a new breed of powerful PRs. Plus the tabloids were gagging for it and there was exponential growth in the women's mag market. *Big Brother*, *Popstars* and *Shipwrecked* creating more and more celebs by the week. A new generation of agents and pluggers bigging them up on an industrial scale.

But inside the tent, I could also detect the hidden agenda. Pushing celeb culture even further. I studied the phenomenon carefully. For tabloid editors, showbiz had started out innocently enough. As a relatively plentiful source of cheap stories. Mainly diary-fillers but, critically, low libel risk. Cheap – as in you don't need to fund a team of six highly paid investigators. To beaver away for weeks on end. To expose wrong-doing in big business. Low legal risk – because if you're writing a story about Madonna's favourite colour, she's not going to sue if you say it's blue when it's actually pink. Neither are you going to slag off Madonna for liking pink instead of blue. If you do, you'll be offside and she'll never talk to you again.

But several strategic factors began to make editors lust after showbiz even more. Firstly, advertisers loved celebrity. Not only was it harmless but marketeers liked to have their products associated with famous people. An unforeseen synergy suddenly took place. Between corporate propaganda, celeb culture and tabloids.

The three sectors fitted well together because they are basically fuelled by the same cardinal passions – fear, greed, grief and lust. Fame is all about status. Many people desire status. Therefore they are attracted to reading about celebrities. In turn, this opening becomes an advertising opportunity. By drawing in showbiz readers who crave status, the admen then sell them products which falsely claim to boost status. Such as big cars, fashionable clothes or beauty products.

In tabloids, women are also used to sell sex. Sex triggers lust. Which is then in turn satiated by a substitute impulse – consumer desire. By constantly appealing to readers' pleasure, instead of their minds, the 'punters' are manipulated. It's no accident that almost all newspaper stories focus on emotion instead of reason.

Showbiz journalism also triumphed because of the PR explosion. The PR industry was basically designed in pre-First World War America to plant corporate propaganda in newspapers. With a view to selling products. Or increasing the power of a new class of industrialists. Propaganda isn't just about wartime disinformation. In peacetime, propaganda is still the main way that the rich and powerful talk to the people. Tabloid newspapers, most broadsheets and the TV networks are primarily vehicles for propaganda. Regarding content, there is no better form of propaganda than celebrity culture.

In the 1990s, PR companies like Freud Communications became disproportionately powerful as the gatekeepers to showbiz. In turn, newspaper editors started sucking up to them. Rebekah Brooks pioneered a new model of story-getting. Firstly she would dig the dirt on a celebrity. Then, through her PR mates, she negotiated a softened-up version of the story to get into the paper. In return for a less damaging story, the celebrity had to confess to parts of the story.

The basic pitch was: 'We'll take out the cocaine bit, if you cough to the shagging.' That kind of thing. The horse-trading lessened the libel risk for Rebekah. The celebs looked slightly less disgraceful. The blackmail model was soon adopted as industry standard. Alongside phone hacking, which conveniently provided the source material for much of this corporate extortion.

Distraction was the other main reason that showbiz journalism got big. If the peasants were looking this way at Jordan's big boobs, then a whole load of terrible things could be slid by them without them really knowing. An age-old trick going back to ancient Rome's 'bread and circuses'. But today it suited businesses, banks and self-serving parts of the state.

Even at the coal face, I noticed these things going on. On the face of it these conspiratorial observations are hard to believe. But later I discovered masses of rigorous academic research to back them up. But at the end of the day, my insights weren't much help. Understanding the daily grind didn't make it any easier.

34

New Editor

My insecurity led to mistakes on two big investigations in India and Pakistan. Just a few months before 9/11, I got a tip about some out-of-control warlord-types. Trying to sell canisters containing small amounts of nuclear material. In the whacked-out areas of tribal Pakistan. The tipster was a mercenary mate I'd met in Albania. A former Royal Marine turned privateer. Now training up Islamic fighters for money. Mick said that he'd spied the canisters in a chieftain's outhouse – ex-Russian stock, left over from the first Afghanistan war in the '80s.

Shacked up in a hotel for two weeks in Islamabad. The bar was Sharia dry. But shadow room service smuggled beers under a dishcloth for cash. Waiting for the call to meet our Mr Big. To turn him over. But on the next shadowy instruction, the go-betweens wanted Mike to go into the mountains first. For a sit-down on the North-West Frontier. Mike got worried. Not wanting to take me. 'Too moody,' he said.

But something didn't smell quite right anyway. Felt like we were being played. Fitted up for an early morning call maybe. By the ISI, Pakistan's notoriously shifty spy service. Relishing the coup of rebranding a couple of doughnut journalists as foreign agents. Alternatively, we hypothesised, our own security agencies might have been using us as pawns . In a bid to frame Pakistan for secretly developing the bomb. Or maybe just a straightforward kidnapping by local bandits. Reeling us in with a bogus tip. Who the fuck knows? It was all madness.

My spider senses were pinging all over the place. Being watched at breakfast and in the street. Panicking, I got up in the middle of the night. To torch a moody passport I'd been keeping on my person, in case of emergencies. The 'book' – a phony EU document from Portugal – was in the name of a non-existent Kosovan asylum-seeker. But with my picture cleverly inserted. Bought illegally as part of a previous sting. But still useful for undercover work. Looked spot-on. But if I got caught with it on this job, trying to buy radioactive material for a dirty bomb in the badlands, I knew it was straight to jail. Don't even pass go. Set fire to it shadily on the hotel balcony.

My secret video recording equipment was also ringing alarm bells. Wired into a foam-packed briefcase which looked like a bomb. Took it apart to look less suspicious. Not to mention the Geiger counter which I'd bought for £500 before we left England. Binned.

Relieved when Mike asked me to go back to London and wait for the call. A few weeks later it came. Disguised as a Taliban, Mike said that he'd got some pictures of the nuclear canisters. But not definitive proof. However, we couldn't invest any more money or time in it. Using an offer to sell us some material on tape, we managed to crash a reduced-strength story into the paper.

Headline: 'How We Bought a Nuclear Bomb for £20,000.'

Bunged Mike nine grand for his troubles. Spent the week dodging calls from earnest Americans at the International Atomic Energy Agency.

The next fuck-up came in India. Two weeks exposing child slaves making fireworks near Chennai, formerly Madras, in India. A great story because the company was called Standard Fireworks.

Household name on bommie night in Britain. Problem was, it turned out to be a totally separate company from its British namesake. The Indians had simply copied the logo. Luckily, we discovered this fact before publication, saving a huge libel payout.

Tipster Paul Samrai got a bollocking. I'm not sure what he was up to but I accused him of making the whole thing up. To wangle a free plane ticket off the *Sunday Mirror* for a family wedding over there. Soon the lawyers banned him from the *Sunday Mirror* altogether, accusing him of mistranslating a tape in Punjabi, leading to a big court payout on a previous immigration sting.

Then my ex-girlfriend Angela got killed in a car crash. Miraculously, her new-born baby from her new feller survived. Went to her funeral and got stick off her mates for splitting up with her. But by then, I'd settled down with a *Sunday Mirror* journalist called Emma Jones. Emma moved into my flat.

Got voted finalist again, for Reporter of the Year competition. The second time in as many years. The *News of the World* kept offering me my old job back – five times in total. Each approach, bumping the money up. Then offering me the post of Deputy Features Editor as a sweetener. Kuttner even biked around a contract to the *Sunday Mirror* offices. Between gritted teeth. To bamboozle me into signing it. When I didn't, they even used a honey-trap to lure me back. Taking me out to the trendy, star-studded Met Bar in Park Lane. Trying to get one of their tasty reporters to make me roll over. The irony was complex. The seductress was none other than the busty Features reporter who Ray Levine had sprayed on to the side of his motorbike. Whispering in my ear that Ray was history. I was the new golden boy. She told me he had been punished for the Beast – demoted back on to the road as a reporter, before being eased out of the paper altogether. But it was all bollocks and none of it would make me go back.

Story-wise, I did an investigation headlined 'Cadbury Dairy Swill', exposing how the nation's favourite sweet factory re-melted stale chocolate that had been thrown out for pigswill, deliberately repackaging the out-of-date bars as fresh Dairy Milks. Even though this was a form of corporate corruption, for me it was no more than a consumer story. I'd begun to analyse stories through Noam Chomsky's 'propaganda model' which says that powerful elites tolerate corruption stories in the papers as 'acceptable dissent'. Even corporations don't like too much dipping into the till, preferring smooth-running systems because they make more money. All very high-brow for a journeyman hack. But true.

Then a shock to my own system. In spring 2001, *Sunday Mirror* Editor Colin Myler suddenly resigned after running a dodgy contempt story. A new editor was appointed immediately – a former *Daily Mirror* exec called Tina Weaver. On paper I should have got on well with her, having lived with her brother once in Bristol. He was a really nice feller. She owned or partly owned the flat I used to rent. Tina had also come up through the same agency.

But we didn't get off on the right foot and then somehow never really hit it off. For me, she was just one of the increasing propor-tion of posh, privately-educated editors that were coming to dominate the mix in newsrooms. Around 54% of Britain's top 100 journalists had come from independent schools – which educated just 7% of the population. The research was done by the Sutton Trust in 2006. Today, all three editors of Trinity Mirror's national titles are public school-educated. The News Desks are pretty much the same. In addition, Trinity Mirror's graduate training scheme provides a disproportionate number of Oxbridge graduates who can and will work for low wages. One day a sniffy executive told me that he didn't like Alicante airport because he had to endure 'too many of our readers there'. How could you write a newspaper for the sheeple – a pretend left-wing one at that – if you're sat in the VIP lounge whilst they flew cattle-class on Ryan Air? The year-on-year ABC figures reflected the 'misunder-standing' between the *Mirror* and its 'punters'.

I realised that the *Mirror*'s left-wing bias was no more than a sham. The *Mirror* was no longer there to 'educate and enlighten' readers, as prescribed by its distinguished Editor Hugh Cudlipp, but to generate income streams for posh people.

Tina liked showbiz. But she wasn't that keen on guns and drugs, child slavery or attacking big corporations. One day I pitched an idea to her in conference.

'Why don't we turn over all these PR firms,' I said gullibly, 'that are controlling everything, all of a sudden? Show them up for being corrupt. Get all those 20-grand-a-year Alice-band-birds on tape, snorting their brains out whilst talking up their A-list clientele?'

Tina snapped back: 'Why bite the hand that feeds us? I've got 96 pages to fill every week and our PR contacts give us stories.'

'Personally,' I said. 'Not once have I ever been given a story by a PR. Never.'

She looked at me as though that was the problem. Like I was a dinosaur who needed to stop fucking about with video bags and villains and start taking out some 22-year-old PR dollies for lunch.

I reacted by going darker. Reverting to type. Retreating into the underworld. Doing even more guns 'n' drugs stories. Recruiting even more hardcore contacts. A former Turkish heroin baron. Big drug dealers of every description. Professional fraudsters. Even hitmen. Reactionary behaviour but I remember a study which said that black people saw themselves through white people's eyes. If she saw me as rogue, scallywag reporter, then that's what I'd be. Play up to it. A lack of self-confidence. Tired that I'd have to prove myself all over again.

I'd had a good run of three-and-a-half years. Been around the world, genuinely trying to change things for the better. Once I'd been a very bad reporter. Holding my trade in contempt. Now I'd actually made myself into a good reporter. Better for the fact that I'd learned from my mistakes. But now the problem wasn't me. I'd have to live with the feeling that my job was under threat.

Tried to jump ship to BBC's *Panorama* and the *Observer*. But there were no jobs. Even to the *Daily Mirror*. After 9/11, the Editor Piers Morgan took an unprecedented and extraordinary decision. Astonishingly, he stopped publishing bollocks. Deciding instead to print a serious tabloid. Changed the mast-head to black. Reprioritised showbiz down the list. Rehired John Pilger as a columnist. The result was roasting. A paper full of hard-hitting stories that journalists loved to write.

But sadly the new-look *Daily Mirror* was short-lived. The Trinity board lost their bottle during the transition phase. Firstly, over the economics. Then, more seriously, over ideology. They couldn't handle that the showbiz crowd had disappeared from the circulation figures. But the relaunched paper needed time to build a new readership. The board couldn't wait. The rug was pulled.

But that was only the cover story. The real threat came when the *Mirror* started openly criticising US foreign policy. The invasion of Afghanistan. The Iraqi sanctions that killed half-a-million kids in the run-up to 'Shock and Awe'. Then even more unforgiveable – questioning the role of America's Middle Eastern hitman, Israel.

Rumours swept the newsroom that US shareholders were 'uncomfortable', demanding that the newly-dissenting Editor be tamed or jettisoned. The *Mirror*'s anti-Iraq War stance was the final straw. A year later, in 2004, Morgan was fitted up. The *Mirror* published fake pics of British soldiers torturing Iraqi detainees. A murky business which the *Mirror* described as a 'calculated and malicious hoax'. Was he black-opped in revenge? That was the newsroom scuttlebutt. Didn't matter. He was gone. Gone. You step out of line, you get whacked.

35

Hacking

The sizzling *Sunday Mirror* decided not to follow the *Daily* experiment. Tina was chauffeur-driven to Labour Party conference – but deep down she was conservative by nature. Staying safe with sex and celebs. The supplement was even rebranded *M celebs*. More stories about shiny, happy people were poured into the paper. But behind the scenes, the atmosphere turned dark. The new Editor Tina Weaver hired in some ex-*Screws* ruffians and scuffians to shake down the likes of my good self.

Mark Thomas was a journalistic enigma. He hardly spoke. How could you be a journalist without basic communication skills? As the new Deputy Editor, his job was to build a Death Star-lite at Canary Wharf. His lack of speech was stressful and unnerving. Subordinate functionaries like me – under-confident and under pressure – felt an overwhelming desire to fill the void. A tedious trick dubbed management technique. Fastidious, Mark was a kind of robo-hack super-functionary.

James Weatherup was an old hand who I was friendly with from my *Screws* days. Now he was being brought into terminate my command. Not that I had much – I didn't have a budget or staff. Tina Weaver crowned Weatherup Head of Investigations – it seemed to me to be a constructive ploy to undermine my position as Investigations Editor. The bullies were back in town. Once more, my mind was sent into a whirligig. I'd buried the Beast deep within my psyche. Now it was creeping back out.

A few years later James left the *Sunday Mirror*. Returning to the Death Star proper at Wapping. Then he got nicked on suspicion of phone hacking. I don't know whether he was 'at it' whilst he was at the *Sunday Mirror*. But I'll tell you a bit about what I do know.

I first heard of phone hacking going on in Fleet Street around 1999 or 2000. But the term phone hacking was yet to be coined. The latest dark art simply was then called 'doing the phones', 'off the phones' or 'listening to messages'. Either way, I thought it was a bit stupid. Not even worth bothering with.

During the early years, phone hacking wasn't a mainstream activity. More of a cult ritual, confined to a small sect of showbiz reporters. To pick up tittle-tattle from celebs' phones. The actual beginning can be traced back to a showbiz desk on a newspaper. I know, because I knew people who worked there. The motivation, as always, was ambition, coupled with pressure from above. But indignation was also a catalyst. The showbiz reporters were getting pissed off. One of their main sources of stories was being choked off. An antiquated dark art known as 'bin-spinning'. As a result, they were losing valuable tips

Rummaging through the bins of famous people and offices connected to them – lawyers, accountants, PR firms – had become a plentiful source of cheap 'diary' stories, especially for showbiz reporters during the Brit Pop years. The practice had started off in Hollywood, before moving clip side of the big moist around 1995. Then embraced into the most receptive and lucrative newspaper market in the world.

One day, I was at the home of a high-flying showbiz reporter. The landline went off and my mate asked me to answer it.

'Hi, it's Benji here,' the voice at the other end said. Well-spoken, deep and slightly slow.

'Sorry, mate,' I said. 'He [my showbiz mate] can't talk at the mo.

'Can he call you back?'

'Tell him,' the man said, 'that I've got a good one on Robbie Williams.'

After putting the phone down I asked my mate who it was.

'It's Benji,' he said.

'He's a good contact – he's the one who rummages through all the bins for us. He's not on a retainer or nothing, but he makes a fair few quid out of us.'

Fleet Street's top freelance bin-spinner was an ex-trainee lawyer called Benjamin Pell. Benji the Binman took his job very seriously. Disguising himself as a recycling technician. Complete with hi-vis vest and van. Doing the rounds within the legal, financial and media districts in London. Emptying the contents of their bins into his van. Before taking the bags back to his pad for sorting. Important documents were pieced back together. Tit-bits phoned into the reporters overnight, just like the call made to my mate.

Showbiz reporters embraced garbology for two reasons. Firstly, because documents were good proof that a story was true. Secondly, and more importantly, because someone else was doing all the graft, while the staff journalists took all the glory in conference.

But even before it really took off, the sun was setting on bin-spinning. Like all good start-ups brought to market, the trade eventually went mainstream, which in turn led to it eating itself prematurely. But for a short while, bin-spinning managed to break out of the showbiz niche, penetrating into rival departments within newsrooms. More often with bigger budgets. Such as News Desks, investigation bureaux, politics and even sport. Not only that, but sweeping across Fleet Street into most of the papers, including the broadsheets. The upshot was that showbiz was losing its monopoly on good stories.

In addition, Benji was getting threatened with legal action

from unhappy victims – including Richard Branson, Elton John and Mohamed Al-Fayed – eventually being convicted of theft in 2000. The rogue sanitation engineer was fined £5.

With bin-spinning gone, showbiz hacks needed to find a replacement dark art. However, a new innovation was already under research and development. A sleight of hand that proved cheaper, cleaner and lazier: phone hacking.

Fleet Street historians are unsure of how reporters discovered that they could listen to someone else's messages. By dialling into a remote-access voicemail system and keying in default PIN numbers. But my showbiz mates told me that there were three sources that came together around the same time. Phreaking was an underground hacking movement in 1970s America. Starting out as a cheeky way of cheating free calls out of phone companies, phreaking soon evolved into voicemail taps. In the UK, the petty criminality was copied by paparazzi and private detectives in the 1990s. At the same time, phone hacking also became a schoolboy prank, popular with teenagers rich enough to own mobiles back in the day.

But one reporter told me how showbiz hacks more or less stumbled on the phenomenon. The person told me: 'I'd first heard of it in 1999. But no one knew how exactly to do it. Then it started by trial and error. I got sent away on a foreign. When I landed abroad, the mobile phone company sent me a text saying: "If you want to access your voicemail back in Britain, ring this long number followed by keying in your PIN number." Something like that. The photographer, who was with me, started messing about, dialling other people's numbers and using the default PIN code to get through to their messages. The first person I ever did was another reporter on my own paper, for a joke. That's because we were on the same network and I knew the PIN code used by our network.

'Other people were doing it around the same time.'

The breakthrough spread like wildfire through showbiz desks for three reasons. Phone hacking was cheap. Showbiz columns don't have loads of money to spend on stories. Nor do they have budgets for private detectives to work on leads. Phone hacking was also ideal for generating 'shorts' – small stories, news-in-briefs and fillers to boost up a diary page quickly before deadline.

But most of all, phone hacking suited the lifestyles of showbiz journalists, generating stories without the reporter ever having to leave the office. Showbiz reporters are often stressed out, tired people. Out all night 'partying' at tin-pot VIP parties. Desperate to pick up gossip. Snorting stripes in cold bogs, to keep them awake and sober enough not to fuck up. So the last thing they want to be doing was going out on stories the next day. Too much like hard work – especially with an angry cocaine hangover. Why bother when you can 'do the phones' while eating a prawn sandwich at your desk?

Phone hacking became a life-saver – or more accurately a career saver. A job-keeper. Many showbiz reporters were young, harassed women, bullied by angrier, sexually aggressive bosses, many of whom were coked-up or coming down themselves. When screamed at for copy, an underling could pull a story out of the hat by 'doing' a soap star's phone before conference. Life-saver. Salary-guardian. Phone hacking fitted in well with those worried reporters who went around with a hunted look in their eyes.

On a political level, phone hacking quickly became a springboard into management, an ideal base on which showbiz journalists could build little empires within newspapers. As celeb culture grew, so phone hacking increased in importance. As showbiz reporters ascended the greasy pole and became the new powerhouses in newsrooms, phone hacking in turn grew in stature.

One reporter told me: 'Mediocre reporters were delivering good stories by doing the phones. So I thought: "If he can do it, so can I." I knew one reporter who couldn't do his job properly. He used to have crack cocaine biked into the office by the firm's couriers. He was a disaster waiting to happen. Then the next minute, he suddenly became a golden boy through phone hacking. He broke three or four very big showbiz stories one after the other. Later he was poached on big wages by another paper. He went on to be a 100 grand-a-year-plus executive. His whole career on national newspapers was built on phone hacking. And he hasn't been nicked yet.'

The rising stars took their magic with them. Soon the newly crowned execs were showing the News Desks, that now worked under them, how to hack phones. Just like bin-spinning, phone hacking went mainstream and all over Fleet Street. But unlike rummaging through rubbish, phone hacking was to endure. Simply because it was less visible and harder to prove.

Even so, I always thought it was a stupid way of getting stories. Practically, it was useless for crime and gun 'n' drugs investigations. Very few of the drug dealers and gangsters I turned over, or got stories off, ever talked business on the phone. Never mind leaving messages. Many of them had taken to not using phones 'for work' at all. Or, at least, switching them off, taking the batteries out and moving the handsets to faraway tables during meetings. Some had even reverted to extremes, using human carrier pigeons to relay messages between villains. Some drug dealing cartels I know even started paying young gang members to use the network of Easy Jet flights around Europe. To pass word-of-mouth messages between cells in the UK, Spain and The Dam. So listening to their phone messages was a non-runner for me.

But I did know of two occasions when phone hacking was used. On both occasions the mobiles of celebrities were hacked. But I resisted getting dragged into the culture of phone hacking – the systematic tapping of phones on fishing expeditions – for selfish reasons. At the time, I didn't know whether phone hacking was legal or illegal. But I knew that if I succumbed, I would inevitably get dragged into doing showbiz stories full-time. I already knew that my bosses were unhappy that I was 'off-message', in that I was earning loads of money plus expenses and generating massive entourage bills for technicians, bag-carriers and freelance tipsters. The editors weren't happy that those resources were going into crime stories instead of showbiz. Ironically, to get involved in hacking would have meant giving in to them.

In addition, I already had a very successful model for story-getting, which I was at pains not to give up:

Step 1. Groom good contacts
Step 2. Get story tips off them
Step 3. Stand the tips up by getting independent and corroborating evidence, mainly using video bags
Step 4. Publish the story
Step 5. Pay the tipsters large amounts of money for their information

A model known as chequebook journalism, much criticised but tried and tested. I didn't need to hack phones like other reporters did – I had more stories than I could possibly work on. The whole point of phone hacking was that it set out to wipe out big tips fees. For me, it would have been self-defeating. I would have lost all my contacts.

On two other occasions computer hacking was also mentioned. One time a senior journalist made it known that he wanted to recruit a computer whiz kid who could hack emails for him. But the hacker turned him down.

On another occasion a private detective approached the paper. The inquiry agent, who had never worked for the *Sunday Mirror* before, claimed that he knew a third party who'd hacked into a celebrity's emails. The private detective then claimed that he worked with a group of hackers. That he was their frontman. The hackers weren't commissioned by the *Sunday Mirror* to hack emails. But they later provided information to the paper that they claimed had been hacked from a computer. Though there was no way of proving that this was true. Private detectives are notorious for lying about the source of their information. For instance, they might say that a document has been hacked to disguise the fact that it has really been been stolen during a burglary, or given to them by a source with a hidden agenda that they wish to protect. The private detective and the 'hackers' claimed their evidence was historic, meaning that it had been hacked from a computer before they had made contact with the *Sunday Mirror*. The private detectives were never used again.

Phone hacking was increasingly being used by freelance photographers, surveillance experts and paparazzi to find out the location of celebrities. I suspected that a couple of secret squirrel freelancers were constantly phone hacking because they were always coming up with big stories with no obvious source of inside information. I only met them on one occasion. On the job, they claimed that they had bugged a hotel room that we were supposed to be watching. I didn't know whether phone hacking was illegal or not. But I knew for certain that bugging a hotel room was. I was always using video bags and I had discussed the law several times with the experts that rented the equipment out. We were always careful not to go beyond what was lawful. The law is quite simple. I can put a tape recorder in a room and record the conversation between me and a target. Just as long as one of us in the room knows that they are being recorded – in this case me. But I can't put a tape in a room and walk out – with the intention of recording a conversation between two other 'third party' people in the room, who don't know they're being taped. That's bugging and can only be done with the permission of the authorities. When the secret squirrels said that they had bugged a hotel room that we were supposed to be watching I walked off the job in protest. I left the hotel in the middle of the night. The next day I got a bollocking.

36

The Final Countdown

Never seen such a sight. Hundreds of naked bodies. Writhing like snakes. On a specially-made, steel-reinforced bed. The size of a small swimming pool. Welcome to the VIP Orgy.

Bankers. Lawyers. Celebs. Olympic athletes. Aristocrats. Politicians. Tycoons. New York socialites. Music industry moguls. A rock star's teenage daughter. Top civil servants. Acclaimed scientists. Russian oligarchy. The ruling elite. Flown in from the four corners. For a once-a-year secret sexathon. In a £15 million mansion, off plush Portland Place. One of those stories that makes you go: David Icke was right after all. Total madness.

Beforehand, I'd wired up the decadent Georgian rooms with secret recording equipment. Now I was disguised as a triple-A security guard. The button hole on my overcoat a back-up micro-lens. Picking up scenes of depravity that I'd thought had died out with the Medici. The bed alone cost £7000. The shabby-chic rooms decorated by film-set designers. Door security were off-duty royal firearms cops. Prince Andrew's bodyguard, who also protected Tony Blair at Chequers. One bi-sexual female copper later stripped off down to a basque and joined in. Phwooar!

Now the pièce-de-résistance. The light from the flickering Louis XIV candelabras wasn't bright enough for a bold, front-page picture. I'd have to take a big risk. Of switching on the main lights. For just enough of an instant. To get off a couple of sneaky shots.

Now! I signalled. As a pair of Manhattan twins splayed out in front of me, in full throes with a famously corrupt English toff, my colleague pretended to accidentally fall over, right on to the ornate light fitting, flicking the knob as he went. For one second, all 64 different positions of the *Kama Sutra* froze. Under the pin-sharp beam of the twinkling chandeliers. Bosh! Bosh! Bosh! Then off into the night.

The hardest thing was going home. Trying to adjust to normal life, hours later. On a Sunday morning in spring. My mind still a whirligig of mad images. One in particular – of two bewitched, ruffled-haired debutantes. Going down on each other, on the dance floor. By now I had two kids. The job was wrecking my head.

My old flatmate and stunt-up fixer Gav got bin-bagged by his girlfriend. Nowhere to stay. No dough. Felt sorry for him when he asked me for help. So I gave him a job as a bag-carrier and news dogsbody. But I found him to be hard work. He wasn't a grafter, to be fair. He'd failed in his ambition to become a famous writer. I sensed growing bitterness and jealousy with age. Gratitude is a burden. Knew from the off it would all go skew-whiff. But what could I do?

Relations with the Editor were still at breaking point. But the tension spurred me on to do some of the best stories of my career. The peasant still strong within me. Fearful and desperate to please. Working undercover in NHS hospitals. First as a cleaner. Then as a kitchen porter. To expose the sub-prison slop they dished out to the sick. Like *Soylent Green* come to life. Then one about the filthy wards left disease-ridden by the freshly-privatised, fat-cat contractors. Whatever happened to the post-war dream? But the Editor was more interested in *I'm a Celebrity . . .* One of the most important jobs in the office had become reality TV correspondent. To stay up all night monitoring *Big Brother*. A coveted, high-status role in the new regime.

On a different tip, I turned over Wayne Rooney. For shagging grannies in a back-street brothel in Liverpool. To get the grainy CCTV tapes, I arranged payment of £200,000 to some extremely sinister organised criminals. Ten grand on top to a couple of identical twin call girls whom the England wonderkid had also 'walloped'. A £5000 bung to another masseuse. An extra £5000 to a swinger called Jim. Tens of thousands more pay-offs to various gangsters, protection racketeers and enforcers. Keeping them sweet and off our case. At one point there was so much money sloshing through various dummy accounts, that Trinity Mirror execs had to check the company wasn't breaking money-laundering laws. Madness.

The videos showed Rooney queuing up to have sex with a £50-a-pop hooker. Dressed as a cowgirl. Personally, I couldn't give a fuck what he got up to. Whether he was shagging mature ladies, WAGs or Coleen McLoughlin, who, by the way, yours truly had 'discovered' to be the girlfriend of the soccer sensation a couple of years earlier. In another showbiz world exclusive. The old magic still there. Personally, couldn't understand why the Editor wanted to get rid of my good self.

The only aspect of the Rooney story that titillated me was the secret glimpse it gave me into modern football. Behind the scenes, Britain's booming organised crime, bloated on record drug sales, was pulling the strings. Coke cartels secretly buying up shares in football clubs, manipulating sports agencies as front companies into vehicles of control. Gangsters blackmailing premiership stars, using mobile footage of them snorting and shagging all over the place.

Kiss 'n' tells had lost their sordid innocence. For newspapers, the genre was no longer just a case of buying up the Page 3 girl and sticking them in a hotel to spill the beans. Professional extortionists had realised that exposés were lucrative blackmail bait.

Getting pro-active. Turning them into highly orchestrated set-ups. Paying honey-trap girls to lure footballers in. Crying cocaine rape. The scandal used as leverage to blood-suck lucrative 'security contracts' out of impressionable, over-cocky young men. Suddenly, behind every roasting story there was a rooting-tooting godfather making the moves. The Queen of Kiss 'n' Tells was soon muscled out of business. A tear came to my eye when I reminisced about the good old days. A rose-tinted RIP to Shirley Ann Lye.

The Rooney story was no different. I couldn't believe how wide the international network stretched. Got calls from crime-lords based in the Middle East and Spain. Shadowy meetings with men with links to Amsterdam and the IRA. I had to fend off five or six crime gangs, private detectives and 'security consultants' to keep the tapes from falling into the wrong hands. Some of them wanting to get the evidence to blackmail Rooney. Some of them Rooney's allies. Trying to buy them back as a 'gift' for him. Of course, without his knowledge. Got followed. Then threatened. My oppo Gav got a slap. From a pizza shop-owning drug lord. The shit scared out of him. The company installed a state-of-the-art alarm system in my new house.

But we nursed the story into the paper. Fending off the *News of the World* in a rearguard action. To keep the scoop tight. The *Screws* Editor Andy Coulson put one of his top assassins on the case. None other than Greg Miskiw. But this time I was ready for him. Employing a former Turkish heroin baron and underworld counter-surveillance expert. To keep tabs on him. Until he was run out of town empty-handed. Greg would later hit the headlines in his own right. For coming back from America to face questioning by police about allegations of phone hacking.

The Rooney scoop led to another Reporter of the Year nomination. Another wasted night on the piss, in the Park Lane Hilton or somewhere. But life at work wasn't getting any easier, despite the big-ups. The knives were still out. I'd fucked up on a story about child-trafficking in Montenegro. The story wasn't mine.

The investigation was done by a freelancer. I wasn't in the office when it was legalled. But as Investigations Editor I took the rap. The lawyers wriggled out of taking any of the blame. The company had to pay out on it. The Editor held it against me.

One day, a short while before, an executive had asked me to download child porn on to my computer at work. Telling me it was for an investigation into a paedophile ring. That much was true. But I refused point blank. Downloading underage sex is a strict liability criminal offence. Meaning there is no public interest defence. Even for a journalist investigating a story. The executive was pissed off that I'd refused to follow an order. Cursing me for not being 'able to handle' it.

Many confrontations followed. Low-level harassment to get me out. Another time the Picture Editor called me a cunt. I had to tell him off. He wobbled like a jelly, backing down the way bullies do. But he didn't like the public humiliation. That's what happens in newsrooms when they want you gone. The editor asked me to turn over TV actor Neil Morrissey. We spent thousands getting into him undercover – but in the end he was so nice that I couldn't turn him over, not that there was any dirt on him – but I just couldn't stitch him gratuitously.

I got offered a job by the BBC. As an investigator for a current affairs show. But I turned it down. Even though I needed an outro. Came down to the money. The Beeb offered £40,000 a year, which sounds like good dough. But when you've got a family in central London, it doesn't go that far. Plus my partner Emma had not long lost her job, so we couldn't take the risk. Instead, I started selling big set-piece investigations to TV. Did a big one for Donal MacIntyre. Buying Semtex in Kosovo. Another one based on book I wrote called *Powder Wars*. The doco was called *Supergrass*.

The desk were still trying to suck me into showbiz. But I kept fucking them off. 'I've written enough bollocks for one life – I can't write any more.' One day I had a bet with a music producer mate I know. He was trying to get some publicity for his next, big dance act. Thinking of paying his PR company five grand a month retainer to plug them in the papers. I told him not to bother. Bet him a grand that I could get him more publicity in a week than he could in a year.

'Most showbiz stories are made up out of thin air,' I told him. 'Just ring up the showbiz desk on any national newspaper and tell them any old bollocks and they'll run it without checking. The stupider and more unbelievable the better.'

Sure enough, the papers were tipped off that a couple of WAGs had joined the band, namely Wayne Rooney's Coleen McLoughlin and Steven Gerrard's Alex Curran. Of course, the completely fictitious story appeared in several papers. Later, the documentary *Starsuckers* used the same trick.

Meanwhile, I'd started a very big and dangerous investigation of my own, into one of Britain's biggest heroin gangs. A corruption scandal at the heart of the British justice system. Going right up to the highest powers in the land.

The story centred around two big drug dealers called John Haase and Paul Bennett. In 1996 the pair had been put in jail for 18 years apiece, after getting caught red-handed with 50 kg of heroin worth £18 million. They were part of an international smuggling network known as the Turkish Connection. But mysteriously, after serving just one year inside, the pair were released. Granted a Royal Pardon by then Home Secretary Michael Howard. An unprecedented act in English legal history. Very fishy to boot.

I teamed up with a Labour MP Peter Kilfoyle to look into the case. Peter's beef stemmed from the fact that two of Britain's most violent criminals – linked to industrial-scale gun-running, numerous shootings and blood-curdling acts of torture and assorted violence – had been released back into his constituency of Liverpool Walton. Fucking the place up again with a recurrent uncontrollable crime spree. The campaigning politician felt he'd been duped by the system. My motivation was simple – ambition. I'd been saying 'no more straw men' for years. Now was my chance to step up and go after some proper villains. Wanting to prove that I could go after weapons-grade targets. Carry out a thorough, truthful, textbook investigation. Multiple layers. Multiple techniques, both straightforward and covert reporting. Under stressful conditions.

Over late-night meetings at Westminster's Strangers Bar, we decided to divvy up the work. Peter would work to reopen the case. By making speeches in the chamber. Lobbying Home Office officials. Pushing Scotland Yard. While I would do the dirty work on the ground. Infiltrating Haase's gang. Going undercover to extract confessions on tape. Digging up old paperwork. Tracking down witnesses.

But the stress was horrific. The gang put a £100,000 contract on my head. One enforcer – linked to several targeted killings since he becoming a hitman aged 14 – told me straight to my face: 'I've thought about killing you twice. You were bringing it on top for John and Ben (Haase and Bennett). So me and Ben had a talk. The plan was for me to come over. Go to your house. And kill you.'

'Even though my partner and kids were there?' I gulped.

'Yes,' he replied.

Numerous threats followed. The Metropolitan Police's Specialist Crime Directorate installed a state-of-the-art alarm system at my house. Doubling up, on top of the one that I already had. The walls were now bristling with panic buttons, multiple sensors and CCTV. The detective offered me protection on the witness support programme. Names changed, move house, all that caper. But I refused.

'How can I?' I said. 'I've got kids. This is where I live.'

But now the pressure was on at home. Getting more nervy and irascible. Thoughts blackening with crime, guns, heroin, murder. When I should have been playing with the kids. Em pissed of, asking: 'What are you doing? This is just an ego trip. Let it go. Grow up.'

But at every twist, the story drew me back. A deep meandering conspiracy into the depths. Involving leaps from the credible to the incredible. Dark powers within the government. Holdalls bulging with millions of pounds in cash. Money changing hands. Thirty-five huge gun caches. Fabricated supergrass evidence. M15. The IRA. Turkish godfathers. Sinkfuls of cocaine and heroin. Warnings from shadowy ex-customs officers. Strange men taking photographs of my house.

But at night I slept lightly. Sounds stirring me into a panic. One point, sleeping with a barely-legal high-powered gas-gun under my bed. That I'd bought on an investigation into firearms. I ended up writing two books about the case. Numerous articles. The police reopened the case. I gave evidence in court. Eventually John Haase and Paul Bennett were put behind bars for 42 years for perverting the course of justice. Making legal history – the first time that a Royal Pardon had been overturned. Textbook investigation. Got a big-up in parliament. Described in *Hansard* as an 'investigative reporter supreme'.

But there was a dialectic tension. The more truthful my stories became, the more I told lies to everyone else. The better reporter I became, the harder I found it to be straight with the people I worked with. Was busy keeping too many balls in the air. I didn't trust my bosses and felt that I had to blag them just to keep my job. The stress was driving me mad. On the cusp of success, the seeds of my downfall were being sown.

37

Freedom Next Time

'Kate Moss is snorting,' Gav revealed.

'I've heard it does go on,' I replied.

Gav was telling me that, for once in his life, he'd had a good tip. About the world's number one fashion influence on Western women. She was out of control on the stripes.

'How can we prove it?' I asked him. Impatient to conclude. The phone ringing. 1001 things to do.

'I know who her dealer is,' he said, eyes looking away.

'The beauty is,' he came back, a trace cockier, 'that I can get them onside. I've had a chat with them. They're prepared to throw her in – for good dough, of course.'

I should have known it was a set-up. There were several warning signs. Firstly, Gav rarely came up with tips. He was not a trained journalist and sometimes found the job hard. For the year or so that he'd been on the firm he'd written little. He found it difficult to work alone. Preferring to have me give him detailed instructions, which was unusual on a Sunday newspaper. Working on the side whenever he could. Making short art-house films. Or whatever the fuck he got up to when I wasn't there to check up.

He liked a bohemian atmosphere. But for me, he was rapidly becoming excess baggage. When he should have been carrying it – for me, on jobs. A drain on resources. Looking back, it'd been a disastrous decision to employ a mate. It's true – never mix business with pity. One day, the Force sensed danger. Gav had intro'd me to a lad in a pub in Camden. Claiming that he was the middle man on the Kate Moss job. But the meeting was moody. Something not quite right. As if the lad was sizing me up. Like a plump chicken, ready for the plucking. But my spider senses didn't register it enough unfortunately. Clouded by the superhuman levels of stress that I was living with on a daily basis.

In the background, I'd started running a Brown Boom mini buy-to-let empire on the side. The preferred middle-class entrepreneurial activity of the age. Clocking up over a million quid's worth of rental properties in a few years. Greedy, London living.

Meanwhile, Gav had been moaning that he wanted more money. Complaining that his wages had been coming up short. Even though that side of things had little to do with me. I was a reporter not a bean-counter. One day he said to me: 'I've been thinking about turning you over.'

Deep down he was jealous. As much as I was filled with avarice and ambition, he was filled with envy for the trappings of success that I'd built up. Like all aspiring writer and artist types, he loved money. Scratch a hippie and you'll find a Thatcherite. Or at least one her yuppies.

Foolishly, I never thought he would. Anyway, I was too busy to deal with details. His threats were just some among many. Including those from the Editor and several of Britain's most dangerous gangsters. I ignored him. Hoping that he'd just suck it up. Like everyone else on newspapers. Now I was too blinded by his snowy Kate Moss tip to worry.

The rumours of Kate's habit had been rife for years. From the grapevine, I knew that several other papers were working on it. Including our sister paper the *Daily Mirror* and the *News of the World*. Sean Hoare, who was now freelancing for the *Sunday*

Mirror, was also on the case. Snooping around the posh pubs on Haverstock Hill. So I couldn't let the tip go. In addition, I had developed a working model that I hoped would satisfy my haters on the papers. Feeding them just enough bollocks to keep them off my back. But leaving me just enough work time to indulge myself manically on my life's work – the big John Haase Royal Pardon story. I'll give you Kate – you let me go up to Liverpool to interview more witnesses.

'OK, how we going to do it?' I asked Gav, a few days later. In a rush, looking around the room. Stopping to vent fury down the phone to someone else.

'The dealer is saying that they're prepared to grass her up,' said Gav.

'Do you mean set her up?' I asked.

'Do you think they'll allow us to get a video bag in there. During a deal. So we can see Kate scoring and snorting etc?'

'That's what they're saying,' Gav assured me. 'But they want to see some money first.'

I should have seen it coming. But my head was wrecked. Worries at work. Job under threat. Editor on my case. Stress of having a young family. Guantanamo-levels of sleep-deprivation. Em was pregnant with our third child. Being run ragged by the Desk. Working almost round the clock on the big John Haase case. More threats. Tense, nervous headaches. Tesco. Lost in B & Q trying to find things. On the phone. Family feuds. Shouting down the phone at everyone. For fuck's sake – what the fuck is going on? All I ever wanted to do was write. Have English O-Level, will travel. Is this the price I had to pay? Where did it all go wrong?

'OK, I'll get you some flash money,' I said. 'I'll get you three grand in cash. You can show the readies to them as a carrot. Tell them that this is what they'll get, if the tip is right. For now. Plus ten times. Twenty times. Or even thirty times more. If they can get us in the room, when Kate is scoring and we can get into the paper.'

Gav smiled. 'Nice one,' he said.

Should have seen him coming. The sly twat.

'But don't, whatever the fuck you do,' I warned him, 'hand it over to them. Or lose it. Or have it taken off you by some daft smack-head. It's only for show. It's only for hypnotic effect. To bewitch the criminal sub-classes into helping us out for the time being. In the search for truth and justice. Or at least until the time we can get control of the story. And start shouting the odds. Now hear this – tomorrow the three grand has got to go back to the paper. It's just for show. D'you get me? No fucking messing about. I want it back . . .' etc.

Gav nodded, Pavlov-style. Smiling and nodding. Never trust a hippie.

I told the new Deputy Editor James Scott the score. He agreed to get the £3000 in cash signed off ASAP. On the understanding that it came back within 24 hours.

'No sweat,' I said, itching to go. In a rush. Mind not on it.

'I'll underwrite personally.' I said. 'If it doesn't come back.'

Handed it over to Gav in my four-by-four at Camden Lock. Surprisingly – I'm sure you can fill in the gaps – the money never came back. Gav disappeared. When he finally surfaced, he said he had given it to Kate Moss's dealers. But the story wasn't very convincing. I listened patiently to the excuse. It involved a lot of shenanigans, him being dragged through a hedge backwards etc. Later, when it all kicked off, the exchanges became very heated.

It was a massive fuck-up. On my shoulders. The excuse the News Desk and the Editor had been waiting for. To wade into me. The Editor came on: 'I'm sick of you. I'm sick of you turning me over. Letting me down . . .' etc, etc. She said some very bad things. I was with Emma at the time, who was pregnant. With the other baby in the car. I went white. Had to alight from the vehicle, half-way down the street and listen to her bollocking on the phone.

Paralysed with stress. Couldn't do or say anything. Phone call after phone call of madness. Had to press the button on this quick. Go nuclear. Stop the ride I want to get off. I phoned in sick. Told them that from now on I was officially 'on the sick'. Saying I was stressed out. Which was true. Spent six months decorating the cellar. Painting the floor pink. Turning it into a kids' playroom. Every now and again, I went in to see the company doctor. Then an expensive psychiatrist in Park Lane. I don't know whether I'd had a nervous breakdown. Or lost my mind. But it certainly felt like that way. I wasn't in the right mind to make rational judgements. But all I kept saying to them was: 'Get me out of here. Get me out of this place. I want to leave this job. It's fucking me up.'

The only time that anyone from work got in touch was to hassle me. I'd forgotten that I was still in possession of the Rooney brothel tapes. A quarter of a million pounds' worth of Trinity Mirror's property. Or not quite. Technically, Trinity Mirror had breached the copyright. Of the original, undoctored tape bought off the madame and the gangsters. Foolishly, the *Sunday Mirror* had sneakily made a copy which was in breach of the contract. I could have really fucked them over. Put it out on the internet or whatever. Sold them. But after making them sweat for a few weeks, I gave them back. Blackmail. Revenge. Not my style.

Six months later I returned to work. On light duties. Then I took voluntary redundancy. But I had to fight to get in the queue for a payoff. Like *Schindler's List*. Trying to get out of there.

For the next two years, I remained an emotional wreck. You name it, I had it. Counselling. Reflexology. Acupuncture. Little pills. From the natural health centre, made from rare weeds. But gram-for-gram cost more than cocaine. Anything to stop me reaching for my M16. Taking to the streets with my top off. Potting-off punters, Michael Ryan-style. Yeah. Get some.

The best treatment, though, was my weekly relaxation lesson. At the local mental health place. Bit *One-Flew-Over*, if the truth be told. But I loved it. Sat there in a circle with people on huge sinkers. Manic depressives. Obsessive compulsives. The acutely stressed. Anxious outsiders. A feller with a phobia of travel. Who'd been building up to a trip to Australia for ten years, coming every week, lying flat out on the floor. Bipolar. Mildly schizophrenic. Self-harmers. The panickers. But, like I always had, I had empathy for the outsiders. I felt more of a connection with my new mates than my old mates in work. Compared to these people, some of whom went into black holes for months on end, I was just a selfish yuppie.

But the breathing exercises. The anger management. The meditation. The talking in a circle. It worked. At least for me it did. Or at least staved off the symptoms. Until I had the opportunity to go deeper. To root out the causes.

To keep the show on the road, I banged out four books, on top of the one that I'd already done. Shied away from freelancing for newspapers. Couldn't face it, in case I regressed. But managed to get into some corporate PR. The dark side – PR gun-slinging. Basically, destroying peoples lives for large amounts of money. Smearing them for big organisations. Doing what I'd always done for the tabloids. But the process was rationalised for added ruthlessness. Dispensing with the niceties of even having to write a story. Just straight to the heart of the matter – to destroy their lives.

I never knew it but there was a whole secret industry out there. Of big corporations who employ black operatives like me. To get at their enemies. Before share flotations. City takeovers. Media battles. The revenge business. All manner of human misery. I never knew my skills were so transferable.

However, it wasn't a good place for me to be. But it was life in the big bad city – I needed to keep the kids in salmon fillets and cherry tomatoes and the like. Or at least I thought I did. I did. Some libel investigations to boot. That's when the legal departments of newspapers employ ex-journalists to investigate 'the other side'. In big-money disputes, over defamatory articles. Ironically, I did one for Tom Crone at News International. A tricky case they were getting sued on. Involving Wayne Rooney's 'auld slapper'. I helped make it go away.

But the madness was never far away. Never quite got over the humiliation of leaving the job. The loss of status. The loss of power. Life outside the corporate order. When you go off work with stress, it's looked on as a form of mental illness. Which it is. Many of my former colleagues, some of whom had never done a good story in their lives, thought less of me for it. But that was part of the problem. I was still seeing myself, my own value, in terms of stories. In terms of my professional reputation. Of what other journalists thought of me.

In August 2007 the kids, Em and I went away for a month. Make-or-break. She was thinking of leaving me. She'd had enough of me always being angry. Sitting up into the early hours. Watching *Performance* on the telly downstairs, on my own. Going to the pictures, again on my todd. Sitting there in the dark. Seething. But we got off. Shacked up in a big-fuck off chateau in Provence, in the South of France. To make things better. To see if I could exorcise the demons.

Then one day, I walked into a book shop out of the blue in a place called Aix-en-Provence. A dark yearning in my soul. Literally screaming out for help. And there, stacked up on top of each other on a shelf, was the answer. A book about philosophy.

'Have that, thanks very much.' Foot down in the space cruiser back to the mansion. Read it from cover to cover in one go. Drinking it in like an elixir. Like being put on a drip. Given a huge dose of mental medicine. Bathing my mind in stillness.

I'm not going to bore you with all the details. Like an alky going on about the 12 steps and all that. But in a nutshell, for the first time in my life the book explained to me what truth was. How important it was to tell the truth. At all times. Speak plainly and in a straight-forward manner. Regardless of whether or not it was in your own self-interest or not. There it was in black and white – the meaning of truth and why it's good to tell it.

Other good tips as well. Patience to reduce anger. Justice to be fair. Courage to get through the day without a hunted look in my eyes. I don't mean having the bottle to turn over a big drug dealer. But to have no fear. Not to worry about the future. Not to worry about things beyond my control – such as my reputation. Or stories about skateboarding parrots.

Philosophy gave me an insight into my madness. The madness of being a hack. No wonder I was fucked up. For the last fifteen years I'd been thinking in an irrational way. What I thought of myself. Linking my self-worth to stories. One week I was soaring – because I had a story in the paper. Getting praise off the Editor. The next I was low – because I didn't have a story and I was getting fucked off by the Editor. Tabloids are like a stock exchange of esteem. Playing havoc with your self-worth. Totally reliant on external events. Whereas what philosophy taught me was to link my place in the world with internal events – what was going on in my mind. Thinking. Telling the truth. Being patient. Being a hack was an unnatural thing to do. Delving into everyone else's life. Running around in circles. When I should be looking into my own. As opposed to living a life of distraction.

When I got back to London, I was a changed person. Sold off all the property. Got into a simpler, quieter life. Turned off the phone. A lot of people think philosophy is an academic subject. About obscure, unhelpful things such as 'is a chair, really a chair?' etc. But my idiot's guide to the subject explained that it was just about thinking about your life. Not going through it on autopilot. Teaching me to think about my opinions and how I behaved. No longer letting emotions, such as greed and sadness, distort the way I thought. Mightn't be your cup of tea. But it worked for me, anyway.

I've got bang into a school of philosophy known as stoicism. Stoicism literally stopped me from going insane. From going right off my fucking head. As I said – of literally reaching for the assault rifle. Running over to Canary Wharf. Taking up a sniper position in my old newsroom. That's how fucked I was. Today I still work for the papers. Mostly crime reporting. But every day, before I go out on a job, I read philosophers such as Epictetus and Seneca. Or Marcus Aurelius who wrote:

'Say to yourself first thing in the morning: today I shall meet people who are meddling, ungrateful, aggressive, treacherous, malicious, unsociable . . . I cannot be angry with any of them or hate him. We were born for cooperation.'

I read things like that to get through the day.

That's that.

End of Story.